MISTRESS IN HER OWN HOUSE

Patricia de Berker

© Patricia de Berker 2005
Mistress in Her Own House

ISBN 0-9548732-0-3

Published by:
Bure Publications
Ferndown Cottage
3 Hillier Road
Guildford
Surrey GU1 2JG

The right of Patricia de Berker to be
identified as the owner of this work has
been asserted by her in accordance with the
Copyright, Design and Patent Act 1988.

A CIP catalogue record for this book is
available from the British Library.

Design & production co-ordinated by:
The *Better Book* Company Ltd
Havant
Hampshire
PO9 2XH

Printed in England

Front cover photograph shows Tunstall Rectory in
1910 with Syria returning from the garden.

CONTENTS

For Paul,
with love

PART I
Africa

CHAPTER 1

Patricia's earliest memories were of the Farm. She could re-enter the vivid storehouse of memory and see again the long low homestead, the sheltering orchard, the big, startlingly purple violets in their wire enclosure, the coiled snake, the Boer handyman Hartenborg, all bathed in golden light. But she had no memory of the silage tank. She often tried to picture it, towering and sinister, and she strove in imagination to alter somehow the way things had happened. But imagination has limitations. It was not until she was much older that she saw a snapshot of the tank as it had really been, an insignificant structure, standing unobtrusively near the other outbuildings.

The Farm, Gaveston, a long narrow swathe of three thousand acres, lay under a wide Matabeleland sky, broken here and there by motionless small cloud islands. It had formed part of a parcel of land which Cecil John Rhodes had given to his close friend Leander Starr Jameson. It had changed hands since then, and in July 1921 it changed ownership yet again and by virtue of a hefty mortgage, became the property of Dr Arthur Pearson. He had come south from the Katanga with his wife Syria to view it, and he described it enthusiastically to his eighty-year-old mother in England. 'This is rather a dream of a place. It is a long, narrow farm in a valley about four miles long and a mile and a quarter broad. The house is at the head of the valley, and looks down over almost all the farm. There is an abundance of bird life and a fair quantity of small game, as well as some big. We saw one huge kudu bull. There is an orchard with magnificent oranges, vines and other fruit, two fresh water springs, and pasture land where cattle could be raised and crops grown. At this time of year it looks like English meadows. To us the place seems like a small paradise. It will take all we have to buy it, but living is very cheap there. Ourselves, three children and a governess could live on £12 to £15 a month, allowing for frequent guests. We shall have twenty native labourers. Some will want to go down with me from Katanga. Matthew and Barnabas will come. We are sure we shall never regret buying it. Any of you who come to visit will never want to leave.'

It was twenty years since he had arrived in Africa as a young doctor, newly qualified from Guy's Hospital, to work with the troops in the Boer War. Their arrival in Capetown coincided with the relief of Ladysmith. 'The enthusiasm all over the bay was intense,' he wrote. 'All the ships decked out with flags, guns firing, rockets going off and steam whistles roaring all over the place. They made a most fearful din. It was as bad as an inter-hospital Cup Final. Cigars and drinks were free in the town to men in uniform.'

Arthur was sent to a big hospital camp in the Karroo near Bloemfontain. He enjoyed life there. As well as work there was plenty of recreation. Most of the local Boer farmers turned out to be far from unfriendly. He was often invited into their homes for a meal, or to play tennis, go riding with their daughters or to smoke a pipe on the stoep with the farmer. He went for long walks in that strange boulder-strewn country, with its sudden huge, piled-up rocks. He made notes on wild life and sketched. Sometimes he took his gun and bagged birds and hares for the pot. He fell in love with Africa. From then on he never settled anywhere else. In 1905 he took up duty as chief medical officer to the the scattered mining communities of the Union Minière in the Katanga district of the Belgian Congo, a vast country, largely unknown to Europeans.

Travelling back to England on leave in 1910 by Union Castle Line, he met Syria Horwood, youngest daughter of a Suffolk country parson. At the age of twenty-five, she had been invited out for a holiday by a brother, working as a mining engineer in the small town of Lubumbashi. The journey achieved what it was discreetly intended to do, which was to give her a better chance of finding a husband than her small parish world offered. It also enabled her to escape an elderly widower who had been pursuing her. She was already on her way home when she met Arthur one warm evening on deck before dinner. It was his birthday, and they fell into polite conversation. They seemed to encounter each other often after that. He was a fine-looking man, broad and very tall, and hardened by a vigorous outdoor life. She was slim and pretty, with a piled mass of chestnut-brown hair and steady green eyes. The prettiness perhaps disguised the determined set of her straight mouth. On reaching England they separated, Arthur to his mother and eldest sister in London, and Syria to the Rectory in Suffolk. He lost no time in writing her a letter nicely balanced between formality and warmth, and followed this up by a visit to her parents. In a few weeks they were engaged. At the age of thirty-four, Arthur was seriously in love for the first and last time in his life. He has just bought the emerald and diamond engagement ring, and is writing to tell her about it.

'As I came back on the train today, I pondered more and more on the wonderful trust and love you show in leaving everything to come with me to Africa, I can promise you, my darling, that I will do my best to deserve it.' He anticipates sharing with her his other love, Africa. It has, he says, grown into him. 'What I look forward to in the Katanga is the time when we can travel together through that country which I entered years ago when it was a land of mystery to white men. It is very dear to me, with its wild wooded hills and windswept pastures, and its beautiful glades. I want to take you to places where I have sat in the moonlight, and felt that sense of the infinite of which I have told you.' He goes on to tease her affectionately, in his slightly pedantic style, for something she has said. "I remember that at the time I proposed to you, my dear said, "You know I haven't got a penny?" I have been chuckling today because I couldn't help thinking that it looked as though you were searching in your mind for my motive in asking you. I don't think, now that my dear love knows me better, she would touch on money for a motive, or believe I want her for any other reason than that I love her altogether, and believe I have found in her my true mate. I do believe that, as I love you now, so I always shall. You are the crowning mercy of my life.'

Syria, daughter of the Rector of Tunstall, took the opportunity to reassure herself about the Christian instruction of their currently unborn children. She had to be certain of Arthur's religious commitment. Arthur wrote back that they would surely have no trouble in teaching Baby about Jesus. He had adopted her idiom, for his family was not outstandingly pious, apart from his eldest unmarried sister, who was a member of the Plymouth Brethren. But he did take marital responsibility very earnestly, and promised her mother that, should the climate of Central Africa not agree with her, he would bring his contract with the Belgian Mines to a close and return with her to England.

There is sometimes a premonitory note in letters to Syria. 'I won't forget what I've got to look for when I get to heaven. And as there's no time there, I shall meet you there already, at once, even if you live years longer than I.' And Arthur has a whimsical humour. 'I always think of you when I first wake, as I do the last moment before sleep, and indeed at most times, but I heard your voice so clearly when it wasn't there. I suppose you were not really in the cherry tree below my window?' These excerpts, scissored out of letters in small bits and pieces, were kept hidden by Syria all her life, and Patricia discovered them after her death at eighty-three, salvaged by some impulse from her almost total destruction of personal papers. She could share Arthur with no one else.

The Reverend Thomas Horwood married them in January 1911, eight months after they had met, in the fifteenth century grey flint church next-door to the Rectory. A path led directly from the graceful old house, through a garden gate, into the churchyard.

Syria, who was prone to small herpes sores on her lip, was chagrined to be afflicted with one on that day.

CHAPTER 2

Soon after the wedding they sailed to Cape Town, and after a honeymoon pause there, journeyed north on Cecil Rhodes' new railway to the Victoria Falls. Thence they travelled with African bearers by safari stages to the Katanga. Arthur resumed his itinerant medical duties and his battle with the killer, sleeping sickness. The work was far-flung but not lonely, for there were friends stationed along the way. Syria took to the life. There were no luxuries here, but there had been none at the Rectory. They always travelled together, spending a few days at each settlement. Syria met Arthur's second sister, May, married to George Watson, a mining consultant. May, an impulsive and cheerful young woman, found herself ill at ease with the reserved, cool-mannered Syria, who in any case much preferred the company of men to that of women, whom she was inclined to write off as superficial. A fading snap shows them all grouped together, under light shady trees. In the background are two or three bungalows, raised on low wooden stilts to thwart reptiles, vermin and ants, and sheltered beneath overhanging thatched roofs. The two women are next each other, clad in ground-length, long-sleeved white dresses, cinched in with a belt. May looks straight ahead of her, almost, but not quite, smiling. Syria wears a slightly disapproving expression, seemingly detaching herself from her neighbour.

A long journey meant overnight camping. The servants set up tents and lit the campfire for cooking. Often a neighbouring headman called with gifts of flour, potatoes and fruit, and logs for the fire. Then they sat back, Arthur with his glass of whisky and soda, and listened to the sounds of evening, the laughter of children in the village, and the calling of pigeons away in the woods. In his diary he recorded these peaceful moments.

The life gave Arthur many opportunities to hunt big game. He slew lion, elephant, buffalo, hippopotamus, and innumerable deer, and took snapshots of them, lying in defeated, crumpled heaps. A few years later Patricia was to look through the albums with puzzled feelings. She was sorry that so many animals had to die, though she admired her father for hunting lions, who, she understood, killed you if you did not get them first.

They returned to England in the late summer of 1912 for the birth of their first child, Grey, at Tunstall Rectory. They did not stay long. Leaving the infant with a nurse and its grandparents, they returned to the Katanga to resume their life together. They were back again two years later for the birth of Peter at the same hospitable house. But four days earlier, the First World War had broken out. It was time to get away while they could. Leaving both babies at the Rectory, they took off once more for the Katanga, where they remained for the four-year duration of the Great War, which scarcely touched them. In 1921 they returned for the birth of their daughter Patricia. Syria's father had died since they were last there, and the new incumbent was her brother-in-law. They had just completed the purchase of the Rhodesian Farm. After the carefree years, they were planning to settle down to family life.

Arthur recorded Patricia's birth in a letter to his future neighbour, Turner. Syria had insisted on having dinner downstairs, ignoring as best she could the contractions she was now having, because she wanted the baby to be born the next day, when a common birthday could conveniently be shared with its eldest brother. However Syria, who got her own way in most things, failed to outwit nature. No other medical assistance being available, Patricia was received into the world at the hands of her father.

This was to be her parents' first experience of living with their children, their knowledge of the first two having been restricted to studio photographs, showing two curly-headed little boys in velvet suits with lace-frilled collars. When they returned to England in 1921, Grey and Peter were no longer picture-book children, and they posed a certain challenge to their parents, especially so to their mother. They found it was not too difficult coming to terms with their father. He was fun to play rough games with, and a good sport if they happened to mess up his suit. He climbed trees with them. Sometimes he took them for exciting drives in a small open car round the Suffolk villages and pointed out to them the War Memorials which were already going up everywhere. These days held happy memories for the boys. Patricia was happy, too, when, later on, her brothers sometimes shared the memories with her. It gave her a proxy fragment of life with her father.

The parents spent several months in England, preparing for the move to the Farm. They had assembled more than a ton and a half of freight. An experienced traveller in the tropics, Arthur had taken care to obtain cases of stout wood or heavy black metal. White ants and winter rains could soon disintegrate them, and render them liable to theft. He was doubtful if some of the larger packages could be got through the homestead door at all. He wrote to neighbour Turner, from whom he had purchased the Farm, asking him to keep an eye on things. Arthur wrote a large number of letters, many of them in typescript, and meticulously recorded them in thick, strongly bound carbon-copy books, where in purple ink on flimsy brown paper, they weathered many decades. He documented every item consigned to his packing cases, and so, as well as pieces of small furniture and ordinary household wares, he recorded a bizarre motley of possessions. One list included, 'One box with small poems inside, one tin of custard powder, two camisoles, one soldier's cap, one roll of coloured veils, one brown coat and knickers, one flannel petticoat, one roll of macaroni, two pairs of combinations, one picture of Tetbury Church, one woollen chest protector, one wedding veil, one old bolster case, one carriage whip, one piece of German aeroplane, one parcel of music, two sponge racks, one drum.' Nothing was easily thrown away in the Pearson family. Syria never jettisoned a piece of string, but painstakingly unknotted from it all trace of former duties and sent it to join similar retrievals in a cotton drawstring bag.

Finally all had been packed away and despatched in advance. Goodbyes were said to Grandmother and Nanny Martin, who had looked after Grey and Peter all their lives; goodbye, too, to the old Rectory where three of Syria's children had been born and where she had spent most of her childhood. The Church authorities were about to sell the fine Queen Anne house, in its setting of wide lawns and magnificent trees, one of the first of many profitable sales, and to accommodate the new Rector more modestly in a smaller house half a mile away down the lane. Then the party, with Miss McCleod, who would fulfil the combined roles of nurse to the infant and governess to the boys, travelled to Southampton and boarded the S.S. *Arundel Castle*, bound for Cape Town. She was to inconvenience her employers by being seasick for too much of the time during the next three weeks. Her main task, which she had to manage as best she could, was to bottle-feed the infant Patricia at regular intervals, to pacify her, and attend to all the other chores of baby-care. Arthur and Syria, who had good sea legs, enjoyed the voyage, and walked the deck together, chatting with other passengers and playing bridge and patience. Arthur was elected chairman of the sports committee and organised deck games. He also took care to keep his diary up to date.

Some of the talk he heard was not encouraging. Farmers told him they had found it hard to make ends meet, that many of them were working at a loss and owners were often glad to get out. Only "one-horse affairs" with minimum overheads were doing well. Arthur did not want to listen to this kind of talk, and discounted tales of disaster, deciding that such farms were not being worked as seriously as he intended to work his. Four days before arrival at Cape Town, Syria started packing, an occupation to which, throughout her life, she devoted great single-mindedness and large quantities of tissue paper. On the last day of the voyage, Arthur recorded that he had just refused to sign a round-robin letter organised by some dissatisfied passengers, requesting a reduction in their fares. He himself had no complaints, and in any case he did not think it quite straight to quibble over a contract previously agreed. Ironically, within a few years, negotiating reduced terms was a frequent necessity for Syria, and one for which she proved to have a talent.

The first news that greeted them on arrival at Cape Town was that the luggage had cost £100 more to transport than expected. Making the best of this, they arrived at the Cadogan Hotel. The change of air did not seem to suit Patricia, and she tiresomely cried non-stop. At supper that evening they met a man whom Arthur's diary unexpectedly describes as a baritone. He told them he had farmed for seven years in Southern Rhodesia, and advised them not to go there. 'He is not the sort to farm,' noted Arthur. A former passenger also called on them, a man who had been warned by the Settlers' Association that farming in Rhodesia was no good at present, and would not go ahead for ten years.

Not allowing themselves to be downcast by these gloomy prophecies, Arthur and Syria left with their little party by the night train for the long journey to Bulawayo, Rhodesia's second city. On the train they met a government vet, who talked to them about quarter evil, a bacillus which was spreading among cattle, and caused gangrene in their limbs. Arriving in Bulawayo after thirty-six hours, they were met by an old friend, Major Robert Gordon, known all over town as Boomerang, after an aboriginal weapon which he had mastered during his previous life in Australia. He had booked rooms for them in the Grand Hotel, and that evening the three of them had dinner together, while Miss McCleod and her charges were disposed of in nursery quarters upstairs. Over dinner they discussed the next move. Arthur wanted to waste no time in getting to his Farm, but none of his native servants had yet arrived from the Katanga. Immediate arrangements would have to be made to engage other labour for the transport of cases to the Farm, and for the purchase of groceries, water coolers, and, intriguingly, twenty yards of rope.

Up to this point, Arthur was satisfied with Miss McCleod, and wrote to his sister Madge in Ealing 'She is ideal. She likes responsibility and has no fear of taking it. Also she is cheerful, and never grouses. We have done well to get her.' They bade goodnight to Boomerang and went to bed, confident that matters were well in hand. Next morning they left Miss McCleod with the children in the hotel, carried out numerous purchases, and set off with their cases on a mulecart organised for them by Boomerang, together with a newly engaged Matabele called Tom. They soon left Bulawayo outskirts behind and entered a narrow red-earth track into the vast heart of the bush. Occasionally they passed a farm, typically a long, fairly primitive bungalow, sheltered from the sun by a verandah, and set in a yard colourful with bourgainvillea and oleander. Close by there was always a welcome tree or two, and usually an orchard, growing oranges, lemons and pawpaws. Beyond the farmstead there would be a wide acreage of cleared land, used for the pasturing of cattle and the cultivation of crops such as mealies. As their mulecart moved slowly on, Arthur and Syria would have often been diverted by families of warthogs scuttling across the track, or by graceful little impala, leaping and curvetting effortlessly on delicate slim hooves. There would have been guinea fowl, frenziedly rushing about to escape the cart wheels. Arthur recorded that they covered the eighteen miles from Bulawayo in two and a half hours, and that they were relieved to reach Gaveston Farm and find shelter from the heat.

They set to work at once with Tom to make the place habitable for the family. Then they called on the Turners, a mile or so away, and were invited to stay the night, a suggestion they welcomed. They spent the evening discussing breeds of cattle.

The next day a serious accident overtook Arthur. It was to have long repercussions. For the immediate present, it delayed his getting to grips with the new way of life at a time when all his energies were needed, though with his customary doggedness, he did his best to take it in his stride.

He had spent the morning scrubbing the kitchen for Syria. As he was opening a kitchen crate with a new cold chisel, a piece of metal flew off it and embedded itself in his eye. Syria at once despatched Tom to the Turners' farm with a note, requesting that Turner come round with a conveyance, and then busied herself packing a suitcase. Turner was not at home, so the services of a more distant neighbour had to be sought. He arrived in his Ford after a delay of two hours, and drove them to Bulawayo. Arthur had medical friends at the hospital, but all of them were out, so he and Syria returned to the children at their hotel, but it was not until six or more hours after the accident that a consultant arrived and examined the eye. It was not yet very painful and Arthur could see out of it fairly well. They decided to have the metal fragment extracted next morning. Syria was uneasy about the delay, but was reassured by the consultant.

At two in the morning, great pain in the eye awoke Arthur and continued unabated. He felt rotten he said, and the eye was much inflamed. They regretted that the fragment had not been removed the previous evening, and then and there Arthur drew up a Will, leaving all, which did not amount to much, to Syria, 'my beloved wife.' At the hospital arrangements were made for Syria to eat and sleep, sharing Arthur's room. After an operation by Dr. Tait, the principal medical officer, Arthur retained his sight, but the eye was still inflamed. Fomentations had to be applied every hour, and irrigation every two hours. The faithful Boomerang called frequently and carried out various missions for Syria. Late that afternoon Syria went to see Matron in her office, and at this interview the seeds of a very poor relationship were sown. Dr. Tait visited his patient at noon and then left. He phoned the hospital at four in the afternoon to say that his car had broken down, and so he would not be returning till the next day. Syria was not accepting this and despatched Boomerang to fetch him. He arrived tardily at seven and irrigated the eye. Then patient and wife tried to settle down for the night.

Next morning Arthur's condition had deteriorated. The inflammation was worse and the pain severe, and the consultant decided he would have to remove the eye for fear of septicaemia. An altercation arose between Syria and the nurse as to who was going to shave the patient, so Arthur resolved the matter by doing it himself. He cut himself and blamed the nurse. He was injected a quarter of an hour before the operation and asked the nurse what it was. 'She became mysterious and refused to tell me,' he wrote in his diary. 'There are quaint people in this hospital.' Arthur was not accustomed to the role of compliant patient, and was seeing things from a new angle.

A few hours after the operation, Matron called and sent down champagne. The quaintness had its ironic side. Syria was teetotal and would have preferred Arthur to be.

That evening a close friend of Arthur's, Dr Travers, came to dress his painful eye socket. This set the scene for another series of scraps between Syria and the nursing staff. Syria was blind to hospital hierarchies and soon aroused the fighting instincts of the Ward Sister. When requested to leave the room while the eye was being dressed, she did so under protest, but took up her post immediately behind the door. She kept a lookout for shortcomings in nursing care and reported to Arthur that when they brought him back unconscious from the theatre, they had allowed his legs to drop off the stretcher with a bump. Furthermore, the stretcher had been accompanied by a large Airedale and a white-haired terrier, which had gambolled around while the four or five nurses were busy chattering, and not, complained Syria, directing the stretcher-bearers properly.

'Oh can the dogs go out!' she had objected. The largest nurse had replied sharply, 'They'll go out in a minute. They're not doing any harm!'

Syria's unpleasant recollections of that week in hospital were sympathetically recorded by Arthur. She was torn between a genuine concern for his distressing condition, and a determination to dominate the nursing staff. The outcome was farce. Only the little ward maid escaped her censure. The eye-dressing sessions were the focal point of the struggle, and hinged upon whether the nurse in charge would allow her to be present or not. For Syria, not to be allowed to do something was a situation that applied only to other people. Arthur was hers, and she had possessed him exclusively for the past twelve years. To find herself treated as any ordinary, run-of-the-mill wife was intolerable. The difficulty was that Sister, too, retained a fine sense of status, and had the authority to use it. She reprimanded Syria for ringing the bell twice for tea because Arthur had been kept waiting after the first ring. Syria did not surrender. She complained about dogs yapping all the afternoon outside the window, exacerbating Arthur's headache. She objected that his drinks were sent in cold and said that he had detected a taste of mouse in his egg flip. It must have been a relief to the hospital staff when within a few days Arthur recovered sufficiently to leave. Matron came in to say goodbye to her patient, and they talked together of their experiences with the British forces in the Boer War. This was a piece of history which Syria was not able to share.

After a few days' rest in Bulawayo, Arthur and Syria, hardly in first-class form, resumed their laborious task of preparing the Farm for the family. They took with them Jeff and Mutt, two young dogs, who immediately ran away. It was Christmas Day. The dogs were recovered, ravenously hungry, on Boxing Day. On December 27th, Miss McLeod arrived from Bulawayo with the three children.

Within the week, Arthur had acquired a horse, a donkey, and forty to fifty head of cattle of mixed breeds. One heifer proved too fierce to milk. They had fourteen oxen for the big farm wagon which would be used every week for conveying produce to market at Bulawayo, whose main streets had been deliberately constructed wide enough to turn a span of oxen in. They also bought thirteen fowls, one of which Jeff or Mutt promptly killed. Native workers were hired, and set up their huts in their own compound on the borders of the farm lands, at some distance from the homestead.

Arthur was imbibing cattle lore piece by piece from Major Gordon. The eyes, he learned, should be far apart, the back straight, and the beef strains shaped like a brick. Other people hinted to Arthur that his faithful friend was in fact no judge of cattle, and that anyone could take him in. Arthur began to realise how ill-equipped he was, in his complete ignorance, to cope with the realities of farm management. It was going to take him some time to know his way around, and he already suspected that one at least, of his neighbours, from whom he had bought livestock and equipment, had taken advantage of him. It was no time for the amateur.

Arthur's eye socket still pained him, and he had to wear an eye shade until the wound had healed sufficiently for the insertion of a glass eye. It was not a cheering prospect, but he made the best of it. The remaining eye had good sight, but his main concern was lest he should no longer be able to shoot straight. The only people who seemed carefree were the two boys. It went quite to their heads to have somewhere so different to roam about in, though they soon learnt that restrictions were going to be placed on their scope for adventure. Even so, there was plenty of fun to be had, and they got on well with Miss McLeod, who did not push them too hard in their lessons. Christmas Day was celebrated a fortnight late. By now, Grey had developed a stubborn constipation, and was treated with Arthur's prime remedy, castor oil. It did not shift Grey, so the next day he was dosed with Glauber Salts. As this was equally unsuccessful, Arthur had recourse to a soap enema. Grey, who had never had this degree of attention paid to his excretory function, was perplexed.

One morning in the middle of January, Syria accompanied Arthur into the orchard, but felt so exhausted she had to lie down there instead of helping to pick the fruit for market. The next day her temperature soared to 104°. She had contracted typhoid fever. She was desperately ill, and it was April before she was able to leave her bed. Arthur nursed her at the Farm with great devotion, perhaps with the memory of her recent fierce care of him scarcely a month before. He hired two nurses to help him with the twenty-four hour task. After a couple of weeks, her temperature fell to normal, but two relapses, so often fatal in typhoid, were to occur. Arthur remembered how he had tended an Army friend in relapse during the Boer War. He had sought to comfort the failing patient and had written his last letter to his mother for him.

The Farm was neglected and new workers left to their own devices while he and the nurses fought for Syria's survival. Red ants invaded the house and he had a job to protect her bed. His one relief was in writing to his eldest sister Madge, in England, about the struggle to keep Syria alive. He told her that the drought threatened to destroy the crops, but he could spare no time for farming. He had been obliged to postpone his quarterly visit of medical inspection to the Katanga mining community, and this held up the only reliable income, small though it was, on which he could depend.

'Syria is in a very grave condition,' he wrote. 'I now have two nurses here and have sent Miss McLeod and the children to a neighbour. She has been in a condition of high fever and low delirium for some days. I can't write about it. I am fighting for a life harder than I have ever fought, and each day losing a little ground. It is terrible. If only I had you here … some new danger is always cropping up. I dare not go far away. I sit and watch from the next room and go in every hour. I try to catch the danger sign before it has gone too far.'

Syria was in delirium most of this time, but the strong constitution of the country-raised girl who had always followed a simple way of life was fighting for her. In his next letter to Madge, Arthur reported:

'The night of the 21st was the worst we had. At about seven in the evening, the condition looked hopeless. I took big risks, and used remedies that are not often employed in typhoid, and by 10.30 the danger was past for the time. Since then, there has been a little improvement each day. The night nurse will go today or tomorrow. She is no good anyhow. We are trying to avoid milk foods and I go out every morning to get a few birds. I only go for about an hour's walk.

This morning I went at 6.30 and was back at 7.30 with one duck, two quail and four pigeons. My shooting is improving and will go all right in spite of one eye. We make delicious soup of the birds, and she likes it best of all she has.

I am planting and carpentering when not wanted, but cannot go far away. We have had four nice calves this week. I am buying ten pigs. Our crops look well. We are very much more fortunate than our neighbours as regards rain. I ought to get £250 for the maize. Goodness knows, we shall want all we can get. This illness has cost me two or three hundred.'

A week later he wrote of continued improvement. He intended to get his children back in a few days, but was expressing disenchantment with their young nurse. 'Miss McLeod does not feel strong. I am afraid she is a washout. She is nervy and lazy. I don't think she will stay two years. She is quite horrified at the idea of walking a mile. I wish I had one reliable help. I am still fighting ants every day.'

This verdict on Miss McLeod was the opposite of what he had written to Madge about her a few weeks before. His initial impressions of people, especially women, were often idealised, and subject later to strict revision. Miss McLeod was possibly finding herself not cut out for the rough conditions of life on the Farm, with its threats of typhoid fever and red ants, and she often complained that the heat made her feel unwell.

Gradually Syria recovered, though as late as August, Arthur was writing to his mother-in-law at the Rectory that she was not yet completely strong. 'After such a bad attack of typhoid, one cannot expect her to be the same for a year. Still, she gets about a good bit, and has begun to ride a little. I have an ideal horse for her. He is perfectly quiet and well-mannered.' Syria remembered Bob fondly for years. She also lingered on the memory of the convalescent piece of toffee which she was prescribed daily.

In fighting to save Syria's life, Arthur was also fighting for himself. Before marriage he had been accustomed to mainly male company. With colleagues in the Katanga, an adventurous outdoor life had been his chosen lot. He saw women as weaker vessels, leading sheltered, domesticated lives. Syria may may have led a sheltered life, but she was not a weak vessel, and Arthur was struck by her valiant qualities. He told her that he felt she was the stronger of the two.

Both idealised the state of marriage, and saw theirs as a model for others. Somehow they contrived never seriously to disillusion each other. Syria backed Arthur at every point, and a powerful loyalty bound them together. Constantly braced for battle with most of the world, Syria did not seem to need to fight him. There was a jealous possessiveness in her loyalty, but he did not notice it. Before Syria, most women had bored him. Syria was never frivolous, and he liked her seriousness in everything she undertook.

By May, when Syria was up again, Arthur recorded: 'Had prayers this morning for the first time.' Syria added in pencil: 'Starting this every Sunday as a sort of Thank You for Syria's recovery.'

Perhaps Arthur should have thought of this himself?

CHAPTER 3

Arthur, with his one eye, and Syria, weakened by her long months of illness, now had to take up anew the challenge of an unfamiliar world. They had had no conception of the difficulties they would have to face. They had arrived in Rhodesia in the middle of a severe drought, and had turned a deaf ear to several warning voices. Not the least of their problems was that, for the first time in twelve years of married life, they were having to make room for their children.

It soon turned out that Miss McLeod did not care much, either for her infant charge Patricia, or for the rough and ready circumstances in which she found herself. She got on rather better with Grey and Peter, taking them daily for lessons. They were both backward for their age. During their life at the Rectory, they had had rudimentary lessons with their Nanny Martin, a kindly country woman who was effectively their mother. She took them for walks on the wide Suffolk heaths, accompanied them at nursery meals, and tended their early illnesses. Once she took them away for a seaside holiday in Margate. It was the only conventional childhood holiday they were ever to have. When he was past seventy, Peter recalled this experience in conversation with Patricia, his eyes lighting up at the rare and treasured memory. After the boys had accompanied their recently revealed parents to Africa, they never saw Nanny Martin again, though they reminisced about her for years.

The boys' way of life was now a great contrast to the old one at the Rectory. It was full of interesting experiences, but these were tightly contained by rule and routine. Their parents' view of children was both simple and severe. They were used to African natives, whom they regarded largely as children, and often treated as such; they were used to animals, and had ways of dealing with recalcitrant dogs. A thieving puppy which continued to steal eggs had a whole boiling egg thrust into its mouth, which was then held forcibly closed. Syria had evolved a method of childcare closely resembling dog care. Children, like dogs, in order to be a pleasure to their owners, must learn the laws of instant obedience. Then their laughter and sense of fun can lift the spirits. But what this pair wanted to do was to run wild, tease snakes, fraternise with the African workers, and explore in their own way all the possibilities of a home that was excitingly different from a Suffolk Rectory. Arthur, watching them, got the impression that, unlike him, they did not have a care in the world, and he rather liked that. But Syria explained to him that they were becoming self-willed and disobedient. They were indeed like the puppies. Arthur acknowledged her judgement and did his best to conform, but some of the fervour was lacking.

The boys liked Miss McLeod much better than their parents did. She was young and light-hearted, and with them she was cheerful, and they did their best to sabotage lessons with her in the outbuilding which Syria had rather grandly designated the schoolroom. But there were other duties, not so easily evaded. Syria and Arthur set them a rota of practical tasks on the farm, aimed at developing a sense of responsibility and manliness, and reinforced by penalties if they were not carried out to the letter. Peter was detailed to feed the dogs, but sometimes he forgot. He disliked washing, and forgot to do so quite often. They both dilly-dallied on their errands, too casual to satisfy Syria's passion for punctuality. Their forgetfulness came almost as high on the scale of misdoings as disobedience. Syria found Grey maddeningly absent-minded. He lost and broke things as though he intended to annoy. Most distressing to both parents was that their sons frequently told half-truths, and even lies, presumably in the hope of deflecting scoldings. Lies were condemned as wicked and contemptible, and attracted the severest penalties.

For Grey at least, there were the good times. He was the bigger and stronger of the two, and his father took him on long treks about the farm lands, pacing distant paddocks to work out dimensions for new fencing, and inspecting the cattle, which needed constant attention. They were forever having calving complications, sickening or falling down, and refusing to rise again. They were to prove an endless source of concern to Arthur.

Sometimes he and Grey climbed together up the side of the stony little stream which, after a rare fall of rain, flowed down the wooded hillside, their path crossed by families of clumsy warthogs or leaping impala. Once in the dusk they lost each other, and Grey, finding that his father had not returned to the house, set forth with a torch to search for him. An attachment was growing between Arthur and the eldest son who so closely resembled him in feature.

Syria, meanwhile, was finding it ever harder to get on with her nurse governess. She began to suspect that Mrs Turner, wife of their neighbour, was alienating Miss McLeod's loyalties. The young woman had taken to spending her rare afternoons off with Mrs Turner. There was virtually no other European female company in the vicinity. A storm brewed over the formalities which meant so much to Syria. Miss McLeod had lent her new friend two pairs of Patricia's slippers and some linen crawlers, without asking permission first. Syria scolded her for this lapse, and followed up by walking over to the Turner farm to express her displeasure. Her neighbour disconcerted her by remarking how good and efficient Miss McLeod was. She took personal responsibility for the loan of the patterns, since she herself had asked for them. Syria returned home, feeling criticised and angry.

Miss McLeod's cheerful familiarity with Hartenborg, the Boer handyman, also rankled. Syria was not pleased to hear, through a chance remark of Peter's, that he had come over to the schoolroom during lesson time, bringing a dyed goatskin as a gift for the young woman. He also came and chatted with her in the evenings. Syria complained to Arthur at what she called hole-in-the-corner behaviour. Grey offended even more seriously than Hartenborg. Arthur had met his son bringing in a bunch of violets for Miss McLeod, and commented tartly in his diary that Syria had succeeded in getting only two bunches of flowers from her son all the week, while Miss McLeod's bedroom vase was never empty.

Miss McLeod was revealing herself as a young lady of spirit, and Syria abhorred spirit in her employees. Miss McLeod was honing the arts of passive defiance and dumb insolence. It infuriated her mistress. Syria required household duties to be performed ritualistically, in exactly the same manner and order as she would do them herself. There was only one right pattern for any task, and that was Syria's pattern. Miss McLeod might be permitted to use Syria's old sewing machine but only on condition that it was replaced in exactly that position which she had ordained for it. Miss McLeod must invariably draw back the verandah curtains for tea, and she must use the side door and not the kitchen door when entering or leaving the house. This last instruction was motivated by Syria's dislike of anything approaching social familiarity with the servants. Miss McLeod's response to the behaviour code was to ignore it, a tactic which proved immensely frustrating to Syria, who was unused to simple silent defiance, and found herself at a loss as to how handle it.

It was in this uneasy state of affairs that, towards the end of September, Arthur deemed Syria well enough for him to leave her in charge of the Farm while he returned to the Katanga to carry out his postponed inspections there. He badly needed the money, and he must have looked forward to meeting again many old friends and colleagues. As well, too, as his sister May and her husband James, there would be Syria's eccentric youngest brother, Alfred, a non-practising doctor and a recently ordained priest, who was seeking an appointment with the Union Minière.

So Arthur set off on the long train journey to the Katanga. Syria and Miss McLeod were left alone together, and it may have been this that prompted the nurse to give notice, her reason being that she could not stand the heat any longer. No one had told her it could be like this.

Syria was shocked. Miss McLeod wanted to leave in December, thus infringing the somewhat feudal terms of her contract, which stipulated that she should stay for at least two years, at the end of which, out of her modest earnings, she would refund Syria the cost of her passage from England. In Syria's regulated universe, contracts amounted to oaths of Biblical solemnity; there could be no renegotiations on personal grounds, and she was taken aback by Miss McCleod's determination to ignore their contract because it no longer suited her. The health excuse Syria regarded as invalid. She pointed out to Miss McCleod with a touching naivety that her reasons for leaving were not fair. Miss McCleod was immoveable, possibly with a growing conviction that the terms of her contract were scarcely fair either. Syria noted in her diary: 'Miss McCleod thinks she is very ill, and liable to break down at any moment.' The subject went underground for the time being. The governess continued to teach the boys and to sit silently with Syria in the evenings, sewing chair covers, and she continued to put the sewing machine back in the wrong place.

Syria was now in the early stages of pregnancy. She felt tired and sick, and tried to rest, but during Arthur's absence she found herself busy from dawn to dusk, actively overseeing the work on the farm. All was not peace. A furious fight broke out between the senior house servant, Matthew, who slept in the kitchen at night during Arthur's absence, and another servant, Kalumbo, who worked in the house part-time. Matthew came upon him and another man at five in the morning in his hut with his wife Martha. He promptly set about beating her, but Kalumbo and his friend rushed to her aid, and belaboured him with a large stick until it shattered. Then they ran off. Matthew returned to the farmhouse, where he found Kalumbo waiting for him. He made a dash for an axe hanging on the wall. Syria, disturbed by the commotion, ran in and managed to put herself between the combatants. She snatched his knobkerry away from Kalombo. Several other men who had crowded in to take sides dispersed on Syria's threat to call the police if there was any more trouble. One man showed defiance, so she threatened him with the knobkerry. She ordered Matthew not to quarrel again before Arthur's return, and dismissed him to do his usual work, but he claimed to feel ill from his earlier beating, and insisted on returning to his hut to rest. He decided to send Martha back to their Congo village by train in a day or two. She continued to insist that all she had done was innocently to invite two men into her hut for an early morning drink.

Matthew, no longer a young man, had suffered sorely at the hands of Kalumbo and his friend. Two days later, as he had not returned to work, Syria went to see him in his hut. He said he was too ill to work, but Syria was not sympathetic. Matthew had let slip that he planned to walk with his wife to the nearest railway station, six miles away. Syria told him that there was no train till Saturday, and he must return to his duties. She was sure he was exaggerating his injuries, so as to avoid being in the house with Kalumbo. The threat of having to encounter his enemy again proved less tiresome than another visit from Syria, and he returned to work.

Despite morning sickness, Syria carried on with her foremanship from around six at dawn to seven o'clock at night. In the Farm logbook she recorded the birthing complications of a cow, together with other routine farm events. Chickens had to have their wings clipped, hens were set on eggs, animal feed was measured out daily to farm workers, and all of them were assigned their work individually. Syria carried out inspections now and again to ensure that they were doing it, and scolded them if she decided they were not. She also ran a regular first-aid service for farmworkers with cuts, bruises, and stomach aches.

There was always sewing and mending to do, and last thing at night, the writing up of her diary and the farm records. There she listed every detail, down to the day's last pint of milk, the last egg, and the last crate of flowers and fruit, to be despatched to Bulawayo market by ox wagon first thing in the morning. Arthur was a meticulous record keeper, and she saw herself as his steward responsible to him for every item. The Farm must not suffer through his absence.

She disliked it intensely when he was away. Underneath the firm exterior, she was apprehensive about her solitary existence in the midst of so many natives, only two of whom, Matthew and Barnabas, did she really know and trust. So she welcomed Arthur's return at the end of two weeks. The sick cow had continued to give trouble. The placenta did not come away after birth, and she had sent to Turner for help. He had prescribed one and a half pounds of salts in six bottles of water. Syria superintended the operation, but it took three days for anything to happen. At last, on the afternoon of his return, Arthur achieved removal of the afterbirth.

CHAPTER 4

Arthur developed a poisoned thumb and a temperature and retired to bed for a couple of days. Syria applied boiling hot fomentations, which came a close second in her pharmacopoeia to castor oil and enemas. They reviewed their accounts together, which depressed them. Arthur noted sardonically that he was reading *A Fool on the Veldt*. A fresh series of mishaps occurred. The fowls and the pigs broke loose, a Friedland cow turned savage in the byre and gored three others, a recently castrated bull calf fell sick, the secondhand plough broke down again. Arthur was at his wits' end at the toll of dead and dying sheep, cows and oxen. Everywhere in the country water was drying up. Arthur had taken on too much livestock and could not afford to supplement the diet of more than a few. Grey and Peter, seeking to do their helpful bit, brought a sick chicken to their bedroom, wrapped it in a wet towel, and put it in front of the open window. Their efforts were appreciated by no one, and they got no supper. Death and disappearance were depleting Syria's little flock of hens.

Among other invalids, Syria took over the care of an orphaned lamb. She fed it for two days by bottle, but then, worried about its constipation, and uncertain how to apply an enema to a lamb, she dosed it with castor oil, which ended its life altogether. At about the same time, Patricia sickened and was dosed with castor oil. She became sicker. She was dosed with more and became very sick indeed, and Syria was seriously worried and summoned the doctor from Bulawayo. She took turns with Miss McLeod to sleep with Patricia at night. Presumably the medication was changed, since Patricia recovered.

The parents decided it was time to further their sons' apprenticeship to farming by teaching them to ride. A donkey was considered the most suitable animal to learn on, and they started donkey rides under the surveillance of the houseboy Jackson. Peter proved unwilling. He was nervous. But his parents were determined to make "a little man" of him, and insisted that he ride every day.

Peter sought to evade this fate with the aid of a few fibs. He was soon found out. Syria was disgusted and Arthur became increasingly irritated by the boys' failure to respond to orders as he had learned to do in his school cadet corps. Peter continued to make trouble about riding, and one dark day Arthur recorded in his diary:

'Peter had to have ten strokes of my rhino-hide whip for leaving the bridle and donkey and getting off and walking instead of riding her. Syria had a row with Grey about his treatment of the fowls. Their first whipping was when Syria was ill, a Sunday morning, I think. I used a small tree branch which I cut for the purpose and broke it on them. Neither cried. Today, when I beat him, Peter didn't cry at first, but he did a little towards the end of it. I warned him that he would have double next time he did it, and he said he would never do it again.' No doubt the threat of twenty strokes with a rhino-hide whip was quite persuasive. Yet Grey and Peter, when grown men, had insisted on the essential kindliness of their father, and had told Patricia how he tried to make it up to them after he had whipped them. Grey was convinced that the force behind the whippings had been mother.

Some rumour of these events reached Arthur's bachelor brother Harry John at home in England, for Arthur wrote back to him, leaving a purple typescript copy in the letter file. 'Don't worry about my being too strict with the boys. Syria is certain I am much too easy-going. You know, one cannot let children of that age tease dangerous cows or try to hit big snakes, or risk their lives in other ways, without trying to impress on them that they will be punished for such things if they don't obey simple orders not to do them. Moreover, in my present circumstances, with children's clothes at the Bulawayo price, one cannot give a child a new outfit once a week because he insists on going through a barbed wire fence instead of round by the gate. Nor does one much like Peter, at the age of eight, to talk about "the damn old donkey'."

Syria and Arthur shared a phobia about swear words, and both had accepted whippings as part of the natural order of things. Syria was the youngest and favourite child of the Rector of Tunstall, and he called her Baby to the end of his long life, but the Bible had taught that the rod should not be spared. When Patricia commiserated with her mother about the beatings she had endured at the Rector's hand,

Syria turned on her sharply. 'He was perfectly right to do it,' she said, 'I thoroughly deserved it.'

The influences brought to bear on Arthur had been less forceful. His father had died when he was seven, and he had been brought up by his mother and several aunts, the youngest and much loved boy. It is unlikely that they ever whipped him. But they made some gesture towards instilling the moral precepts of the times. A child's story book had survived which reinforced them, a tattered volume which Arthur had inscribed in clear, childish writing, with his name and the date, 1884. He was ten years old. It was the story of *Blind Willie* by Catherine Crowe. Its rulings on Right and Wrong were severe. A well-to-do family, who live in a beautiful villa near London, receive their young, blind, and orphaned cousin to live with them. The blindness is the result of smallpox. The trials of life had already left their mark on Willie's nature, 'and no kind friend had ever taught him the necessity of subduing his sinful passions.'

On his arrival at Roselawn, three-year old Annie whispers loudly that she does not like him on account of his "gate white eyes." Her brother, cousin George, a fine, open-hearted little fellow, just eight years old, who was never in a bad humour, tries to heal the offence she has given to Willie. He unfortunately employs a tactic which has already caused his mother great distress. He does not always speak the truth. If he thinks he can save another child from punishment by telling a fib, he does so. His kind Mamma is very sorry to perceive this fault in her son, and points out to him the sinfulness of his conduct in the eyes of God. Just now he tells Willie that Annie has asked him to say she is sorry for having vexed him. As Willie can clearly hear her laughing in the background, this carries no conviction, and he bemoans the fact that no one cares for him. His young relatives hasten to assure him that they pity him.

Next day, Willie, who has disrupted his cousins' lessons, is scolded by Mamma. She dismisses his complaints about his blindness, saying, 'We cannot understand why God does everything, nor is it right that we should wish to know. But the Bible says, "Whom the Lord loveth, He chasteneth." Now Willie, the Lord has chastened you, and He has done it, undoubtedly, for some good purpose. Perhaps, if you could see, you would never think of turning to Him. You might live in neglect of your Bible, and at last die unrepentant and unforgiven. And then what follows? Endless punishment in the lake that burneth with fire and brimstone. Does not this prove that the Lord loves you? He has chastised you in mercy that you may remember that there is a home in Heaven where sorrow and sickness never enter.'

'I wish I was there,' murmured the boy.

'Perhaps you will have years of suffering and sorrow to undergo before that time arrives,' continues his mentor complacently. 'You must learn, dear Willie, to curb your sinful passions. Then, but not till then, you may be comparatively happy.'

Mamma then turns her attention to the cheerful George, whose conscience has nagged him into confessing that he lied to Willie the day before. 'I am very sorry you have been so wicked, George,' she says. 'I had hoped that you were nearly cured.'

'But I will be, dear Mamma, I will be cured of this fault. Only say that you forgive me!'

'How can I believe you?' she replies. 'You told me the very same thing last time. But I forgive you, and I hope He will too. A liar is certain of being hated and despised by his fellow men, and also of the wrath of God, in this world and the next. Pray every morning and evening for assistance.' Patricia found something almost endearing in the sudden descent from the moral to the banal when Mamma, having heard George promise that he would try always to deserve her praise, replies, 'Do, dearest, and remember that another Eye beside mine is upon you. Now go and put on your hat.'

George's chief joy is his dog Pluto. Mamma urges him to give the dog away, to see if he is capable of sacrifice. Having extracted this painful promise from him, this quirkish lady relents. But not for long. Pluto has accidentally, (it is to be hoped) swallowed poison, and George is called upon to pronounce the death sentence on him. It is his dog, so it is he who must take responsibility, and if he cannot bear to pronounce sentence, he will know he has condemned Pluto to die in agony.

They have to learn early, these children. Three-year-old Annie has her arm pinched hard by her mother to teach her not to tease spiders, accompanied by the taunt, 'I think Annie is a nasty ugly thing and I do not like her, so I will kill her.'

The baptism of a baby sister offers another lesson to be learnt by Catherine Crowe's young readers, an opportunity not to be wasted.

'Your little sister came into the world with a very wicked heart. When the clergyman took baby and sprinkled her face with water, he did it as a sign that God would wash that wicked heart in Christ's blood and make it fit for Heaven.'

There may have been little overt violence in Arthur's *Little Willie*, as there had been in the whippings at Tunstall Rectory, but the obsession with sin and punishment was much the same.

Arthur himself was the perfect mother's son. The youngest of five brothers, he was the straightest of the straight, and excelled at school. He was a particularly good shot, and appeared in browning photographs of the Shooting Eight for 1892 and 1894. He was the centre figure, holding the ball in the school Rugby team, he was the handsome Sergeant Pearson in the school Cadet Corps, wearing a peaked and sharply pointed helmet rather like that in the German Army. He was a solemn youth, with a heavy brow and a very direct expression. Some of the other boys wear a smirk, but not Arthur.

Syria and Arthur were now fighting, though not quite admitting it to each other, for financial survival. Labour relations were often a problem. Arthur, accustomed to the notoriously autocratic attitudes towards Africans in the Congo, had not come to terms with the proud Matabele tribesmen of Rhodesia, descendants of a warrior race, and traditional farmers in their own style, who formed the bulk of his work force. He and Syria seem to have regarded most of them as chronically lazy and mendacious. Arthur coolly recorded, 'Kicked Jim in the shin and hit him for a lie this morning.' It was the dogs-and-children, rough and ready treatment.

Constant minor thefts took place, despite the precautions Arthur took in locking up stores and implements. From time to time he searched the workers' compound, finding various missing objects that they had stolen, or perhaps merely borrowed from each other. After such occasions, they were rounded up and scolded. The industrious Syria, unable to make allowances for more easy-going characters, continued to lose patience with the servants. The two principal houseboys, Matthew and Barnabas, who had come with Arthur from the Belgian Congo, threatened to leave if they did not get a pay rise. They had a keen sense of fairness, and they complained that new workers were getting higher pay. Status differentials mattered. Syria showed a ruthless hand with one African who arrived late for work. She sacked him on the spot. Was it a coincidence that later that day the newly repaired plough broke down as soon as it was put to work again, and that a worker accidentally threw away six bags of selected mealies?

A chronic problem was ants, which continued to make their way into the house. Arthur burned sulphur under the spare room floorboards, and Syria creosoted the verandah.

Occasional respites remained to them; brief hours which they could enjoy together, as in the old days in the Congo. Six months after their arrival, they took the day off. Starting soon after dawn in the bullock-drawn wagon, they travelled to the annual Agricultural Show in Bulawayo. The Farm was showing mealie seed, oranges, lemons, grapefruit, tangerines and limes, and their mealie seed won a first prize. This was an opportunity to exchange ideas and experiences with other farmers. No one was having a good time, for rainfall had been the poorest on record, and their Farm, with its two springs, had fared better than many. Arthur and Syria lunched with Boomerang at the Grand Hotel, and were able to put their troubles behind them for a few hours.

There was another peaceful day a few weeks later. They went down their valley, and while he worked on fencing, she sat on her folding stool and sewed. There was always mending to be done, and the re-fashioning of new clothes from old for the children. Patricia recalled some of these creations, especially the heavy pique cotton frocks, encrusted with broderie anglaise, which had been made for her out of her mother's Edwardian afternoon dresses, and which hung so stiffly on her small frame.

Throughout the next months, many visitors came and went, some staying several nights. There were old friends from the Congo, and farmers from isolated homesteads who offered help and advice. They also offered cattle and farm equipment at bargain prices. Arthur continued to suspect that, as a novice farmer, he could easily be taken advantage of, and perhaps had been. But they all kept up a friendly front, and sustained as best they could a tradition of mutual support through hard times.

CHAPTER 5

The loss of an eye had not deprived Arthur of one of his greatest pleasures. He had been a keen shot and a hunter of big game, and he now found that he had not lost his skill with a gun. When he arrived in Africa at the beginning of the century, he had travelled much in the bush in the course of his medical duties among the copper-mining communities. His favourite mode of travel was by bicycle, riding with his heavy gun strapped to the bike, and accompanied by several Africans who jogged along on foot. He became adept at negotiating twisting native paths, where high elephant grass crowded in and sharp senses and quick reactions were vital. His first lion was very nearly his last, and he published a description of the encounter in *The Empire Review*, a popular journal of the day.

Descending a slope quite fast on his bicycle, he suddenly found himself almost on top of a lion and his mate who were lying in the grass to the right of the path, and within a couple of yards of it. The animals and he caught sight of each other simultaneously, and the pair sprang up with deep growls, looking at him. He dismounted and tore at the straps fastening the rifle to the machine. Fortunately for him the lions decided not to take the encounter any further, and, still growling, turned away. He thought later that it was the bicycle that had put them off the attack. His Africans were still well behind him along the path. He glimpsed the lion, now separated from his mate, at the summit of a nearby ridge. He assumed the lioness would be close at hand and decided to follow the spoor to try for a shot. Suddenly he heard deep grunts behind him and turning, saw the lioness coming at him at full speed. He dropped to one knee and aimed at her chest. She fell, but got up again. Then he heard the voices of his Africans nearby. The lioness made off into the long grass. To his alarm the Africans appeared and started running in the direction where she had first fallen. Arthur tried in three different dialects to call them back, but they did not understand his warning. He ran towards them and at that moment the lioness came out, with hair bristling and retracted snarling lips, showing her great fangs. The farthest men shinned up their nearest trees, but she leapt upon the third and pinned him, screaming, down. Arthur was afraid of hitting the wrong target, but aimed high at her shoulder, hoping for the spine.

She rolled off the youth and lay motionless. Arthur pulled him up and told him to run up a tree, which he did, despite his injuries Arthur then climbed up another tree, and, uncertain whether the beast was yet dead, fired another shot at her. Coming down from his perch he ascertained that she was lifeless. All the Africans came off their trees except the injured one, and Arthur had to go over and coax him down personally. One blow of a paw had broken his shoulder bone, into which the mighty claws had dug deep. Within six weeks the wound had healed.

Other big game adventures published by Arthur in *The Empire Review* were all somewhat in the style of boys' magazines. When Patricia was about six, Syria used to read them to her after tea, when, as often as not, Patricia was seated on a low native stool on the skin of that very lioness, now a truncated mat, for while it hung out to dry, a leopard had taken off the head and a hyena the tail.

It would be at least another half century before animal numbers became so decimated that there was a reversal of attitudes towards big game hunting. All the same, while proud of the Big Game Hunter who had been her father, Patricia used to feel a pang as she looked through albums full of browning snapshots of him and his native helpers, all posed proudly around the corpses of dead animals. Her mother told of how she had once tried to become a hunter too. She aimed at an impala, but on seeing it brought down by her shot, she had uncharacteristically burst into tears, and run behind a boulder. She never tried again.

Big game seldom came near Gaveston now, but there were many deadly snakes, and there was an abundance of bird life. Arthur was elated to discover that his aim had not been impaired, and nearly every day he brought home pheasant, guinea fowl, and pigeon for the pot. Sometimes he bagged a hare.

August 22nd was Patricia's first birthday, and as her brothers' birthdays were also in August, they were all celebrated together on the same day. Grey's feelings about his sister were lukewarm. He had been told to expect a special present for his birthday, which was on

August 23rd. He had been asking for a clockwork train, so his disappointment on being presented with Patricia was keen.

On this three-in-one birthday, Arthur and Syria took their sons for a walk around the farmlands, and the boys showed them an African eagle's nest which they had found. Arthur fostered Grey's growing interest in birds and noted: 'Grey is certainly going to be a bird naturalist of some standing. His knowledge of birds is uncanny at his age.' In the afternoon the children were, for once, allowed into the kitchen to help make sweets and cakes. It was a happy day, but typically, that very night, troubles bore down again. A cow had started to give birth in the morning, but had made no progress by nightfall, despite Arthur's efforts to help her. She groaned all night, so at dawn Arthur took up his gun and shot her. The calf would have been a fine little Hereford bull.

Making renewed efforts to run his disastrous farm at a profit, Arthur consulted a soil erosion expert who suggested a system of shallow trenches gently sloping downwards from the long hill. Gums to provide shade for cattle would be planted in the centre of the valley meadow. Arthur also went exhaustively into the choice of crops.

Soil analysis had shown a deficiency of phosphates, but the remedy recommended by the expert was not, as Arthur had supposed, artificial phosphates, but a rotation of crops, to include a sequence of maize, velvet beans, monkey nuts, sunflowers, and sweet potatoes. But Arthur was not hopeful. An acquaintance in Bulawayo, fresh out from England, a young man with three small children, asked Arthur if he could recommend him to go ahead with the purchase of a farm on a working capital of £3,000. 'You might as well commit suicide,' was Arthur's ominous reply. He was speculating now in terms of ten years ahead, although fearing that it might soon become necessary to sell up and turn to doctoring full time in Elizabethville.

He had never worked in an ordinary practice and harboured doubts as to whether a doctor with a glass eye would be acceptable, especially to the women patients. But a partnership had already been offered to him by a colleague practising in the town. He was not much drawn to the idea. It would be very different from work in the wilds, and he felt reluctant to embark on this kind of doctoring.

Another problem for Arthur was that he was not used to seeing himself as a man who made errors of judgment. He had become something of a model for his colleagues. He could be relied on not to make mistakes, and was generally respected. Some, Patricia's mother had hinted to her, had even spoken of him as a possible future leader of his country when it came to the self government that was being planned for Southern Rhodesia. But now, with a growing family and a fourth child on the way, he had to accept that this time he had made a serious mistake. He had set out, insufficiently capitalised, to start farming, about which he knew nothing, in a country which was new to him. As was his way, he had done all that doggedness and determination could do, but in vain. Back and forth he footslogged on his unrewarding territory, his boots wearing out, and unable to afford a new pair, calculating the cost of cattle feed, mealie seed, the planting of eucalyptus trees, the possibility of more intensive dairy farming; still hoping that he would not have to admit defeat. He had not realised when he bought the Farm that it was situated in a region where the rainy season often failed, causing havoc to crops and cattle. If he had chosen the Eastern Highlands, where the climate was similar to that in Britain, matters might have turned out very differently.

He tried to joke it off in letters to England. 'The old oxen are deciding that life is not worth the living, and anything young with a poor constitution has also come to the conclusion that it is not worthy of a place here.' To his brother Harry John he wrote more confidentially, 'Cattle are dying all over the country. As it is quite likely to be two months before we get any rain, I may lose half my stock. I bought at the wrong time, as many another man has done. We make nothing on fowls and vegetables, and our pigs cost us about twice as much as they fetch. Everything is at bottom level.' In his diary he admitted that he was very worried indeed as to how they were going to get any sort of income out of farming.

CHAPTER 6

Miss McLeod suddenly confirmed her threatened intention to leave within the next two or three weeks. She and Syria still sat in silence most afternoons and evenings, sewing and mending. Miss McLeod was proving a dismayingly determined person, who insisted that since her health was being undermined by work conditions, and her nerves affected by Patricia's constant crying, she would not be well enough to go straight to another job when she left the Farm.

She would, of course, seek medical advice, but if the assessment of her health proved as she expected, she would decline to pay a penny towards the cost of her fare from England. She considered she had given them good value for their money anyway. She had worked extremely hard, had virtually no holiday, and had had sole responsibility for the children much of the time.

Syria accused her of dishonourable behaviour, but Miss McLeod had become strangely impervious to Syria's disapproval. A few days after their second Christmas, she left the Farm after an unpleasant exchange the day before, when Syria had told her that neither she nor Arthur wished to have anything further to do with her, and forbade her to have any more contact with their children. Since there were barely twelve hours left for Miss McLeod under their roof, this penalty could have had a limited effect. These disturbances did not make life any easier for Arthur. But he cast no blame on Syria. It suited them both that he readily accepted her point of view.

After Miss McLeod's unhonoured early morning exit, Arthur and Syria were left alone with their children for three whole days. Nothing like it had ever happened to them before. They did their best. Conscientiously, they woke up sixteen-month-old Patricia, day and night, at prescribed intervals, to give her bottles of Glaxo milk mixture, which she angrily rejected. They laid her down in a darkened room for long afternoon rests which brought on noisy protests. Glaxo, in addition to a variety of laxatives, still constituted her main diet. Arthur was worried and annoyed at her refusal to accept the proffered bottles. They gave her cups instead, and she threw them on the floor. They took it in turns to mind her, and this interfered with Arthur's farmwork. They tried to bath her in the big galvanised iron bathtub, and she screamed again until Arthur found a way round this by putting a flower in the water. They inspected her excrement and found it defective, and gave, listed carefully in Arthur's diary, first magnesia, then grey powders, and finally castor oil. This produced a prolapse of the bowel, her third, for she had had two previously while in Miss McLeod's care.

Constipation re-establishing itself, Arthur gave his daughter another enema and recorded with puzzlement, 'Her condition must be far from right.'

Patricia often perplexed Arthur and caused him loss of sleep, yet he was captivated by her baby ways. He wrote fondly about her to his mother in England; 'She has a portion of the verandah to play in, and she and Peter play hide and seek. One hears all the time the pit-pat of her feet and a constant series of joyous squeaks. It is the funniest sight to see Patty hiding. If her face is round a corner, she considers she is hidden, no matter where her body is. She has a little basket which she takes round everywhere, and collects things. Our diary, a packet of envelopes, or Peter's boots - anything goes in there and is conveyed to some secret spot. She talks quite a lot now. "Pinkie," her favourite plaything, is a shawl, and she drapes it round her neck and minces up and down like a Bond Street shopper swanking. When she gets angry she beats us and throws things at us. She swears sometimes. Also, when she has had enough milk, she throws the cup on the ground as far away as possible, and then looks round and says, "No! No!" in a very severe manner, before anyone else can say it.

She is quite happy with a "book," which is generally a trade catalogue, and sits down on a little stool and reads it very gravely out loud, generally upside down. She often has a ride on the donkey. She sits in her cot in the afternoon and preaches sermons to the pictures on the wall.

I jammed a finger in the door just beyond the nail. Of course I sat on the floor and screamed, till Patricia came up and kissed it. I suppose she is like any other kid at her age.' Arthur was discovering for the first time what a kid of that age was like.

He often carried her with him on his long rounds of the farmlands.

Patricia pondered these long-ago happenings, and cursed the amnesia of early childhood which had stolen all these memories away from her.

On the day that the new nurse-governess arrived, Patricia was in temperamental mood again, and Miss Arrowsmith's first night at the Farm was punctuated by her maddening screams. It was soon clear that Miss Arrowsmith, like her predecessor, was better suited to older children and did not care much for babies. She put a cheerful face on things to begin with. Grey and Peter soon came to like her. She was a sociable, outdoor type of young woman who enjoyed riding and meeting people. But life for the boys continued to have its ups and downs. One morning Peter told no less than two lies about cleaning his teeth. Caught out and punished for this, his nerves gave way and he collapsed into one of the uncontrollable screaming fits he had been going in for lately. Grey, the apparently unheeding, pursued the absent-minded course which so infuriated his mother. She was convinced that he lost things on purpose to annoy. Even his constipation seemed deliberate, so stubborn that purgatives and enemas had little effect. Sometimes he annoyed both parents by dawdling over the chicken feed and not getting back to the house till eight o'clock. He seemed not to notice the irritation he caused.

Syria suddenly forbade Peter to help with the fowls any more. He had confidingly told her of the nice times he had been having with the African boy Waili at the hen coops. Waili had been so friendly and had lifted him up and told him all sorts of interesting things. Syria, unlike many white settler mothers, did not allow her children to have ordinary informal contact with natives. So Peter, without knowing why, lost his new black friend.

Syria and Arthur now decided that the time had come for Grey to be sent away to boarding school, to be pulled into better shape. He was despatched in mid-January to a boys' prep school some miles away on the other side of Bulawayo, and soon reported back by badly written letter on his unhappiness there. His parents read this as evidence that the medicine was working. He would soon get over his homesickness and school would make a man of him. Ironically, the last thing that Arthur needed at this time was the burden of school fees, and they faced together the fact that, after barely a year of struggling with difficulties they had never anticipated, they would have to sell. They began to discuss with the ever-helpful Boomerang who knew everyone in Bulawayo, the business of finding a buyer. It was all proving too much; the prolonged drought, the constant pathetic deaths of their ailing livestock, the breakdown of second-hand equipment, the petty thefts, the unrewarding labour for them both, in their attempt to wring some return out of the land. Their financial base was turning out to be seriously inadequate. Syria's pregnancy, coupled with her lack of affinity with the labour force, were further problems. They had trusted in the simple principle that hard work is crowned with success. They had worked incessantly and were confronting failure. It was essential to provide for their family, the years of carefree fostering on grandparents half a world away were over. Life was no longer a pioneering trek together in the wilds.

So they prepared a retreat. Arthur felt he had no alternative but to follow up the plan of a general practice partnership with his friend in Elizabethville, though with misgivings. He was desperately tired, and plagued with headaches.

CHAPTER 7

Syria and the new nurse-governess soon got across each other. Miss Arrowsmith showed the same signs of independence that had so irked Syria before. She was also following the fatal path of friendship with neighbour Mrs. Turner.

One of the puppies disappeared. The surviving one, now almost fully grown, continued to attract ever more desperate penalties. Beatings had not cured him of eating eggs. He had even been caught recently with a china egg. Syria persevered with pushing a scalding hot egg into his mouth and holding it closed, but he seemed to have developed an immunity to punishment. He moved on to eating two eggs at a time. He was beaten, chained up, and given a mustard egg. Curiously, it never occurred to his owners to supplement his diet. A couple of weeks later, Arthur noted that the dog had begun to have spells of paralysis in the legs. No more is recorded about this unfortunate creature. Probably Arthur shot it.

A more serious threat to egg production came from a snake which was getting into the hens' enclosure and killing the chicks. Syria moved the coops to another position. Peter was still required to carry out his set tasks with the chickens, but punctiliousness had never been his strong point. Arthur recorded briefly, 'Peter had to be shut up as a punishment for disobedience and rudeness re his nesting boxes.' Peter's aversion to these particular duties was chronic. One disastrous morning he managed to break all the eggs he had collected. Two days later he cried because he had to go to the fowls barefoot, on account of his having gone out in his only pair of boots before breakfast when told not to. In view of the proximity of snakes, this seems to have been a hazardous punishment.

There was fractiousness all round. The governess was found crying one morning because Patricia had howled for half an hour, and she didn't think she could stand any more of it.

Minor disasters, and not such minor ones, followed each other. Cattle broke into the cement at the water dip as it had not been laid in accordance with Arthur's instructions. The livestock continued to sicken and die. Spring hares got into the monkey nuts. Peter on his morning round found a cobra half inside a chicken coop. Syria's horse got the strangles. Farm machinery disintegrated. Nails turned up mysteriously in the mealie seed corn Arthur sent to market. This really pained him, for it seemed to cast a shadow on his integrity. Was it the revenge of some disaffected farmworker? The 'boys' were always muddling their orders. Arthur went the rounds at least twice on most days to follow them up.

Early in March there came a break for him, when he had to leave again for a fortnight's duties in the Congo. This was now his only dependable source of income, and the change of scene and encounters with old friends were what he needed. As she had done previously, Syria proved herself an industrious steward She was now nearly seven months pregnant, but she was up and out at dawn, unlocking and giving out farm equipment, packing fruit for the Bulawayo market, scolding, chivvying and supervising. She was wryly amused when Matthew confided to her that her special name among the Africans was, "Grumbling Mumma." Grumbling was, as she saw it, her duty, but she found humour in the nickname, and she was fond of Matthew, whose work she seldom felt moved to grumble about.

During Arthur's absence, the rain fell at last, and heavily. The wind blew strongly and the water windmill began to lean sideways. In the night the kitchen chimney fell in, and the wall with it. First aid repairs were carried out next day by Mr. Turner.

Matters were not helped by Patricia's refusal to go to sleep in the morning and most of the afternoon. Syria regarded sleep for most of the twenty-four hours as a young child's proper duty towards its parents. It was certainly a convenient one. Patricia was now eighteen months old: and by dint of incessant noisy protest and digestive upsets she was getting her way over the daily stream of Glaxo. But too much pram and cot and insufficient exercise were getting on her nerves. This added to the discomforts of the household, and of her exasperated young nurse. Syria herself had had no experience of babies or toddlers. Routine and discipline were, she knew, necessary in any situation involving children, but it worried her that her daughter cried so much, and she began to have doubts about the nurse's handling of her.

Arthur had a good break on the Congo trip with his old friend and colleague Mr Moore, familiarly known by his African name of Kasempa. There was a brotherly affection between them of many years' standing. Kasempa and his cheerful wife were certainly not teetotallers, and Arthur felt free to enjoy a few drinks with them. Syria did not approve of strong drink and had always done her best to rescue Arthur from his sundowner habit. Now he seldom indulged at home. Not long before this trip, Arthur had typed a letter to his friend, leaving a telltale little purple typescript copy which Syria must surely have overlooked. She would not knowingly have allowed it to survive. It contained a strangely equivocal little passage in which the facetious element fails to disguise some resentment at her attempts to reform him. It would have cast a shadow across her firmly sustained ideal of their perfect marriage, where both thought and acted as one. 'Yes, my wife has the frozen aspect these days. It used to be a word and a blow, but now it is a blow and several words. This is since someone (was it you?) wrote and told her that you and I carried on something shameful with the booze when I found you alone at Panda. I scarcely dare say a word now. Only yesterday she threw the cat at me because I suggested that all eggs sent into town for sale must be absolutely fresh to maintain a good name for the place. She then laid me out with a letter weight.'

At dinner in the Club one evening, Arthur noted down Mrs Moore's drink score, intrigued doubtless by the contrast with Syria. She got through a sherry, a whisky, some Chablis, a glass of champagne, and finally a glass of beer. She would outlive them all.

When away from his depressing farm and in the company of old friends, Arthur's hopes of financial survival rose. He discussed with Kasempa the feasibility of sending frozen meat from Rhodesia to the Congo. There was also the matter of several terraced houses he had invested in at Sea Point, Cape Town. On this Congo trip he met a similar investor who had just turned down what seemed a very good offer of £2,000 each for his houses, thinking that much more could soon be asked for them. The area was destined to become a goldmine for investors later on. It was part of the irony that haunted Arthur's financial speculations that after his death his Sea Point property, as well as the Farm, were to slip through Syria's fingers, profitless, at the time of the thirties slump.

When he went home, he forgot to take with him a small piece of uranium ore which Kasempa had given him as a curiosity. It was then worth ten shillings (fifty pence) a pound, A Greek was reported to have stored six sacks of this ore, worth about £450, in his house. He got a prison sentence of six months for this illegal appropriation from the mine.

Arthur arrived back at Gaveston in mid-March, the start of the cool season. He came at lunchtime, and after the meal he lay down while Syria unpacked his things. Then they walked round the farmlands together, inspecting the new gum plantation, the cattle, the pigs, the mealies, and the broken windmill.

They climbed to a lonely spot about a quarter of a mile away from the house, where Arthur remarked that it would be a wonderful place to lie forever. It was at the top of a lightly-wooded hill, overlooking many miles of Matabeleland. The muted golds and soft greens of the veldt faded into misty distances. He was only forty-six, yet premonitions of separation and untimely death seem to have haunted them both. They had covered this ground as far back as the first year of their marriage, when Arthur, had written to Syria in his blunt, straightforward way: 'I think when a man has done his best for others throughout his life, the approach of the Great Reaper cannot really hold terrors for him. The only terror in death must be the parting from those he loves, and it is for such a little time. When we think of eternity, such a very little time. Somewhere, somehow, wherever the first has gone, the second will follow. One of the fundamental laws of science is that matter is indestructible; it can only change its form, and the spirit is certainly greater than matter. Your talk of separation makes me write this. To the one who lives, there will be no longer any fear of death, for death will offer the best chance of re-union. To the one who goes first, the thought is more terrible, but some consolation arises in the belief which seems natural to us and which is expressed in the Bible that after death there can be no more Time. "A thousand years is as a day." If this is so, there is almost no separation for the first one to go. It could be but momentary. So it would seem that the first one to go has the easier part. I write of this because you do. But we may hope for long years, and with their advent, riper thoughts.'

Patricia was touched by Arthur's ingenious arguments for allaying Syria's anxieties. Yet this early preoccupation with death seems strange. Strangest of all was a dream Arthur had recorded in which he was forcibly pushed into a van labelled "Death." Arthur's father had died when he was a young boy of seven. Syria had gone short on the care of her own mother through invalidism. So they may both have experienced a heightened fear of loss.

Syria cut the paragraphs out of Arthur's letters, together with the description of his dream, and kept them hidden away all her life. When she was eighty-three, and a few months before her own death, after a long life of remarriage, stepchildren, a second widowhood, and all the tribulations which her unbending character had drawn down upon her, Syria told Patricia, in a rare moment of confidence, that once more, after a silence of many years, Arthur was visiting her in her dreams.

During the next week Arthur was busy with a hundred things. Repairs to the windmill and the damaged kitchen roof were put in hand. There was a long report to be written on his Congo inspections. There were accounts to be brought up to date. There were arrangements to be made to help a recently widowed sister-in-law in Cape Town who had been left almost penniless by the long illness and death of Arthur's eldest brother. Arthur felt it to be his family duty to contribute what he could in the way of financial help, and to persuade her reluctant brother to do the same. He outlined to her plans to get her two daughters started in nursing training.

On the Farm there was haymaking to superintend on top of the usual duties. Heavy rains had now set in, making walking around the lands a sticky business. Arthur remarked to Syria that soon they would need fires in the house. There were hundreds of mealie cobs to be set out to dry when the sun shone. He developed a sore throat and made himself up some medicine, thinking he might have a touch of malaria. It did not occur to him, nor would it have done to anyone else, to connect his malaise with the small piece of uranium ore that he had carried around in his pocket for several days, and then forgotten to bring home. He needed to rest, but there was no time.

There were some mealie cobs remaining in the nine-foot cylindrical silo near the farm buildings, and these Arthur decided to clear out completely on March 26th. It would be about half a day's work. There was access to the mealies via a small trapdoor at the base, through which they could be raked out, or through an opening from the top of the silo whence a vertical steel ladder led down to the floor inside. Arthur decided to clear the remaining mealies with a native helper via the top opening.

He had had time to write one more letter home to his sister in England which overflowed with his pride and delight in Patricia. 'She is a remarkably happy baby, regarding everything as a huge joke. She maintains an angelic outlook on life and is always happy. She is a great pleasure to us all. She is a very cheery little soul and can amuse herself for hours with her playbox toys, talking to herself and them. Her little tricks of speech and imitation give us lots of fun. She loves animals and has no fear of them, but is afraid of motor cars. She likes a rough and tumble with Peter too. It is difficult to teach her not to do a thing which is prohibited, as she thinks it a great joke to imitate her instructress and look severe and say "No!" with a sharp toss of her head. Then when she has made us laugh, she drops the stern manner and laughs herself.' Ordinary, loving descriptions of an ordinary, happy child, thought Patricia. She could not see anything in common between the way her father saw her and the unpleasing impression she had left upon her nurses.

She was also pleased to read on and discover that her usual place at mealtimes had been beside Arthur. He had obviously been a friendly neighbour.

Peter as well as Patricia must have been happy to have their father home again. While he was away. Syria had made Peter write Arthur a letter, and had felt compelled by stern principles to punish him for crying and messing it up. He had had to write out Lines. This was a tedious form of punishment in which the miscreant had to copy out some short, moralistic phrase over and over again. In this case the "Line" would have taken some such form as 'I must take more trouble,' or 'I must not lose my temper.'

Arthur's personal diary ends on March 25th, but for the next day Syria takes it up in his voice, although for style and content, it is quite different from what went before. It is as though she felt herself to be so completely Arthur's alter ego that they still thought as one. And so, for March 26th, it was granted to Arthur to speak from beyond the grave. The entire journal is, in fact, in Syria's handwriting. She had copied Arthur's original so as to be able to censor out any parts which she wished no one to see. The last of "his" jottings for the 26th anticipates a storm with Miss Arrowsmith:

'Miss Arrowsmith practically gave Syria notice this morning. Upset Syria very much. Syria meant to tell me this later on in the day.'

The diary for March 26th finally gives up the pretence of writing in Arthur's name, and Syria takes over:

'Re Peter: the schoolroom doorweight fell on his fingers and he was screaming. Arthur teased him by saying, "Baby, Baby Bunting!" It was good for Peter. They were his Daddy's last words to him. At Arthur's last breakfast with me, he had picked Patricia out of her playpen and put her on his knee while he had his breakfast. I remember so well his looking over to me in a mischievous way, as though he expected me to scold him. But I didn't.' Syria probably had a 'rule' about not taking toddlers out of playpens. She clearly felt glad that this time she had been forbearing. She kissed him as he left the house, a memory she treasured, and he told her he would be back at about 12.30, and that in the afternoon they might drive together to Bulawayo, taking guavas to market.

He went to the silo and let the native boy Joe down through the trapdoor from the top. He had not reckoned with the poisonous carbon monoxide gas that had accumulated beneath the last mealies at the bottom of the tank. Joe began to lose consciousness, panicked, and called up that he was dying. Arthur squeezed his head and broad shoulders through the narrow top aperture, and tried to pass a rope down to Joe who was already recovering consciousness now that the ground level aperture had been opened and was letting in fresh air. In his attempts to assist Joe, Arthur fell in himself. Perhaps one-eyed vision interfered with his sense of distance and space in that upside-down position. He crashed headfirst onto the floor with such force that his glass eye fell out and he broke his neck. He probably died instantaneously from the fall, but it seemed at first that he had merely lost consciousness as Joe had done.

Africans came running to the house in great agitation, calling for Syria, who ran out to the silo, sized up the situation and at once made the native carpenter enlarge the hole at the top. She then got two men to haul her up to the aperture and lowered herself into the silo down the vertical ladder, quite a feat for a woman seven months pregnant. Arthur lay on his face, with Joe unconscious beside him. The air in the tank was still bad but the fumes were dispersing. Syria fastened a rope round Arthur's waist and he was hauled out, and after him the unconscious Joe, who soon recovered. Arthur was laid down and for the next five and a half hours Syria worked in relay with Mary Arrowsmith in an ever more despairing attempt to bring him round by artificial respiration. Dr. Travers arrived late in the afternoon from Bulawayo, examined Arthur, and pronounced him dead. His neck was broken and he must have died instantly. He was laid under the kitchen table, and there Peter, overlooked in those hours of catastrophe, found him as he wandered around, frightened by the cries of the servants, the absence of his mother and his governess. He must have been hungry too, so into the kitchen he went. He saw his father lying prone under the table, and then he understood what the servants were calling out to each other: 'Bwana is dead. The Master is dead.' A lifetime later he recalled to Patricia, 'You can imagine, I felt pretty low.'

Arthur was buried the following afternoon in the place on the wooded hill where he and Syria had paused on their walk a week ago. It was a bare twenty-eight hours after his last job on the farm. Syria had packed Peter off to stay with the Turners and then, unable to sleep, had sat up writing letters until dawn. To her mother in Suffolk, she wrote a perfectly clear, detailed description of the whole event. She was already outlining practical plans for coping, and for staying on for as long as it should take to sell the Farm, though, 'I would like to leave this place of tragedy at once. I hate it. But I should lose a lot by a forced sale.' She cannot sleep in their bedroom any more, 'That big, lonely room would drive me mad.' She goes on: 'Poor little children. I can only just manage to mother them, and shall make a poor father too.'

She is thankful that death must have been instantaneous. 'No pain, no thoughts of anxiety. For these two only comforts I do thank God, I only hope his spirit is not now suffering for us. I cannot bear to think it is. His sweetness deserves only rest and peace now, after all the worries we have had. There are no more for him.' The letter has the ring of disinterested love, and a powerful determination, from the first, to carry on.

A small party of mourners arrived next day for the funeral, together with the local magistrate, a white policeman, a native interpreter, and Archdeacon Harker, who would conduct the service. The legal formalities were first completed. One of the Africans who had been present at the scene of death gave official evidence which was duly recorded before the magistrate, and the Archdeacon then preceded the heavy coffin to the grave. Twenty-four Africans took part in getting it there, with frequent changes up the steep hill path. Syria must have found the procession not unlike that of Cecil Rhodes to his lonely grave in the Matopo Hills, twenty-one years ago. Rhodes, too, had died on March 26th, and had been carried in procession by African bearers.

So Arthur was committed to rest in the African earth to which he had been so strongly drawn, which had cost him so much fruitless labour and finally his life. The solemn words from the Book of Common Prayer were uttered and drifted away over the land that had defeated him. 'I am the Resurrection and the Life. He that believeth in me, though he were dead, yet shall he live.'

Whatever Arthur's beliefs were, they must have been those of a straight and uncomplicated man.

That evening, after the grave had been filled in, Syria made her solitary way back to it, and personally arranged the wreaths over it. Peter was brought home from the Turners next morning, and Syria at once took him up there. 'Peter,' she wrote in her diary, 'cried very bitterly, and was so sweet, yet so practical.' Two days later, Grey arrived back from his boarding school, to pay his respects to his dead father.

'Is there nothing we can do to bring him back?' he asked his mother.

'Nothing,' she replied. 'Nothing at all.'

'I feel only half,' said Grey.

CHAPTER 8

Syria immersed herself in a frenzy of letter writing and farmwork. The packing and despatch of produce for market, and details of her medical attentions to the workers were meticulously recorded in the Farm logbook. Some ailments were not so minor. One youth developed diphtheria.

She was as stern with them as ever, probably more so. An inefficient worker was sacked on the spot. He had been one of those who had given evidence to the magistrate before the funeral. The Farm diary carried on exactly as before, with no hint of what had happened. She was still Arthur's steward, as she had been a month earlier when he was away in Katanga. There were complex business matters to attend to in Bulawayo. The pressure of all this deadened feeling. She had not yet reached full awareness of what had happened to her, of how her life in the future was going to be completely different. It was as though she had struggled up after a blow that had almost felled her, and was carrying on in a daze. Routine had always been important to her, now it was essential. Feeling was deadened, but not for long. Years later she told Patricia that on the day of Arthur's death, Patricia had cried uncontrollably for a long time. For several hours no one could spare a minute for her. But at last Syria was able to go to her and picking her up, she walked round with her in her arms trying to soothe her, and this, she said, had given her something so immediate and ordinary to do that it had carried her through the last hours of that long day.

From now on and for many months, Syria avoided the bedroom she had shared with Arthur and slept with Patricia in the night nursery. She also made permanent arrangements for Arthur's two trusties from the Congo, Matthew and Barnabas, to sleep in the kitchen at night. Except when one of their old friends came to stay, Syria, Mary Arrowsmith, Patricia and Peter were alone with their native workforce in the comparative isolation of the Farm.

Friends were greatly shocked by Arthur's untimely death. It was ironic that the seminal work on modern hygiene standards in native mining compounds over which he had laboured for years in collaboration with a Belgian doctor, was published in almost the same week as his death. He never saw it. Reviews in the medical journals were laudatory and it was recommended by the London School of Tropical Medicine for its practical approach. The book continued to sell until the last copies were demolished in the London Blitz of 1941. Obituaries in the British Medical Journal for May 26th 1923 and the Pall Mall Gazette of April 17th, followed close upon the book reviews. That in the B.M.J. must have been written by a close admirer. It recognises Arthur's medical achievement, but gives a particularly glowing account of his personality. It was probably from the pen of Dr David Forsyth, one of the earliest British psychoanalysts, who had once tried, though unsuccessfully, to persuade Arthur to share his psychoanalytic interests. He wrote to Syria: 'How very deeply I feel for you. Arthur was my oldest and best friend. I know what a fine and loveable character he had, and I think I can understand what his death must mean to you.' He offered his help in any way possible: 'I shall be only too happy to do anything in my power, in memory of so dear a friend.'

Syria had helpers nearer at hand. In addition to the Turners, to whom she could and did turn at any time for practical aid with broken or heavy machinery, there were relatives in the Katanga and friends such as Boomerang, who came to stay now and again, relieving her loneliness and advising on financial matters, all of which had previously been dealt with by Arthur. Her own youngest brother, Oswald, a strange, maverick person, part priest, part unpractising doctor, arrived from the Katanga. Syria's brother-in-law, George Watson, a mining engineer with the Union Miniere, hatched up a scheme whereby his wife, May, Arthur's youngest sister, would come and stay with Syria for six months to keep her company, while Oswald would step into Arthur's shoes in the Mining Inspectorate, and, himself a doctor, albeit an unpractised one, would earn for Syria what Arthur would have earned. This chivalrous plan was rejected at once by Syria. 'I would not have this for anything,' was her tart comment.

As for accepting May as a companion, that was completely out of the question. There had always been a coldness between the two. May could not understand the rigorous personality of the woman her favourite brother had chosen to marry, and Syria had no intention of sharing her mourning with Arthur's sister.

She was stunned for weeks. Throwing herself into hard work as she did, she became rather too busy. She strove to direct personally every activity undertaken on the Farm. As this was impossible, her inability to delegate led to troubles with her workers, though there was a short period of truce immediately after Arthur's death. She found time every day to cut fresh flowers and take them up to The Hill, as the place of Arthur's grave was now called. Miss Arrowsmith had for the time being given up complaining about the hardships of her working day. She ceased to threaten notice and consented to stay on for another year. Syria planned to take over most of the care of Patricia, handing the infant soon to be born over to a second nurse. This would clearly be facilitated if Patricia would obligingly spend the greater part of the twenty-four hours asleep. Syria would do all in her power to bring this about. Grey could then be brought home from his expensive boarding school and taught with Peter by Miss Arrowsmith.

Three weeks after Arthur's death, Syria received from Grey what she described tersely as a very poor letter. He had absent-mindedly begun it "Dear Mummie and Daddy". She wrote to the Headmaster to complain of her son's thoughtlessness and their omission in not having noticed it, and Grey received a reprimand from the Head.

She began to emerge painfully from her numbed state. Relations with Miss Arrowsmith and Turner deteriorated. Miss Arrowsmith, a sociable soul and oppressed by the mood at the Farm, spent every bit of her spare time with the Turners. On one occasion she had had to spend a night alone with her charges at the Farm while Syria was away on business in Bulawayo. The day after Syria's return from her night out, Mr. Turner came over and after some embarrassed delay, when it was not clear to Syria why he had come, he gave her advice about not leaving Miss Arrowsmith alone at night. Syria got on her high horse. 'I told him that no one need worry as to that, that I had lived twelve years in Africa and quite understood the conditions, and should no more dream of leaving Miss Arrowsmith to sleep here alone than I would do so myself.'

Patricia had been surprised to read this, for her mother had always treated lying as a deadly sin. Yet her diary for the previous day clearly records her night spent away in Bulawayo. It was of course a sophistry. Miss Arrowsmith had not been left literally alone in the house, for Matthew or Barnabas would have been on guard in the kitchen. But Syria must have known perfectly well that a young woman, fresh from England, would feel alone and nervous in such circumstances. Unlike Syria, she had not known Matthew and Barnabas for twelve years.

Turner was not reassured by the response he had had from Syria, and two days later, she received from him a letter, the content of which she did not commit to her diary, but it greatly offended her, and she noted haughtily, 'I have filed it, a rude letter and in bad taste. It has resulted in my deciding to do without his assistance in the future.' It was a hasty decision, and one which she was soon forced to break. For the present, she took on another worker, a European named Geoffrey Carter, young, and as it soon turned out, inexperienced.

That same week, Miss Arrowsmith broke down once more, complaining at having to call Peter at six thirty in the morning. Syria, never one for compromise, stated simply that she liked Peter to get up at six thirty. Miss Arrowsmith retorted that she thought it made life a perfect toil. Later, noted Syria, she apologised for being rude. Outspokenness always spelt rudeness to her.

At the end of this trying week, Miss Arrowsmith asked permission to go away for a weekend, saying that she felt she needed a break. Grudgingly Syria let her go, but considered the request unreasonable for Miss Arrowsmith had already been away twice in less than four months. Her other helper, the white overseer Carter, was also not reaching the expected standard. He had taken over some of the duties Syria had been shouldering, and was not doing them well enough. He unlocked the tool store and forgot to lock it up again afterwards, thereby running the risk of pilfering. He was also, she felt, too familiar with the native workers; how therefore, she asked, could they respect him? Worst of all, he was showing signs of closer friendliness towards Miss Arrowsmith, and would wander into the schoolroom for a chat with her. Peter, who had earlier discovered how to earn favour with his mother by sneaking on the puppy's misdemeanours, now sneaked on Carter who received such a dressing down that, observed Syria, he nearly cried.

Three weeks before the birth of her youngest child, Syria suffered from false labour pains. This followed upon a particularly bad night. The African wagon-drivers had returned drunk at midnight from Bulawayo and were making so much noise that Syria became alarmed and went to wake Barnabas who was asleep in the kitchen. Nothing more happened, but Syria could not stay in her bed and finished the night on the sittingroom sofa. There were to be other such nights, the labour pains passed off next day, but the episode unnerved her.

More trouble brewed with Miss Arrowsmith. Syria ordered her to report back if Carter continued to call upon her in the schoolroom, but recorded, 'She rather plainly showed she disapproved of the rule.' That night they fell out over Patricia's sleeping times She was refusing to spend two hours in the morning and another two hours in the afternoon asleep, on top of a very extended night. She was now coming up to two years old, an active and observant child, and a lively talker, as her father had noticed several weeks before. She needed more exercise and more company, but Syria needed her to go to sleep, and looked to Miss Arrowsmith to arrange this. Patricia had become a fractious challenge to her exasperated nurse. When Miss Arrowsmith was rebuked for failing to organise Patricia's daytime slumbers satisfactorily, she had what Syria described as a stormburst, and accused her employer of heartlessness. Syria had become excessively exacting. Her confinement was imminent, and her loss was oppressing her. On May 19th, her diary records, 'My darling's birthday. He would have been forty seven.' That night, rats kept waking her.

Miss Arrowsmith was proving herself a girl of mettle, and proud. An unpleasant episode occurred a few days later, when Boomerang arrived unexpectedly at lunchtime with four friends. The dining room table would conveniently seat no more than six people, so Syria told Miss Arrowsmith to take Peter and Patricia out to the back verandah and have lunch with them there. After lunch she sent Matthew for the nurse with instructions to bring Patricia and join them for coffee.

Miss Arrowsmith refused to come, so Syria went herself to fetch her. But the young woman refused to budge. She objected, she said, to being made to act the part of the housemaid bringing in the baby.

'This,' wrote Syria, always careful to get her figures right, 'is the fourth time in less than fifteen months that she has shown her temper, and in each case over nothing. I am tired of it, and do wish I could get someone in her place, but I am bound hand and foot, for if I send her away, I have to lose the £17 her fare cost me from Cape Town, and I can't afford this.' It was a replay of the McLeod predicament. No matter how small the salary a nurse received, she was expected, when she left, to reimburse her employer for the cost of the journey to the employer's home.

Syria continued: 'I cannot possibly be left here alone. She hates her life here and lets me know it, and of course it is bad for Patricia, who feels the moods of those looking after her.'

Miss Arrowsmith was sensitive about her social status at the Farm, and felt that Syria treated her insultingly. The next day she had her revenge. Bringing in a pair of Peter's pants, she held them up to the light, and asked if Syria had done anything about getting him a new pair as it was a waste of time to mend them. Miss Arrowsmith then released her poisoned dart. 'She remarked in a spiteful little way that she should really like to keep them herself as a curio. I said she should not do that.' Patricia could imagine the ice in her mother's tones. 'I said I would keep them myself, and I did not think it at all a nice idea to wish to keep them as a curio.'

That night Syria sat up late, mending Peter's ravaged pants. Her darns were meticulous and she would tackle wide empty spaces undaunted rather than throw anything away.

At about this time, Syria decided at last to allow Peter to give up the enforced donkey rides which had cost him numerous chastisements and so many tears. He had earned good marks for reporting back to his mother about Carter's continued visits to Miss Arrowsmith in the schoolroom.

Sympathetic female company appeared at last in the motherly person of middle-aged Sister Marcus, who had been recommended for attendance at the confinement by one of Arthur's medical friends.

He had chosen well. She would stay at the Farm until four weeks after the birth of the baby. Syria came to trust this older woman, and was comforted by her presence. 'Sister Marcus is a sweet-natured lady and a skilful nurse who looks after me well. She is exceptionally good with babies and loves them.' Sister Marcus was good with their mothers too. She seemed to understand Syria's predicament, and to be generous and kind.

This was not how Syria experienced most women. She acknowledged the Sister's professional competence, and allowed herself to be discreetly mothered.

CHAPTER 9

On June 8th, Syria walked the quarter mile or so up the wooded hill to Arthur's grave, and spent some time there. Labour pains started after lunch and her diary records: 'After a short and frightful time a boy was born at a quarter to eleven in the evening.' Miss Arrowsmith redeemed herself by sitting up and making tea for people. Arthur's friend Dr Travers arrived from Bulawayo in the late afternoon. During the next week various guests came to offer congratulations, and Miss Arrowsmith made it her job to look after them. Syria still rested in bed. Miss Arrowmith showed special initiative one afternoon when she had a table taken out into the garden for tea. But Syria was displeased, for she had failed to ask permission. However, the young woman was learning, and had her own ways of parrying a scolding. Syria was growing wary of her sharpish temper which, once roused, she took no trouble to conceal. She came openly to the point these days, unaffected by Syria's icy responses. "Answering back" or "offering cheek" was for Syria the height of insolence, but this time her fighting spirit was weakened by her confinement, and she wrote in her diary: 'Miss Arrowsmith made me feel I had committed a faux pas.'

A week later, Grey returned for the school holidays. His mother commented drily, 'His accent is not so bad as when he came home before.'

Young Carter continued to displease Syria, so she gave him notice. Turner had been largely replaced by Gould, another farmer. Later Syria fell out with him too, but for the present he was a reliable help, superintending the cattle, arranging for the castration of bull calves, and seeing to the harvesting of mealies and the regular despatch of fruit crops to market.

Two weeks after the birth of her son, Syria got up for one and a half hours. The next day Miss Arrowsmith, feeling that she had done well by her employer during the past weeks, asked for a few days off in Bulawayo as soon as a new nurse, engaged to take over the two youngest children, should arrive. Her own role would then be simply that of governess to the elder boys. Syria, taken aback at this request, felt it to be unreasonable and said so. Miss Arrowsmith then came out with everything that was on her mind. 'She became excited and lost her temper, her voice trembled and she went white. She said several times she couldn't understand me; that I was a most inconsiderate person, nothing but work here all day long; that she never had any time away from the children, had given up all her afternoons lately, and hadn't been to town for eight weeks - had had a most trying time here, hated her life and said I never realised anyone wanted to enjoy themselves and that she wasn't exactly Methusalah. She had been warned from Cape Town not to come by someone I didn't know who had heard that Miss McLeod had no time off while she was here. Everyone had told her she ought to have a weekend off every month, and she had been advised to get this from me in black and white; claiming she was entitled now to a fortnight's holiday.' Miss Arrowsmith finished by naming two other employers who would have treated her better.

Syria retorted that she thought it a great pity Miss Arrowsmith had ever come. The girl took fresh exception to this, saying she had only stayed on because Syria had begged her to. Syria knew, and Miss Arrowsmith knew too, that at the bottom of this lay Syria's unwillingness to pay her nurse's fare back to Cape Town, which she would have to do if she dismissed her before the two years of the contract were up. Syria had convinced herself that she was quite unable to afford it.

The altercation became very frank on both sides. Miss Arrowsmith was not cowed by Syria. 'She pointed out to me how cheerfully she had done her work. I said I thought she did well the things she liked doing, but I didn't think she had the temperament for babies.' Miss Arrowsmith defended herself angrily against this accusation, claiming that Patricia had been a most difficult baby.

The row broke off for the night, and Syria agonised over her own position. She was convinced of the correctness of everything she had said, but thought that once or twice she had been a little unfair. She carried this concession back to Miss Arrowsmith next morning, but justified herself by saying that she had been driven to criticism by some of Miss Arrowsmith's remarks, especially those about her cheerfulness at work. Syria added primly, 'In my opinion, it is quite in the ordinary duties of life to do one's best as cheerfully as one can.'

Miss Arrowsmith now opened up a new battlefront, saying that Syria was planning to use her to save money by getting her to teach both boys instead of sending them to school. Syria retorted, 'I have thought the thing well over and believe it to be as broad as it is long, and if anything, school would cost me less!'

'Now you're making me feel in the way,' countered Miss Arrowsmith. She proceeded to lay down her own terms. She required a whole week's holiday in Bulawayo. She would agree to resume teaching both the boys again after that. Syria sought to regain the initiative by demanding that she teach them for twelve unbroken weeks. Miss Arrowsmith became angry again at this new attempt to tie her down, and accused Syria of not knowing how to treat a governess, probably because she had been used to natives for so long.

Accustomed as Syria had always been to getting her own way, she fought a stiff rearguard action: 'I said it was a pity that I had not been coached in the correct way to treat a governess.' But in the end she had to capitulate and promise Miss Arrowsmith a weekend every month. She found it outrageous, for the word "holiday" had no meaning for her. She also felt very sorry for herself, wondering how anyone could treat a new mother so harshly, only two and a half weeks after her confinement. Miss Arrowsmith's holiday would coincide with the departure of kindly Sister Marcus, who had understood Syria so well.

In the course of that night, Syria decided that she would try to induce Miss Arrowsmith to leave of her own accord, thus relieving her of the contractual obligation to refund the fare. With this hopeful strategy in mind, she went to Miss Arrowsmith's room after breakfast and told her that if and when she left, Syria would write to several potential employers she knew in the Union who might give her a good post or find one for her. But her nurse would have none of this tricky favour. She told Syria that in view of her comments the day before, she had already decided to leave after all at the end of the month, and added that she wouldn't work anywhere through the good offices of people who were friends of Syria.

Syria accepted this decision with mixed feelings. There was relief at the prospect of the tiresome Miss Arrowsmith's departure, and there would be no need for her to pay the fare to Cape Town, but it would mean the extra expense of sending both boys off to boarding school.

That evening Grey cried tears of anger because his governess was leaving and he would have to return to his hated school. In the hope of changing this latest decision, he proceeded to tell his mother and Peter as many unpleasant things as he could think of about the conversation of the boys. He had been right in assuming that lavatory jokes would shock Syria, but she was equal to the challenge: 'I told them that as far as their own conduct was concerned to try and copy their Father, and act so that neither he nor I need be ashamed of them. And they promised.'

The moral icon was in place. This little scene may have earned the boys some favour, but they quickly fell from grace. The very next day, revealing that they were learning something from the ways of their school, Grey and Peter belaboured one of the younger and smaller African boys with a stick. The boy complained to Syria, who recorded: 'I whipped them both and sent them to bed for the rest of the day.'

The new baby's nurse, Miss Stanhope, whom Patricia was to remember simply as Nanny, arrived to take care of the two youngest. Sister Marcus left, and Syria was bereft. 'Miss her dreadfully,' she wrote. The next day, July 4th, was her birthday. 'No one knows,' she noted sadly. 'Perhaps Arthur does.' Religious faith faltered in the face of silence.

Continuous activity kept her going. Letter writing played a big part in this, as it always would do. Also commanding much of her attention was the daily correction of her two older children. "Punishment" is a word which crops up often. It was meted out for unacceptable language, carelessness, lies, and mischievous pranks.

'Punished Grey for cutting Patricia's ball into strips. Punished Peter for saying "Damn" twice.' Syria's obsession with the evils of swearing was surpassed only by her fascinated horror of masturbation, and she was constantly on the lookout for evidence of this malpractice in all her children.

The two boys left the Farm for their boarding school in mid-July. Grey was miserably homesick, but Peter, embarking on his first term, was too excited to say goodbye to anyone. After their departure. Syria discovered that all was not well with her eight-week-old baby. It was the new Nanny Stanhope, a baby-lover, who alerted her to the fact that he was not taking his bottles properly and was steadily losing weight. Up till then Syria had been too distracted by the Farm and other problems to pay the infant much attention. Nanny reported that she had overheard someone say he was going downhill and would probably not survive. She urged that medical advice be called in. Syria was stung into action. She saw herself losing the child who, she now came to see was Arthur's last gift to her. Years later she was to say to Patricia: 'I felt that something of Arthur himself had gone into him.' She had realised vaguely that he had not been thriving too well, but this was looking serious. From now on, he was to take precedence in her affections over her other children. However much she and Nanny Stanhope were to fall out with each other, Syria felt a bond with her for having, as she saw it, saved her baby's life.

Noticing for the first time how thin he was, she at once added an extra bottle to his diet, supplementing it with a pinch of soda bicarbonate, one of her favourite remedies. She sent to Bulawayo for a doctor and for Sister Marcus who had only just left. Dr Travers came and examined the infant and pronounced him to be suffering from mitral heart murmur which was affecting his liver function and circulation. The news galvanised Syria. As for the infant, George O'Reilly MacArthur, he was henceforth fussed over and cosseted day and night. Sister Marcus stayed on a while, ostensibly to keep a medical eye on his well-being, but even more on that of his mother. The baby was quite ill for a few days. He was still weak and sickly and unable to absorb nourishment. Syria never breast fed any of her children for more than a week, complaining that they hurt her too much. To begin with, Sister Marcus and Nanny took it in turns to sit up all night with him. He was swaddled in cotton wool, and only half of him was washed at a time. He was lifted out of his cradle as seldom as possible. He still weighed less than his birth weight of nearly two months before. Never one to balk at vigorous measures, Syria gave him soap and water enemas, fearing the deadly effects of constipation. The doctor called from Bulawayo every two or three days and tried to balance George's diet with a combination of nourishment and stimulants. He was given drops of brandy in his bottles. He persisted in looking a very bad colour, and for a few days no one dared be hopeful about him. Syria kept watch in the intervals of her Farm tasks. But with the awakened feeling for the baby came a forlorn depression, and nearly every night she cried herself to sleep. Sister Marcus comforted her, and at bedtime she brushed Syria's long thick hair for her. After a fortnight, the baby stabilized, started to take an interest in his bottles and put on weight.

This relieved Syria sufficiently to allow her to assume the farmer's duty of visiting the Annual Agricultural Show in Bulawayo. This year it was opened by Prince Arthur of Connaught, son to the late Queen Victoria. Boomerang conducted her round the exhibits, among which Gaveston had taken four firsts and one second. The Major sought ardently to cheer her up and humbly suggested himself for consideration, in due course, as a second husband. He was firmly, though very politely turned down. Years later, Syria told Patricia that she could not have contemplated marriage to a man who drank several whiskies every day. She had almost managed to break Arthur of his sundowner habits, but Boomerang was not a man who could be prevailed upon to reform. He tried, as he escorted her around Budawayo, to console her by reminiscing about Arthur, but this only emphasized her loneliness. Sister Marcus gave her much more comfort.

On her return next day to the Farm, she was met with the good news that the baby had put on three more ounces. The following morning Miss Arrowsmith bade goodbye to her fractious charge Patricia and to her dissatisfied employer, and disappeared for good from the life of the Farm.

A curious little incident had involved Patricia and one of the native servants. Msombalowa was seen by Nanny Stanhope lifting Patricia out of her pram and making a fuss of her. He was summoned before Syria and told that on no account must he ever do such a thing again. The youth probably had younger brothers and sisters, perhaps even a child of his own. Like most Africans he would have been fond of children. There was a dearth of loving men around now. Patricia must have enjoyed this rare kind of attention. A few months later, when she had crossed the threshold of memory, she used to wonder why none of the tall, black African house servants in their bright white robes, ever spoke to her. She would have liked them to.

CHAPTER 10

Syria was sometimes disturbed by a rat in her bedroom. She often felt nervous at the night sounds of the African farmworkers in their compound a hundred yards away, laughing and shouting in intoxicated merriment. 'I am very sorry for you,' Matthew told Syria. 'The Farm needs Bwana.' But their endurance was wearing thin. Syria without Arthur was too exacting an employer. She could trust Matthew and Barnabas because they had been with Arthur for so many years, but she had no talent for trust, and even less for understanding the point of view of an employee. But the trusties were becoming restless, and told Syria they wanted to return to their homeland. Syria urged them into an unwilling agreement to stay on until she had sold the Farm. They could not keep their promise. Two weeks later they gave her a month's notice. Syria felt ill-used. She was too put out to try to persuade them further, and commented in her diary: 'It puts them on the plane of animals.' She was obliged to change this harsh judgement when, two weeks later, Matthew relented. He told her that he missed Bwana every day, and again that he was very sorry for her. He offered to stay on for three more months, and he persuaded Barnabas to stay too. Syria accepted this as no more than her due.

But the truce remained an uneasy one. Another episode occurred which nearly overturned it. One morning Matthew stayed away from work to console his wife Martha who had just received a message from her people in the Congo that her mother had died. Syria found this trying, as she wanted to get a wagonload of produce off to market and Matthew's help was important; but she conceded that he should stay and keep Martha company for that day. A little later on, Matthew came to the house to ask Syria for a pass for Martha and her children to leave with the wagon for Bulawayo whence she could catch a train to the Congo. Syria supplied the pass. But just before the wagon left Martha herself came to the house to tell Syria that she wanted Matthew to accompany her home. Syria was not having this. 'I told her she must either go quietly off in the wagon, or stay quietly here, but Matthew could not go. I went later and told Matthew this, and told him to tell her she was not to upset everyone just because her mother is dead.'

A silent battle of wills ensued between Matthew and Syria over the next two days, and astonishingly Syria won it. Matthew again said he would stay on with Barnabas until Syria left, and it was arranged that when Meg, Barnabas's wife, had her expected baby shortly, she and Martha and the children would travel back together to the Congo without their husbands.

'Feel very much relieved,' wrote Syria. To her this seemed the only proper solution.

Several other African workers had already left, all finding one reason or another, and none of them satisfactory in Syria's eyes. Joe, the man for whom Arthur had died, may have taken it ill when Syria ordered him to get rid of his dog on pain of a drop in wages if he 'disobeyed'. He and the dog left to find employment elsewhere. Three more insisted on leaving at short notice, though she told them that they had to stay another three weeks. She was forced to give in.

Finally, before his promised three months were up, fresh trouble broke out for Matthew, and this time it proved too much for him because his personal honour was at stake. It had always been the custom for storage cupboards containing farm tools and some of the workers' own personal possessions to be locked up at night. One night a workshop was broken into and £4 worth of Matthew's clothes were stolen. At the same time, the keys which were kept by Syria, disappeared. She sent to Bulawayo for the police. The next day another worker, Country Inn, returned the keys to her, saying he had found them in a farm cart. Matthew's clothes did not turn up, the police delayed their arrival for two more days, and Matthew, convinced that Country Inn was the culprit, became impatient. At last a trooper arrived and spent an afternoon questioning the workers. He came and went a couple more times and finally took Country Inn away with him for further questioning in Bulawayo. After three days in gaol, Country Inn was returned, together with a letter from the police corporal who said he believed the man was guilty but could not prove it.

Matthew, profoundly offended at what he saw as a failure in

justice, left the Farm on the spot, after many years of loyal service. 'I did my best to calm him back to reason, but I couldn't and he ended by saying that I mustn't stand any longer, that I must have my breakfast. He refused to continue to work in the same place as Country Inn for even one more day.' Matthew departed at once without the usual present, his return fare, the wages due to him, or food; a loss calculated by Syria in terms of money equal to the considerable sum of £25.

'He went off after nearly thirteen years, with not even a clapping or a salute, just "Goodbye Mama," with his back to me.' His honour was deeply affronted, and personal loyalty, already tried to the uttermost, could count no more. It never occurred to Syria that, with the cloud still hanging over Country Inn she could have dismissed him and so shown respect for Matthew's sense of honour. But she was touched by his departure in a way which went unexpectedly deeper than the inconvenience it caused her. 'The boy is like a friend,' she wrote, 'and I am very fond of him,' and then, as a characteristic afterthought, 'I put away a lot of my plate when he left.' Only Barnabas of the original trustees remained.

Syria now had the digestive, and even more absorbing, the excretory functions of two young children to attend to. George O'Reilly MacArthur's bottom became very sore and Syria applied neat methylated spirits. She noted: 'Baby cried most dreadfully.' It was upsetting. At the same time Patricia became 'not well at all.' During the next twelve hours she was dosed twice with bicarbonate of soda, then with castor oil and olive oil. Following this medication, Syria noted that she cried almost continuously. Both the children's medications seemed perfectly calculated, with the best of intentions, to worsen their original condition. The doctor, summoned from Bulawayo late in the evening, diagnosed Patricia as suffering from enteritis, and an enema was added to her other therapies. She must have had a robust constitution, for she survived them all. Sister Marcus was sent for and stayed two nights. She succeeded in calming things down, and most essentially, in soothing Syria, brushing her hair again at bedtime, and lightening momentarily her burden of loneliness.

With the new Nanny Stanhope, there were the usual ups and downs. They often got on each other's nerves, particularly when Syria reverted to her imperious mode. But about her treatment of baby George, Syria never found cause to complain. Nanny's obvious devotion to the infant spoke strongly in her favour. Where Patricia was concerned, as with Miss Arrowsmith and Miss McLeod before her, matters were very different, so much so that Syria, not normally averse to strict discipline, became uneasy. Nanny found her a very difficult child, given to sudden noisy rages and uncontrollable bouts of crying. At times, her nerve broke, and shortly after Patricia's second birthday, Syria was moved to reprimand Nanny for losing her temper with the child and slapping her. The more Nanny slapped and scolded, the more Patricia screamed. 'Nurse was quite rude to me, saying it was no good always giving way to her; she'd give a lot of trouble if so, and it was simply that Patricia was in a very bad temper. I said, 'You mustn't talk to me like that, Nurse, and put my arms round Patricia until she stopped crying, which she did at once. She is very irritable and difficult today because she is cutting two big double teeth. It isn't good to let her shriek like that. I left in a few minutes, feeling very ruffled and bothered.' Even Syria could not help noticing that Patricia had not had much luck with her three nurses. But she and Nanny made up their difference in a way that would never have been possible with the other two.

'I took a cup of coffee to her and found her sobbing on her bed. She said she was sorry she had lost her temper. But that she did love the children, and I knew it, didn't I? I put my arms round her and forgave her fully, and told her I should think no more about it. I asked her never to slap Patricia, and told her it was a wise rule never to strike a child except in cold blood.'

There was a rather patronising quality to Syria's forgiveness, but it did not entirely obscure a genuine sympathy for Nurse's overstrained condition. Then she went back to mending and writing letters and crying herself to sleep. The grim sense of duty, which bore so heavily on others, was directed equally sternly towards herself. In some way it saved her from sinking further into depression, and kept her going. The fracas with Nanny recurred fairly often, when Nanny retaliated by going into a sulk. Patricia's earliest memories dated from this period. Almost all of them related to her Nurse, Mother was only remembered once, seen from behind and wearing a hat. She recalled Nanny as a bustling little person, impatient and hard to please. This did not particularly upset her. Things happened in a certain way, and that was that.

As she had done with her previous nurses, Syria now worked up an anxiety about Nanny's behaviour with Hartenborg. She considered that she was becoming too attached to his company, so much so that she would stroll along with him, apparently deep in conversation, neglecting her older charge, Patricia, whom she allowed to lag many yards behind. There was some substance to this criticism, for there were deadly Black Mambas, puff adders and cobras on the Farm. Patricia remembered vividly a walk where she dawdled behind on her own, while Nanny and Hartenborg, some way ahead, climbed into a low wire enclosure to pick violets. Patricia spotted a snake, coiled up under a nearby tree, with its vicious little head reared high out of the coils. Patricia called out in panic to her Nurse, who merely told her crossly to stop making such a fuss, and went on picking violets. Patricia never forget her huge fear of the snake, nor could she understand why her Nurse paid no heed.

Syria despised Hartenborg for a low-grade white, though one who could be very useful to her when properly under her control, and even indispensable when Nurse departed for a week's holiday and Hartenborg slept on the verandah, in her absence.

'I was without fear at night for the first time for nearly a year,' she wrote.

She remained a jealous guardian of her status as employer. She could not bear Nurse to take any initiatives for which she had not previously sought permission. She was angry when, having been absent for a night visiting Grey and Peter at their boarding school, she returned to find that Nurse had persuaded the house servant to unlock her bedroom and had entered it to show Arthur's photograph to a Nanny visiting on her day off from another farmstead. 'I spoke severely to her,' wrote Syria, who retained a life-long passion for locking things up. Not only had Nanny breached this taboo, but she had shared Syria's most prized possession, Arthur, with someone whose suitability for this privilege Syria had not been in a position to monitor. Similarly, she scolded Nanny for opening the Farm mailbag which had arrived while she was away for the night in Bulawayo. 'Although,' noted Syria acidly, 'she knows well that I dislike my mailbag being opened without my permission.' Other people should expect to wait about for their own mail in such circumstances.

Yet there seemed to be a mutual tolerance, verging on fellow feeling, a latent kindness between the two women, which sometimes moderated Syria's haughty style, and enabled them to survive under the same roof. Nanny respected Syria's gritty courage, and Syria recognised a devotion to the care of Georgy which she was convinced had saved his life.

Syria was tolerating Patricia better at this time. Her gentler side was most readily aroused by suffering, ill-judged though some of her ministrations might be. So long as she could see Patricia's black moods as caused by the pain of toothcutting, she could put up with them. She had never had anything to do with a teething child, and was distressed by her daughter's miseries. 'Her whole mouth and gums are dreadfully inflamed,' she wrote. She flew to various remedies, not just one, but several at a time. So she had immediate recourse to her usual favourites, including glycerine, bicarbonate of soda, and castor oil three times a day. Memories of the dread castor oil treatment hailed back to Patricia's earliest days. It was handed out, a dessertspoonful at a time with a segment of orange, and could be relied upon to exacerbate a stomach upset for as long as it was administered. Syria remained oblivious to any connection.

But as well as dosing Patricia, she now sat and talked with her, sparing time from her busy day. This was the medicine that helped them both.

CHAPTER 11

Grey and Peter did not fit into boarding school. During his father's lifetime, Grey had written home, making it plain how unhappy he was, but his parents made light of his complaints. When Peter, as a result of Miss Arrowsmith's defection, accompanied Grey to school for the first time, he had been very excited, but Grey had wept. Now they were returning to school again. 'They were both very sweet and very sad,' recorded Syria. That did not disturb her, it was natural for them not to want to go back, and she accepted the tribute of their sadness at parting from her. But when she visited them three weeks later and stayed the night with the headmaster and his wife, she found both her sons looking pale and unwell. She also took an intense dislike to the headmaster's wife. She felt herself treated in an offhand way at being seated halfway down the big table at dinnertime. 'She then took us all to see a bonfire after dinner, and we stood looking at it and hanging around for so long that I collapsed and sat on the ground.' Syria's way of showing displeasure took various forms of expression. Her hostess abounded in defects, but the one which disquieted even Syria was her approval of Matron's handling of the miserable Peter. Bedwetting had set in not long after he began school. 'Matron asked me in front of Grey and Peter if I knew that Peter was incontinent, saying that of course she had scolded him and tried to shame him out of it by exposing his weakness to the other boys in the dorm.' This she did by holding up his wet sheet in front of them all. Peter's morale crumbled, and he became a licensed object for bullying, though Grey did his best to protect him. Uneasy about this, for she could not bring herself to interfere with the course of discipline, Syria returned home.

Previously Peter had been only an occasional bedwetter, and Syria had not made an issue of it. But when he returned home for the Christmas holidays, he drenched the bed night after night.

While the boys were still away Syria had to go into hospital in Bulawayo for an operation on a toe joint distortion caused by the wearing of ill-fitting shoes in childhood. She took the opportunity of this trip to register as a voter for the new Rhodesian Parliament, the country having just been granted Dominion Status, She was in hospital for three weeks, paying fifteen shillings a day, reduced from a pound on account of her being a doctor's widow. For years she took financial advantage of this status, nor did eventual remarriage deter her from continuing to claim a reduction in medical fees on behalf of herself as well as her children. It was a useful perk.

In hospital she recalled poignantly her stay there with Arthur two years earlier when fate had dealt him its first blow. She had many flowers and visits, particularly from the dependable Boomerang. Relations with Matron and the nursing staff teetered, but just held.

While in hospital Syria received a cable from England with news of her mother's death. She had lost both husband and mother within less than a year of each other. Background figure at the Rectory though her mother was, Syria had been devoted, and often referred to her fondly as 'My little Mother.'

Her parents now rested together in one big square grave in Tunstall churchyard. Her father had preceded her mother there by a few years. Until she was a very old woman, Syria travelled across England once a year to visit their grave and tend it. The memorial stone records the deaths of this couple of mid-Victorians in a place of utter peacefulness, sheltered by the grey fourteenth century church tower. On it is incised a biblical text: 'Sin abounds, but grace does much more abound.' Patricia's grandfather had at last hit on a formula for getting the better of sin.

On returning to the Farm, Syria had a warm welcome from Nanny, "the dear babies" and the houseboys. She had been told to lie up for the next fortnight, but of course did not do so. On Christmas Eve she packed presents and went to bed, feeling tired and sad. The first thing in the morning she was up again and on her way to Arthur's grave. While she was out, Nanny, Grey and Peter decorated the breakfast table for her as a surprise, the sort of simple gesture that brought the best out of her. In return she made them a trifle, a pudding at which she excelled, and which was always arranged in a shallow mauve Art Nouveau bowl.

This recipe, in its bowl, was to appear on special occasions down the years, and was inherited by Patricia who carried on the trifle tradition as the favourite pudding of her own children. In the afternoon, the family made toffee together, and a valiant attempt was made to keep spirits up on this first Christmas Day without Arthur.

At this time, Grey had a dream about his father which he related to Syria. 'Daddy came into the room and asked him how he was getting on,' she wrote, 'and he said, "Rather well, I think." I was very interested and glad he had dreamed of Daddy, but I felt a bit left out of the story, and said was I there, and did Daddy talk about me at all?' Grey tactfully restructured his dream: "Oh yes, Daddy talked a lot about you. You were there with him."

'Which,' continued Syria, 'of course is just as it always was, and the children thought of us two as one, and as being always together.' This was not in fact how it did appear to Grey, as this early dream hinted even to Syria, who was not happy until he had rearranged it. Grey made it quite clear to Patricia in later years that he had always felt them to be very different people, and this had been obvious to him when he and his father were doing things alone together on the Farm. In losing his father, he felt he had lost half of himself. But he was as yet a long way from the time in the future when, as a young trainee pilot in the War, he had told Patricia, 'Sometimes I've hated her so much I could have killed her.'

The Christmas truce was short-lived. Syria's notions of how to treat young boys rather resembled those of the mother in Arthur's childhood book *Blind Willie*. The boys simply accepted what came their way, having no conception of any alternative. So on Boxing Day, Grey was in disgrace for breaking Syria's favourite malachite stalactite and forgetting to tell her. For this oversight he was forbidden to enter the sittingroom for a week. Syria favoured staggered punishments, strung out over several days. They made a longer-lasting impression.

Peter offended too. 'He called Patricia a devil before breakfast. I punished him.' Peter's use of "horrid words" in front of Patricia was also reported back by Nurse. 'He pretends they are said in innocence, but I know better now. It is just Peter's duplicity, I fear.' Grey and

Peter then 'confessed' together to having repeated 'some of those rotten low things that boys at school use, to Hartenborg and Nurse.' Perhaps they had hoped to influence their mother against sending them back. Everyone, from Nanny downwards, seems to have been trying to deflect blame from themselves by telling tales on someone else.

Nanny herself had come in for a scolding. 'I told her to lengthen her dresses, and not to go in to Grey again after I had put him to bed.' Grey was now a well-grown lad of twelve. Unhappy about Peter's torments at school, he spoke to his mother again about his persecution there. Grey was tall for his age and able to look after himself, but Peter, two years younger, was on the small side, his charming, almost girlish features, framed in golden curls. He was the perfect victim. But Syria was still convinced of the virtues of a tough school life for boys: 'I expect the teasing does him good.'

Peter had almost stopped bedwetting during the holidays, but at the approach of term time she wrote, 'Peter gave way to his trick again. I shall take a cold sponge to him tomorrow night.' She was now certain that he bedwetted deliberately. Like so many of her remedies, the cold sponge was more likely to worsen the condition than to cure it, and of course it satisfyingly combined punishment with treatment. Grey, too, was getting on her nerves. He was not biddable like his brother. 'Gave Grey a good talking to for being rude and absentminded, and resenting any correction. He is very irritating at times'.

Soon they were gone and off her hands. There had been the usual misery on leaving home. 'Peter cried when he went to bed, and couldn't sleep for hours. Next morning the children very sad at leaving and both nearly crying at breakfast.' But by these evidences of their attachment, they wiped out the debit account of their misdoings during the holidays. Even so, Syria was not let off lightly. A few days later she refers to 'sad letters from Grey and Peter. Feel dreadfully fed up and tired of everything.'

She was in an unenviable position financially. Arthur had paid over £6,000 for the Farm, a price which, unsuspected by him, was grossly inflated. He had taken out a large mortgage, and had spent too much of the remaining capital on the venture. At the time of his death he had almost decided to give up and go into general medical practice.

Now there was even less money and no breadwinner. By some fortunate intuition Arthur had taken out a life insurance policy shortly before his death, and small though it was, this was to provide Syria's capital for the future. She hoped soon to find a buyer for the Farm, and Boomerang was doing his best for her in Bulawayo. Several came to look, but no one stayed interested for long.

The problem loomed of the boys' education when they returned to England. Grey's godfather was reasonably wealthy. Syria wrote to him to enquire whether he would be willing to pay Grey's fees at public school. It was a great relief when he consented to do so. It was hard for Syria to hold out the begging bowl. She must have seen no other way of getting Grey educated in a manner she considered acceptable for Arthur's son. It was probable that help could have been forthcoming from inside Arthur's own family, but this would have given them power over her, and that she could not tolerate. Arthur's family was large and matriarchal, and cared for its own, including those who entered the family through marriage and were willing to throw their lot in as honorary members. But the daughter of the patriarch of Tunstall Rectory found this position inappropriate for her. Peter would have to be educated by other means, and on her return to England, Syria was to negotiate sponsors for a free place at Christ's Hospital.

There was no one for Syria to talk to frankly about her chronic unhappiness, Nanny would have been sympathetic, but Syria was too reserved to confide in her, and in any case believed in maintaining a distance between herself and any employee. There was a brief relief when Cedric Johns came to stay for a few nights. He was Patricia's godfather, and had been Arthur's friend and admirer, for Arthur had succeeded in curing him of sleeping sickness, a rare achievement. Syria led him off to The Hill to inspect Arthur's great granite stone, which lay across the grave like a lid. On it was incised an obituary, ending with the Kiplingesque sentiment so typical of Syria, and of Arthur too:

IN MEMORY OF MY HUSBAND ARTHUR
WHO WAS BORN MAY 19th, 1876,
MARRIED ME JANUARY 4th, 1911,
AND PASSED ON BEFORE, MARCH 26th, 1923.
HE PRACTISED IN HIS STRAIGHTFORWARD LIFE
AND IN DEATH THE CREED WHICH WAS HIS,
TO DO UNTO OTHERS AS YOU WOULD BE DONE BY
AND TO PLAY THE GAME.

Syria's Anglican faith did not seem to be helping her much now, but she listened gratefully to Cedric. 'He believes one's loved ones gone before are always near to us, and that Arthur was near us all the time we were talking - feels quite sure of it. He commends me on the way I am carrying on. He comforted me in some measure by his own conviction of Arthur's presence, but I still feel that I don't know what to think, and everything is silence and uncertainty to me still.'

Acquaintances in Bulawayo who belonged to a Spiritualist circle claimed that messages had come through from Arthur, and invited Syria to join them. She refused. She would have nothing to do with what she regarded as wrongheaded practices.

For someone as nervous as she was, it was surprising how little diplomacy she showed in her dealings with her African workers. She scolded and chivvied mercilessly. She reached a peak of cold fury with one man who had arrived hoping to find work. She told him to set up his hut in a certain place, but word reached her from Hartenborg that the man had the reputation of being "an out and out rotter," and she marched off for a further interview. His hut was not where she had told him to put it. When she found it in a different place, she ordered him to be out and away by that time next day, when his hut would be destroyed. 'He trembled with fear,' she wrote, 'and the next day I went to see that his hut had been destroyed.'

During Nanny's three-week holiday, a young woman came over temporarily from Bulawayo to help in the house while Syria took over the care of her two children. It was the first time she had ever taken sole charge of any of her offspring for more than a day or two. She soon found Patricia's constant grizzling very troublesome. Up till now she had excused her on the grounds of tooth-cutting, but Patricia remained perversely cross, and cried intermittently much of the day and at all hours of the night. Syria could see no good reason for it, and hit on a remedy which worked quite well. She exiled the wailing child to an empty bedroom where her former nurse, Miss Arrowsmith, had slept. She had noticed for some time that Patricia was afraid of this room. She called it 'Googie's 'oom,' and shuddered. 'What is she afraid of?' wondered Syria, seemingly forgetting that Miss Arrowsmith had never taken to Patricia. She discovered that if she locked Patricia into this room alone, she stopped crying very quickly. Patricia had begun screaming for her mother several times a night, so on these occasions she was removed from her cot and locked away in the dark in Googie's room. Ten minutes in there usually did the trick. Patricia told her mother that she never wanted to sleep in there and that she didn't like that room. But for Syria, Googie's room proved the perfect solution to her problem.

The first anniversary of Arthur's death came round, and Syria wrote in her diary: 'Patricia quite unexpectedly at breakfast this morning said "Daddy's gone bye-byes, Mummie. Say Daddy, Mummie."

I said it, yearningly.

"Patricia likes dear Daddy, Mummie. Mummie likes Daddy, Say Daddy again, Mummie."

And I said it again. I think Arthur must have known and heard.' She struggled on, trying to keep her flickering faith alight. She came from a family loaded with parsons, and she never railed against her faith, and remained a churchgoer all her life. But Patricia came to suspect that her mother had an agnostic streak. Till the day she died, she kept on her bedroom wall the prize-winning sonnet of the 1926 Rhodesian Esteddfod, which dwelt on Nature's compensation for the pain of unbelief.

Patricia and Syria eventually grew quite close in this brief period of Nurse Stanhope's absence. The night-time crying ceased and Patricia's vocabulary began to include many endearments, much valued by Syria, which clearly reflected the language that Syria was now using towards her. 'Patricia very adorable tonight; called me many times 'Patricia's little darling Mummie.' Patricia had touched the springs of affection in Syria which she never did with her latest Nurse, who reserved all tenderer feelings for "Baba Bud," her pet name for the baby brother. It was because of him, she told Syria, that she agreed to accompany her and the babies back to England. There was certainly little financial incentive. Syria told her flatly that her wages in England would be less than at present, between £36 and £40 a year. She would also have to wear uniform, and be expected to address Syria as "Madam". Nurse hesitated on hearing these conditions, saying that it was a low wage, and she was not sure that her father would approve. In the end she signed the contract which Syria had drawn up.

CHAPTER 12

In the early April of 1924, Syria removed Grey and Peter from their hated school and accompanied them by train on the two-day journey to Cape Town. They would never see the Farm again. Grey lived up to his harum-scarum reputation by losing both his school hats. Syria found his absent-mindedness as unbearable as ever, and let him know her displeasure. But her irritation never made the slightest difference. For years he continued to lose, mislay and break things, including a valuable pair of binoculars which he managed to leave on a train. At Cape Town, after a night's stay all together in one room at the International Hotel, Syria deposited her sons on a steamer bound for Southampton. She inspected their cabin, tipped the steward, almost certainly inadequately, and asked a woman occupying a nearby cabin to keep an eye on them. The boys had the time of their lives. The unknown woman never came near them, and they found themselves gloriously liberated for three weeks.

Syria spent a couple of days in Cape Town before returning to the Farm. She visited Sea Point to take a look at the cottages which Arthur had bought as an investment. Building was going on at the site and sales were under way. Then she went to the Queen's Hotel where she and Arthur had once stayed, and enquired after one of the managers they had met there. An elderly man, he was still there, and he earned one of Syria's supreme accolades when she recorded: 'He was kindness and good taste itself when he realised who I was. Said he would have liked me to come and stay there as his guest.' But there was some sadness in the encounter. 'He insisted on having me to lunch as his guest. The son came too, and the whole thing broke down my control, I am sorry to say. The sights of the place are all so poignant, and bring back dear memories.'

Patricia's memories dated from this time, three or four months before her third birthday. She hung onto them and often rehearsed them in her mind, not allowing herself to lose them, her last tie with that place of sunlight and flowers. They appeared to her like coloured snapshots, clear inner pictures of people and places, events, impressions, even distinct snatches of thought. A favourite memory was the fragrance and flavour of 'mealie-meal,' which she had in a bowl of milk for breakfast on the verandah. The golden beads of corncob shone as they lay in heaps on the plate. She retained almost no memories of her mother. Nanny was the presence who ruled her life. She conveyed an air of impatience and faint displeasure, though she had the redeeming feature of singing songs to Patricia when in a good mood. But Baba Bud, that pale bald creature, was still her darling, and Patricia knew quite clearly that she herself was an awkward child who interrupted Nanny's love affair with her brother. She tried to be particularly nice to him, having observed that this was the best way of winning Nanny's favour. It did not always work.

There was the occasion when each of them was immured in separate playpens, alone in the room and out of reach of each other. Georgy was not doing anything at all. Patricia could see that he was not interested in his stuffed cloth ball, which was coloured a dull pink and white. Her own ball, in white and vivid scarlet, was much more interesting, and she was sure that both he and Nanny would be pleased with her if she gave it to him. So she broke through a weak corner of her playpen, ran over, and dropped it into his. Just then Nanny returned and dragged her away, scolding hard. She hadn't noticed how kind Patricia had been to Georgy, and that silly creature didn't seem to have noticed it either, but sat on there, dumbly staring. The African carpenter was sent for, and he set about repairing the pen, and Patricia knew that, unlike Nanny, he did not mind in the least that she had broken it. He went on working, saying nothing to anyone.

She broke out of her mosquito-netted cot too. She was bored by rest-time which went on and on with nothing to do. Across the room and through a crack in the drawn curtains, she spotted Hartenborg in the sunny garden. She had sung all the songs she knew several times. She wished she didn't have to be shut up in the dark, and Hartenborg was that interesting creature, a man. The African servants, following Syria's orders, would not speak to her, but Hartenborg did. They had conversations while he was gardening. So she rose up in her cot, broke easily through the net, climbed out and ran across to the window. She did not have time to call out more than a few words, for suddenly Nanny was there again, with her scoldings.

There was another indelible memory which involved the playpen again. Patricia had been incarcerated alone for some time. She had already spent a long and unproductive session that morning on her chamber pot. Now she realised that she needed it urgently, but it wasn't there. She called, but no one heard. There were a few wooden bricks with her in the pen, so she hurried them together in a shape that seemed about right, and used them as a pot. She was distinctly pleased with this bit of inventiveness. But Nanny, when she turned up, was quite extraordinarily angry. This made Patricia angry too. It was her clearest realisation so far of the unfairness of things. Nanny seized her fiercely, marched her out of the room, banged down a chair in a lonely spot right at the end of the passage, and shouted, 'You can sit there in silence for ten minutes.' Patricia hated punishments which exiled her from people, and she hated not being allowed to talk. More, she felt very strongly that this punishment was not deserved. She did not agree that she had been naughty. She had tried to be helpful, and she thought, very clearly, 'Nanny expects me to cry, but I'm not going to. I shall pretend I don't mind. She won't like that!' She stuck out the ten minutes, and decided she was no longer a baby.

Her memories of the larger life outside the farmhouse walls were mixed. They were sunlight, warmth, and the massed colours of bougainvillaea and oleander, and she remembered vividly walking with her ugly but dear white doll, Daisy Dimple, under trees that seemed to soar forever into the blue sky. There was the day when the calf, given her by her godfather Boomerang, fell ill. They all walked to the cattle compound. There was a crowd of Africans there, and one of them came over and reported that the calf had just died. Patricia knew that death meant an end. She had lost her calf.

One fine morning Boomerang came to take her and her mother for a drive in his car. He sat with Syria in front, a bowler hat perched on his head, and Patricia settled into the back seat next the open window. It was one of the gaunt vehicles of the early twenties, with a hood that could go up or down, like a pram. Today it was up. Apart from Hartenborg, Boomerang was the only white man who appeared regularly in her life; the only sort of man she was allowed to speak to. They drove off down the narrow, red-earth lane leading towards the open veldt, which stretched away in all directions, a world of great spaces and tawny light. Here and there were clumps of trees and dense green tangles of bush. Suddenly she saw, far off a dark cloud, moving low and fast, coming closer and blotting out the sky behind it. 'Locusts!' cried the grown-ups. The dark cloud enveloped them, and one daring insect flew in at the window as they drove along and settled amusingly on her godfather's hat.

One sunny afternoon, Patricia was invited to a tea party. She and Nanny were driven by a neighbour, Major Sharpe, to his farm a few miles away. He had been a close friend of Arthur's in the Katanga, and they had migrated to Southern Rhodesia at about the same time. Sharpe had moved more cautiously, establishing his farm one step at a time. He had bought only three or four head of cattle to begin with, and had concentrated on developing a hardy strain. He became widely known for his first class herd of pedigree Friesians, and also for his keenness to experiment with new ways of farming that looked like being an improvement on the old. Among other successes was his method of cultivating a higher quality of mealie seed. This lay in the future. At the time of Arthur's death, they were both beginners.

Patricia was very interested in Major Sharpe's legs. They seemed to be done up in brown bandages. These were puttees, worn by the Army in the Great War, and later adopted for country use. When Patricia and Nanny went over to their farm for tea, they were greeted by his friendly wife and led towards a shady corner of the garden. 'Here come the twins,' said Nanny to Patricia. 'Make friends with Tom and Tony.' Patricia was pleased to see two little boys being urged towards her. They would make a change from Georgy. She ran towards them. But Tony and Tom were not at all pleased to see her. They hid behind their mother and began to cry. Patricia was surprised and disappointed. Why should they cry when they saw her? And why were they allowed to go on behaving in such a silly way? She tried for a little longer to make friends, but it was useless. They did not like her at all. Their mother sat them on high chairs and gave everyone a good tea, but Patricia felt affronted by the twins' refusal to play with her. They were as big as she was, but clearly, they were just big babies.

Tom lost his life in the Rhodesian Air Force during the Second

World War. She met Tony again seventy one years later. He was now a seasoned farmer who had inherited the farm where he was born. He was known throughout the district for his fine herd of Friesian cattle and for his innovative methods of improving mealie seed. With his wife and family, he had survived all the rigours of the war for Zimbabwean independence. Tony and his wife showed Patricia and her husband great hospitality in that same farm where she had gone to tea with Nanny. Tony took her back to the Farm, Gaveston, which was up for sale yet again, and led the way up the steep, stony hill, now overgrown with light-leaved trees and rustling with small bush life, to where, at the top, she stood once again beside her father's last encampment. Tony's Matabele farm workers had cleared a way through over-grown parts of the path uphill, and, unasked, had lined each side of the last twenty yards leading to the grave with a low wall of small boulders. All the men who had worked for Arthur must have died long ago, but some ancient tradition of respect for the dead man on his lonely hill had lived on. The boulders seemed to Patricia a gesture of kindly courtesy to the daughter who had come from the other side of the world to be with him awhile after a lifetime away.

Nanny took her two charges out for a walk most afternoons. Georgy was now in the pram where Patricia herself would have liked to ride, but was seldom allowed to. She often took Daisy Dimple with her. She was stiff and plain, and certainly had no dimples, being covered, except for her painted face, with white hair, like a goat. Patricia had never seen a person like her, not only because she looked so odd but because her clothes were sewn onto her. She happened, all the same, to be very fond of Daisy. Her other doll, Pinkie, was also strange-looking. She was deep pink all over, being made out of coat, and she had thin limbs that flapped out of a very stodgy body. Her bonnet was trimmed with soft grey fur, and her face, like Daisy Dimple's, was painted on. Patricia wished that Georgy would not grab Pinkie whenever he got the chance, and chew her fur with the corner of his little dribbling mouth.

On their walks, Nanny and Georgy were interested chiefly in each other and Patricia often hung behind. There was one particular moment, to which she sometimes returned in later years, when trying to recapture the feeling of Africa. She had paused, leaning against a tree trunk, her head back, looking up through reddish-gold leaves into the blue sky. The trees seemed to climb up and up and far away from her. A strange sensation passed through her, a wave of wondering who, where am I? Perhaps it was one of those moments when one slips out of time. Perhaps it was simply a sense of being a part of nature. Patricia was too young to be able to find any words for it, but she felt something unforgettable, and at rare intervals in her life, she recognised its fleeting touch again.

Syria was now actively preparing for departure to England. She was cataloguing books, tools and stock, and pressurising Boomerang to find a buyer for the Farm. He had done his best, but without success. Eventually a short-term tenant was found, for two years at £200 a year. Farm implements and tools were left for his use, and Syria made a meticulous inventory of them. All these deals meant legal expenses, and Syria was shocked when the final account arrived. 'I was bracing myself to bear about half the amount. I have been very wrong to go to him so much. I never realised that everything was charged for. It is due to culpable childishness. One buys experience dearly. I'll be more careful in future with the money Arthur entrusted me with.'

She practised being careful with money for the rest of her days.

She made a last visit to Bulawayo in the horse-drawn wagon, noting that the journey took exactly two and a half hours. On her return to the Farm that evening, she found that Patricia's face was badly bruised, and was told that she had fallen off her chair and onto her face.

In the course of time, Patricia had four children of her own, and though they fell about in various ways, no one ever fell from a chair straight onto his or her face. It seems an improbable explanation for such an injury. Syria did not question it.

During her last days at the Farm, she gave Hartenborg another sharp scolding for slacking on the job of making the Africans work harder. To the end, he never won Syria's approval. She was particularly affronted when he told her she ought to remarry. 'For this impudence I rebuked him severely.' The rebukes were probably impressive, for Syria adopted Biblical idiom on such occasions. Work must have been scarce, or Hartenborg would hardly have stayed. He often went into a sulk, and pointedly failed to do what she asked of him. The fact that she never showed appreciation of his efforts could not have helped. But Syria was not one to link effects with causes.

Georgy's first birthday was approaching, and Syria was relieved to learn, after the baby had been given a check-up by Dr. Travers, that his heart was now in perfect working order. She nonetheless continued to treat him as a delicate child. To lose him would be like losing Arthur all over again.

Carried away by all this activity, Syria's grieving was pushed to some extent into second place. She was even able to write in her diary of a motor trip in the Matopo Hills with friends. 'Had a lovely picnic.' But she still cried in bed most nights, and Patricia did not help by returning to her shrieking fits. 'She sleeps well, but is very irritable and gets into sudden furious rages.' Nanny still found these outbreaks a great trial and complained to Syria that her daughter was extremely naughty and troublesome. Where Patricia was concerned, Nanny's tolerance was in short supply. Syria's response was to order Nanny back to her room, rather like another troublesome child. Nanny cried and apologised, and was graciously forgiven. When apologies were forthcoming, Syria was always mollified.

She continued to try to adminster enemas to Patricia, who now resisted them with all her might. So Syria was forced to abandon her ultimate weapon against costiveness. She did not give up easily, and there were some severe struggles first.

Syria felt insulted by the type of approach from a stranger that might have amused another woman. During a day in Bulawayo she lunched alone in the Grand Hotel restaurant. 'A man, probably a bit drunk, tried to talk to me and offered me a drink, after which impertinence, I succeeded in choking him off completely.'

At the beginning of August 1924, seventeen months after Arthur's death, Syria paid her last visit to his grave. It was a hot morning, and she spent some time there. It was hard to leave. Then she turned and made her way back down the stony hill to the Farm, which had promised so much and destroyed so much.

Thirty years later she visited Arthur again. Originally she had wished to be buried there with him, but the passing of so many years, ending in a small cottage in a Somerset village, had led her to abandon this hope. She asked only that the words from Psalm 95 be incised on her own gravestone: 'In His hand are all the corners of the Earth.' She explained this directive to no one, but Patricia understood that her mother was saying that, in death, distance no longer divided them.

There was a send-off group of friends and neighbours on the station platform at Bulawayo. It included the doctors who had looked after Arthur and Syria and their children. Their wives came too. Boomerang was there. He and Major Sharpe had undertaken to keep a watching brief over the Farm and its tenants, and most important of all, a task they would never be able to fulfil, to seek out a purchaser.

Dr. Travers, who had been such a constant support, was combining business which he said he had in Cape Town, with the arduous pleasure of accompanying the family down there. He had chosen this unobtrusive way of helping Syria with a difficult journey, She had with her both young children, their Nanny, and a vast quantity of luggage and impedimenta, including several pieces of furniture. The train guard was very annoyed at the amount Syria confronted him with, and it needed all Dr. Travers' diplomacy to smooth him down. The journey was made in comparative comfort for Syria had rented a coupé, and they had a whole compartment to themselves. They set off on the Sunday and arrived in the early morning of Tuesday. Patricia remembered it as a long blur of unpleasantness. She felt sick, and retained no memory of Mafeking, where her mother took her off the train for a few minutes and went for a walk with her along the platform. It was a few days before her third birthday.

On arrival at Cape Town, Nanny Stanhope took the children to a room in the Grand Hotel for a wash, breakfast and rest, while Syria made final arrangements for her mountain of luggage at the docks.

Later that day they went on board. Patricia followed her mother up a steep ladder onto the liner. She was not used to stairs. There had been no staircase at the Farm and she felt very nervous. But there was no alternative. She knew she had to go on. So she persevered, keeping as close as she could to Syria's heels. For long afterwards she had nightmares about going up and down flights of impossible staircases.

PART II
Suffolk

Patricia was just three years old when she made the voyage from Cape Town to Southampton with her mother Syria, the infant Georgy, and their Nurse, who spent all her time now with Georgy. Patricia was sharing a cabin with a near-stranger, her mother. Syria must have felt keenly the contrast with the voyage out in 1921. Then she and her husband, Dr. Arthur Pearson, had travelled first class, and he had organised deck sports. They had envisaged a promising future together on the 3,000 acre Rhodesian farm he had just bought, and saw no reason to worry about the size of the mortgage. Now she was leaving him alone in his hilltop grave on that farm, and was retreating back to England. The farm was up for sale, but there were no buyers in sight. Her two older sons, Grey, aged twelve, and Peter, aged ten, had already returned, and were staying in London with Arthur's relatives, whom Syria would shortly join.

She led Patricia by the hand round the big P. & O. liner. Patricia was having to get used to stairs. There had been none at the farm. Their cabin let in little daylight and was dimly lit. She slept on a bunk opposite Syria. It seemed odd to be going to bed on a shelf. She often felt sick, as she had on the two-day train journey from Bulawayo to the Cape. When she was feeling better, Syria took her to the big saloon where she was surprised to find plates and cups sunk into niches on the table. She began to get used to her mother. One evening when she was lying awake on her shelf, Syria gave her a ginger biscuit. She did not like the taste, but was pleased to be given the biscuit. She hardly set eyes on Nanny or Georgy, and she did not miss them at all. Syria took her for walks around the deck, and sometimes they sat down to watch the sea, which was turning grey, to match the sky. It was getting cold. Patricia hit on the idea of feigning illness because when she was sick, her mother was especially kind. So while they were walking round the deck, Patricia suddenly sat down and made herself look ill. The ruse was not a success. Syria sent for the ship's doctor, and Patricia was laid out on her back and her naked stomach was subjected to his proddings. This was distressing, because she knew already that nakedness was a shameful state.

Syria herself was having a more interesting voyage than she had anticipated. It started out unpleasantly. She suffered from seasickness for the first thirty-six hours, and had a quarrel with Nurse who, also seasick, was weighed down by the care of Georgy, his nappies and his feeding bottles. There were no facilities on board for dealing with infant hygiene, and Georgy was fractious.

'I will never again travel with young children if I can help it,' wrote Syria in her diary. 'The washing provides big problems.' Nurse stuck grimly to her task, but was disillusioned, and distinctly curt. 'I let her go to church,' wrote Syria, rather grandly, 'But that evening I took her to the Reading Room, and when I spoke to her about her rather abrupt manners - I do get a bit fed up with only getting a handle to my name once in the twenty-four hours – she was very rude and told me she was tired of all this nonsense and wished she had never come. There was no fun to be had on the boat and she disliked it very much.' She offended Syria by telling her that she had never wanted to come and had only done so to oblige her. She wouldn't stay a day longer than six months, and, by the way, she didn't need lessons in manners.

Syria felt ill-used. She assured Nurse that she should leave as soon as she could find someone to replace her, as she did not care to keep people working for her unwillingly. She reminded Nurse that she had said she wanted to come because she was so fond of the children. It was ridiculous of her to be so annoyed with the boat. No one could help it being an unsuitable place for children. Nurse then cried, and her tears softened Syria's heart. She took her for a brisk walk round the chilly deck and tried to cheer her up. But she felt 'dreadfully disappointed in Nurse,' as she thought she had found a faithful treasure in her. As events turned out, she had, but not the kind of treasure that would meekly submit to scoldings and aspersions on her manners.

'But one blow, more or less, doesn't have much effect on me now,' wrote Syria, resignedly.

It was a fact that for Nurse, permanently closeted with Georgy, these were hard times. For Syria, things were looking up. Despite the low spirits into which she had settled over the past months, she found herself beginning to take an interest in the people around her. There were two or three male passengers who came and took Patricia and the baby for walks, and both children attracted pleasing admiration. It was undoubtedly the pretty, aloof young widow who was the source of interest, and she had several friendly invitations to join a game of bridge. One unhappy husband insisted on confiding his marital troubles to her. This displeased Syria, who promptly wrote him off as showing bad taste, the worst social offence in her book. This individual managed to persuade her to act as mediator between himself and his wife. Syria accompanied him reluctantly to their cabin, but the mission was not a success. 'I am afraid I annoyed her and I left quickly.'

Another man asked her advice about his baby's sore bottom. Syria suggested treatment with neat methylated spirits, undeterred by any memory of the screams which this had elicited from Georgy. 'He was very grateful: but his wife was chilly about it as usual.' Perhaps she felt that she, and not Syria, was the right person for her husband to consult about their baby's bottom.

The most interesting encounter was with the ship's Captain, Commander Herbert Porter. He had noticed her as soon as she came on board, and lost no time in inviting her and the children to tea in his cabin. Syria was impressed and found him a charming man. Soon afterwards, he invited her again, this time to his cabin after dinner. He must have known his manners, for he asked her if she minded coming alone. Syria did not mind at all. For the first time since Arthur's death, she had found a man who stirred her. 'It ended in a very wonderful evening, which we both enjoyed.' Similar visits were to follow. The Commander was obviously attracted to Syria, and she allowed herself to respond, at least to a point which did not offend her moral standards. The day before the liner dropped anchor at Southampton was a busy time for them both, but they managed a last stroll along the deck and, he promised to phone her in a couple of days in London and arrange a date.

Syria was definitely interested, but there were difficult times to be got through before their next meeting. She made her way with her little party to Ealing to stay with Arthur's unmarried sister Madge, his bachelor brother Harry John and their unmarried cousin Ethel. This elderly trio lived together in a comfortable three-storey Edwardian house in a tree-lined road. The front garden was small and unremarkable and very different from the one at the back which was long and rambling, with a feel of the country lingering. There was a big lawn with seats, and an ample area behind given over to the cultivation of vegetables and soft fruit bushes. From the raspberries, strawberries and gooseberries she grew there, Aunt Madge produced large quantities of jam and bottled fruit. Syria went there because it cost her nothing and was convenient but there had always been a latent antagonism between her and the two women, particularly with Ethel, who was impulsive and indiscreet and a great favourite with her nephews and nieces. Madge was kind, but a certain aloofness held her back from the closeness which all children enjoyed with Ethel. Harry John was no less popular than she was, but popularity with children was a suspect commodity with Syria who felt that it must have been bought with too much indulgence. But being a man, and perhaps an echo of Arthur, Harry John escaped her censure.

The day before Syria's arrival at Pitt Avenue, her older sons Grey and Peter, who had been dotingly cared for there since reaching England three months earlier, had been despatched to Suffolk, to stay at the new Tunstall Rectory with Aunt Edie, Syria's eldest sister, and her husband Ayscough, who had succeeded their grandfather as Rector. Syria spent two nights at Pitt Avenue, where she deposited quantities of luggage. She also met Commander Porter for a sedate teatime date at Fuller's Tearoom in Regent Street. Then she left the two youngest children with their Nurse at Pitt Avenue and joined the Tunstall contingent. Grey and Peter looked remarkably well, but Aunt Edie reported them as rather spoiled and a little difficult. They had obviously made the most of the months spent under the indulgent eye of the trio in Ealing. Syria viewed Edie's report with suspicion. A spoiled child would have to be unspoiled. Her forebodings were confirmed when she found among Grey's belongings a letter written to him a day or two ago by Cousin Ethel. She made a stern entry in her diary:

'It plainly shows she does not understand how to play the game between a Mother and her children. Grey and Peter will never be allowed to stay at Ealing without me again until they arrive at years of discretion.' She lost no time in seeking to demolish Cousin Ethel's influence:

'I and the children had a very sweet talk together about the whole matter, and I pray to God it has resulted in drawing me nearer to my own and Arthur's dear firstborns, rather than the leaving of that subtle wall of division and misunderstanding between us which was otherwise bound to be the result of such a letter.'

Cousin Ethel disapproved strongly of the methods of child-rearing at the Farm, which she had been hearing about from Harry John. She attributed their severity to Syria's influence, as did the other two. They knew their Arthur, and were sure it could not have been him. But Ethel unwisely had not only conveyed this opinion to the two boys, but had developed it in her letter to Grey. Syria brooded over it but did not take immediate action.

She now had two immediate tasks before her. One was to find a house to rent, preferably not far from her sister Edie, and the other to place the boys in boarding schools. As Grey's godfather had undertaken to pay his fees, it remained only to find the school. This was not easy, because Grey's patchy education had left him below standard for his age. She found an unpleasant little house to rent in Southwold where she proposed to settle for the time being, and decided to get Grey private tuition from a crammer until such time as he was ready to take the entrance exam to a public school. The one she had in mind was Epsom College where his godfather was on the board of governors.

Settling Peter proved easier. He had always worked harder at his lessons and at pleasing Syria, and she was successful in enlisting the three sponsors who were necessary for him to obtain a free place at Christ's Hospital. His enuresis problem had cleared up within a short time of his leaving the Rhodesian prep school where the matron had held up his wet sheets for the other boys in the dormitory to jeer at.

Syria took Peter down to Christ's Hospital for his first term. It was a harrowing experience. She wrote, 'It was a dreadful half hour before leaving him, as he broke down completely, my poor little darling, and hid his head on my shoulder and cried so. He cheered up bravely, however, and we got him into his uniform, and he looked fairly brave when I left him. I found time to visit his Housemaster and his Matron. Maidservants helped them change their clothes, and called them "son" all the time.' Syria does not seem to have been struck by the irony of this.

She went back to stay with a friend in Golder's Green. That night she cried herself to sleep. Reading this years later recalled to Patricia the misery of her own first weeks at boarding school, two hundred and fifty miles from home, and how she had penned desperate letters to her mother, begging to be taken away.

'Don't you worry,' said Syria's friend. 'You're suffering more than she is.'

Patricia's earliest recollections of the new country, England, were not cheerful. They arrived in November. The sun never shone, and there seemed to be little difference between night and day. She disliked train travelling. The peculiar smell on trains made her sick. There were cavernous railway stations, dark and chilly. The streets were crammed with high, dingy houses. Motor cycles were particularly startling. There was endless movement from place to place. But she came to like her elderly relatives in quiet Pitt Avenue, and to feel at home in that house and garden. Aunt Madge was dressed in black, with white hair parted in the middle, fastened at the back in a bun. She had been a beautiful, calm-faced young woman with classical features, but Patricia only knew her as the oldest person she had ever met. She was very different from Syria to look at. To Patricia, her mother looked perfect, with her green eyes and her thick mass of chestnut-brown hair, fastened up with tortoiseshell combs. But although she found Aunt Madge plain, she liked the kindness in her face and her cheerful, encouraging voice. She gave Patricia big flat buttery toffees which they had made together in the kitchen, and she gave her more than Syria would have allowed. She did not know what her aunt made of Georgy, but she certainly liked Patricia and never scolded. Sometimes Aunt Madge stopped what she was doing, and gazed at Patricia fondly, and suddenly hugged her. One day Patricia came to realise that it was her dead and favourite youngest brother that her aunt was seeing in her. She was already hearing over and over again how like her father she looked.

The house began to feel like home. It had landings and staircases that went up and up, but there were cosy carpets, a big white fur rug, shining golden lamps, and many paintings on the walls, for her uncle was an artist who had made a creditable reputation for himself, both as a water colourist and as a painter in oils. His speciality was pert little girls of about nine or ten, with long legs and shingled hair. He belonged to a generation who did not need to read a prurient significance into this. Many of the paintings of these charming children were reproduced on the covers of women's magazines in the 1920's, and Patricia fancied, quite mistakenly, that they were pictures of her. Queen Mary was also said to have bought one of them.

The house smelled pleasantly of flowers and caster sugar, which Patricia enjoyed pouring onto her porridge at breakfast time from a tall silver caster. In the back regions there was the big kitchen where they made toffee and Turkish Delight. There was a scullery, where washing up was done in a glazed sink. In one corner of the scullery stood a copper for the weekly boil-up of household linen, and next it a mangle with rollers for squeezing the water out of the washing. Airing of laundry was done on a couple of pulley-operated runners which ran the length of the kitchen, close to the ceiling, and imparted a warm agreeable smell.

The kitchen was the headquarters of a cook and housemaid, but Aunt Madge spent a good deal of her time there, for she loved cooking cakes, jams and sweets. She also preserved, in large glass bottles fruit grown in the garden. Tinned fruit was not for her. Patricia enjoyed, working with her in the kitchen, a place that was entirely new to her. One of her favourite jobs was dusting down with icing sugar the Turkish Delight they had made.

Aunt Madge was an expert needlewoman as well as cook, and she set to work on a dress with two frills for Patricia, which lent itself cleverly to lengthening, so that Patricia was able to wear it for two or three years. It was made of cream-coloured Liberty silk, covered in small pink roses and blue-green leaves, and Patricia loved it so much she felt like eating it. Syria did not make clothes, though she would mend them until there was practically nothing left of the original garment.

Cousin Ethel, the third member of the Ealing household, was almost as old as Madge. She had a little stoop and a squarish face. with loose wrinkled skin looping from chin to neck. Her voice was rather deep and hoarse, but with a slight laugh in it. She often read Patricia stories from the large store of illustrated children's books which she kept by her.

Nanny was hardly to be seen these days, for now she was free to spend most of her time with Georgy, the child for whom she had crossed the oceans.

Much as Patricia loved being with her aunts and uncle, she could not get used to the dreariness outside the house. The sun seldom shone, and sometimes there had to be walks in dingy park gardens with no flowers. Then her mother arrived back at the Ealing house. Immediately she had taken possession of her bedroom, she altered the position of the main pieces of furniture, as was her custom when she went to stay with anyone. People became resigned to the sound of heavy objects being dragged across the floor shortly after her arrival. She never sought permission, but simply set about altering the geography of other people's rooms. She completed this operation by pulling the bedclothes off the bed, and remaking it to her own design.

Rest time in the dark was now enforced. Patricia submitted unwillingly, for she found herself quite unable to produce the required quota of an hour and a half's sleep, and neither Pinky nor Daisy Dimple, the dolls she had brought with her from Africa, were allowed to keep her company for Syria reasoned that Patricia's long conversations with her dolls would keep her awake.

The day came when the little group left Ealing and moved to the cramped, ugly house in Southwold which Syria had rented. On the way they picked up Grey from Tunstall Rectory. Now he would have to settle down to hard work with a crammer. Patricia remembered the Southwold house with abhorrence. It was not a home, although it was the place where she had to live. The rooms were small and badly lit. The ceiling of the children's bedroom leaked and no amount of repairing cured it. Trunks and boxes were stacked in the hall and in the corners of rooms. Hard white light glared through rattling sash windows, and damp permeated everything. Life seemed one long shiver.

Patricia returned often to the lost home inside her head, with its sun and space and flowers. It was a memory she held onto.

The Southwold house was not only an uncomfortable place, it was an unhappy one. Nanny was cross and silent with Syria, and sharp altercations took place and were recorded verbatim in Syria's diary. She was already having difficulty in retaining the services of various part-time helps, who came to assist with cooking, cleaning and mending. Most could not be relied upon to return after a day or two, and one was inconsiderate enough to allow a miscarriage to interfere with her regular attendance. Nanny had not had a day off for weeks, so Syria graciously granted her a half day on her birthday, with the bonus of time-off in the evening so that she could go to a local dance with Evelyn, one of the part-timers.

'She set off with Evelyn, having been told to return by nine thirty.

She appeared after eleven thirty. I asked her why she was so late, and she said, "I was at the dance".

I said, But I told you to be back at nine thirty. She said, very rudely.

"I'm not going to be dictated to like that. I've never been told before to be back at nine thirty."

I said, Don't speak to me like that, Nurse. Go up to your room!

She said, "I won't go up to my room!"

I said nothing, but later superintended her warming of my baby's food and left the night nursery without a goodnight. I am worn out and wish I and the children were all able to die together. Life is too hopelessly full of difficulties.'

The next morning neither of them spoke to each other. On the third day, Syria broke the silence by requesting an apology from Nurse for her rudeness. Nurse retorted that she saw no reason to apologise. Syria wrote angrily that she remained quite rude in her manner, and very sullen and obstinate. She told Nurse to think things over for two weeks, and if she still did not wish to stay, she could leave in a month. She disposed of Nurse's presence over those two weeks by sending her off with the two children to stay with the obliging Aunt Edie. The atmosphere calmed down, and Nurse agreed to stay on for a while.

Meantime, a storm was brewing up between Syria and the Ealing aunts. Syria had taken great offence at the letter Aunt Ethel had sent Grey a few weeks ago. She could not rest until she had extracted from him exactly what his aunt had said to him. At a firelight supper, she relaxed his guard.

'He said he knew he oughtn't to have done it, but he'd asked his aunts to call him Arthur as he couldn't bear his name of Grey. I asked him carefully why he didn't like Grey, and since when he had disliked it, as he had never told his father or me of this dislike. I told him that I did not want him called Arthur. That was his father's name, and I had chosen that he, Grey, should bear it too, but had said to his Daddy that we would never call him that. There was to be only one Arthur. We would call him Grey, and in this he had been honoured by being called after Daddy's best friend. I told him that no one but his wife was ever to call him just "Arthur".'

Grey told her then that it was really the aunts who had asked why he couldn't be called Arthur, like his father, and who had rather made him feel that he didn't like his mother. 'True, he had gone on to say he wished they hadn't made him feel like that, and that it had always been Ethel who said such things, and not Madge or Uncle Harry John.' Ethel told him that they had to be careful what they wrote to Syria as she was a rather jealous person and didn't understand children. Grey had said to her he agreed about that.

I said I might often be cross and strict with him, that I had to be both his Daddy and Mummy to him, that I did it all from loving motives, and that I understood him better than a distant cousin, for he was actually a part of me and Daddy. He said he thought Ethel had spoiled him, as she used to come in after they were in bed about every ten minutes; that she had of course been very kind, but it wasn't right for her to have said the things she'd said about me. I said 'No, she hadn't played the game, and that kindnesses were as nothing compared to this.' It seems that Peter was with him in all the above. He seemed much relieved at having confided in me, and I said I felt we should be truer friends for having had such a talk. He had his tub and I heard his prayers and read him his *Little Pillows*, and when we had our goodnight kisses he dearly said he wished it could last all

---

* *Little Pillows* A child's devotional book.

night. His parents are fine lovers, and their eldest-born is truly a part and parcel of them in this respect.'

But the glow of that cosy scene did not last long. Two days later, Syria found Grey so careless and disobedient over his table manners that she sentenced him to breakfast in the scullery for the rest of the week. This was one of those staggered punishments she favoured. The miscreant was overshadowed by his wrong-doing for as many days as the penalty was renewed.

Reminded by this event of Aunt Ethel's treacherous innuendos to Grey, Syria penned a barbed letter to her and showed it to her sister for approval. Edie advised her not to send it, remarking that she would be very upset to receive such a letter herself. This advice was ignored. Aunt Ethel's cause was immediately taken up by a more formidable opponent. In terms of cool frigidity, Aunt Madge could equal Syria when she chose, and she chose to do so now. Syria found herself well advised to restrain her spleen in future. She did not wish to go so far as a permanent break with Arthur's sister.

When she was older, Patricia discovered that the whole Ealing household, as well as further outreaches of Arthur's family, deplored Syria's child-rearing methods. They had been none too happy about Arthur's either, and Uncle Harry John had written to him in Africa querying the beatings he had been administering to the boys with a rhino-hide whip. But they knew their Arthur, and united in attributing the general direction these matters were taking to Syria's powerful influence. It did nothing to endear her to them, but they wanted very much to remain in touch with Arthur's children.

CHAPTER 14

By now, Syria had assembled a platoon of domestics who came and went, cleaning the house, clearing out the kitchen range, laying fires, ironing and washing, cooking and mending. It was only a small house in an ordinary small town, but about five women seem to have been occupied in its upkeep. This did not prevent Syria from feeling overworked and exhausted. She did some of the cooking and mending herself, and took the children over from Nurse for half a day a week, to allow her the few hours that hardworked individual had managed to wrest from her employer as a condition of staying on. And Syria was forever writing letters and doing accounts. Every penny, literally, had to be accounted for. Nor did she sleep well. The nights were often broken by Georgy's toothcutting howls and Patricia's bilious attacks. Grey took the entrance exam to Epsom College and failed. Cramming had to continue. Syria went to London and managed to fit in another teatime outing with Commander Porter, who was briefly back in England. They had a walk together afterwards and she promised 'faithfully' that she would go on writing.

Then she set off to Edinburgh for a fortnight's stay with Patricia's godmother. She noted that Grey had accepted her recent departure more cheerfully than she had expected.

Eleanor Donoghue, her hostess, was the wife of a fashionable lawyer. This undoubtedly was a source of satisfaction to Syria. She collected names with handles and prided herself on being an arbiter of taste, and she appreciated the social tone of the company she met with in Eleanor's house. But she found herself and her friend moving away from each other.

'I inadvertently made a confidence to her which I regretted afterwards. I wished I had not said what I had, and regret in myself this too much talking phase which I find I am liable to fall into since my great loneliness came to me. It is natural but unwise.' Reading this, the adult Patricia found it hard to imagine that her mother had ever done too much talking. She seldom perceived in her any tendency to confide, though she liked to cull confidences from others, with a subtle stealth that they did not notice till too late. Patricia herself fell for this technique at first, but over the years she learned to defend her own privacy, and, even while regretting it, found that she could not tell her mother anything about herself which mattered to her.

Syria suffered one or two crushing migraines, but the visit was a restful change of scene. She appreciated the leisurely breakfast in bed brought up by the maid, and the social round took her out of herself. She also wrote many letters, and did some mending for her hostess. She tried on a few nearly new surplus clothes of Eleanor's, which she consented to accept. When she returned to her leaking house in Southwold, she was given a welcome which heartened her by Nurse and the two children. The change had benefited everyone.

There were disappointments in store. Grey had failed his common entrance exam for the second time, and an appointment with a person unnamed in her diary was not kept. This was almost certainly Commander Porter, about whom she had dreamt all one night in Edinburgh. References to him become cryptic. It really was too soon for her to think of remarriage, and he, despite the strong attraction he had obviously felt to begin with, might by now have detected warning signs. They continued to meet occasionally for some years, for Patricia, at the age of ten, remembered him, a tall good-looking man who took her and her mother out to the London zoo, and to tea in Claridges afterwards. That was on a glorious summer afternoon in 1931, but Patricia never saw him again. He had helped Syria to realise that romantic interest in a man could return, despite the disaster of Arthur's death.

She continued to oppress herself greatly with the many tasks that she felt obliged to perform from early in the morning until midnight. Nurse herself was labouring almost non-stop. She was now allowed a few hours off over weekends, but one of those hours had to be spent in church. Her employer expected it.

As well as looking after Patricia and Georgy during the day and often during the night, for Patricia was a restless and complaining sleeper, she had to take thirteen-year old Grey out for walks. He continued to get on Syria's nerves, not being one to pay attention to little details, and when scolded he became morose. Unlike Peter he was not on the lookout for ways of being helpful, and the scoldings often ended in tears. The solitary lessons at the crammers gave no opportunity for finding companions of his own age. He often made mistakes through inattention. Syria could not overlook mistakes. 'Thou shalt not make mistakes' was for her the Eleventh Commandment. It was laziness and it was a kind of disobedience. He made it so difficult for her to idealise him as the firstborn Son of the Father. She took him out to the shops to buy an amber pendant as a Christmas present for herself. Patricia remembered that pendant. It looked like a huge drop of Golden Syrup suspended from a gold chain. Syria must have made a substantial contribution towards its cost. She would finger it, saying, 'Grey gave me this.' It was perhaps an attempt to restore in herself a better humour towards Grey.

Peter did not come home for Christmas, for Christ's Hospital was having a bout of chicken pox, for which three weeks of quarantine was ordained, and Syria observed all quarantines to the letter. So once more Aunt Edie at Tunstall was called upon to take him for the first half of the holidays. It was Syria's regular practice to separate the contagious child from the rest, and later, following this principle, Patricia was to find herself dumped several times with no warning on strange households, not all of whom were pleased to have her.

Having disposed of the contagious Peter, Syria made the hazardous decision to take the other children and Nurse to Ealing for Christmas. It was not a success. 'A real Ealing situation had materialised by 8.45 a.m.' she wrote, the day after arrival. 'The usual thing. My arrangements for sleep, etc., etc., etc., for the babies pointed out very politely as being criticisable. Grey has "the Ealing attitude" pretty badly developed, and left the house with Ethel for church with no kiss for me, and a defiant air. Patricia was very rude to me (in her baby way) at being put to bed at 10.45 am, and Baby shrieked and shrieked.' Grey enjoyed his visit. Aunt Ethel treated him to two shows, *Treasure Island* and *Peter Pan*. Aunt Madge never entered a theatre on account of her religious principles, for she was a Plymouth Sister, but she did not impose these on others. Christmas Day came, and after breakfast the children were given their presents.

Grey did not manifest sufficient gratitude to satisfy Syria. She was not one of those people with a happy instinct for giving the right thing. That night Nurse was very sick, bur Syria was unsympathetic, for she saw it as entirely Nurse's own fault:

'She had been up with Cook's family the night before and, confessed, after close questioning, that she had had sweet port to drink and a nut or two. Cook, however, told Madge that she had gorged on two sausage rolls and turkey for her supper. I am sorry Nurse has this habit of misleading one, as it makes me feel uncertain of her. But she is better than most are in this respect, I suppose, so I said nothing.'

Patricia was crying a lot and getting "rather spoilt," and Syria decided to take them home two days after Christmas. She collected Peter from the Rectory en route. During the following week Peter had the misfortune to almost overturn the pram with Georgy and Patricia both in it. Although Syria herself had once managed to overturn it completely when Georgy was in occupation, and to give him a bruise on the head, she was not disposed to deal lightly with Peter.

'He did it by carelessness, so I sent him to Coventry and gave him lines to write out. Had a scene with him as he told lies the old way which had so disgusted Arthur and me.'

Syria now had to contend with three liars, Grey, Peter and Nurse.

Aunt Edie's home at the Rectory where Peter had spent Christmas was a relaxed place, which contrasted markedly with the atmosphere at Southwold, where everyone, including the querulous "babies" and the part-time workers, was on edge. Things had calmed down to some extent by the time Peter was due to return to school, though shortly before his departure, he was sent from the lunch table for vulgarity to Patricia. But on the day he left, Syria's softened mood, helped by Peter's obvious reluctance to leave home and herself, led her to refer fondly to "My Peter." It was never "My Grey." Once more that irritating lad had shown himself as "very non-committal." He was learning to look after himself in a way she didn't care for. Peter never learned it at all. Grey did cry on the eve of Peter's departure, but he cried out of sympathy for Peter, who was sobbing his heart out. Grey's life was quite bizarre for a big strong boy of rising fourteen. His mother "put him to bed," as early as 7.30 when that suited her, or as late as 9 or 10 if she wanted company. She was developing an ingrained disapproval of the person he was.

In her eyes, he was headstrong, lazy and not affectionate enough. He still needed breaking in. She had to be father as well as mother to him, and the late Rector of Tunstall had shown her what a father's duty was. She found herself better at being Grey's father than his mother.

Early in March she took him to Berkhamsted, his father's old school, where Arthur had distinguished himself by every kind of schoolboy achievement. His likeness was to be seen still in school portraits of the football team, the Officers' Training Corps, and the shooting team, gazing tall, earnest and upright, upon the little world he had conquered. At last Grey found a school willing to accept him, unpromising scholar though he might seem. He sat and passed the common entrance exam there and then, and Syria had a reassuring and "nice" talk with the Headmaster, Mr. Greene.* Financial concessions were agreed, and Grey's godfather would be paying the balance. He would enter school next term, Mr. Greene's commonsense was to prove of value to Grey. In the meantime there were two months for him to survive at home. Syria inspected his leisure reading and disapproved. 'I made him start reading Gilbert White's *Selborne* to me after lunch as he spends all his spare time on infantile stories.'

A fracas ensued in the matter of a financial transaction, managed by Grey, of a threepenny loan from Nurse in order to repay a twopenny loan from a local boy. Grey's problem was under-capitalisation. Syria took this rather clever legerdemain very hard. She scolded him so harshly that he broke down in tears, and then confided to her diary that if it hadn't been for the Babies she really thought she would have done something desperate. Further evidence of Grey's moral deterioration came to hand the very next day. Nurse unwisely told Syria about Baby having fallen on the back of his head while he was with Grey the previous Sunday, and how Grey had not confessed to it till Monday. The pram was becoming a dangerous place for Baby. Grey was being steadily edged into a climax of compulsive confessions which did him no good at all. It was to be some time before he grew wiser.

* Father of the writer 'Graham Greene'.

Syria was relentless. Less than a week later she brought her biggest guns to bear on this intractable boy: 'Grey was very rude at breakfast, and I told him I'd have nothing more to do with him till he apologised. This he didn't do until I was leaving him for the night without kissing him.' He had succeeded in standing up to her for a whole day, but the outcome was inevitable. The lying apology, ruthlessly extracted, would always in the end serve up to Syria the submission she required.

Patricia was barely three and a half but already Syria had marked her down as a budding rebel. 'Had to whip my Patricia this morning,' she noted. The offence was not recorded. The most humiliating part of this unpleasant chastisement was the bum-stripping.

The impression of never-ending darkness continued. Nurse would take them out for a walk during what Patricia took to be night time, but which turned out to be day. Sometimes life in the disagreeable Southwold house was exchanged for a spell at Aunt Edie's pleasant Rectory. She and Georgy were parcelled off with Nurse while Syria went on her travels. It was good at the heart of the gentle Suffolk countryside with the easy-going Aunt and Uncle Ayscough, the Rector. They had a gardener called Alfred, and Patricia and Alfred enjoyed each other's company. She sang to him all the songs she used to sing to the gardener Hartenborg in Africa, and which she had learnt from Nanny, who sang a lot when she was in a good temper. For years afterwards, the ageing Alfred remembered Patricia as the little girl who sings.

She loved her big Uncle Ayscough, who used to come up and kiss her goodnight in bed. She put her ragdoll Pinky to bed in the empty black grate in her bedroom because it reminded her of the bunk she had slept in on board ship. She was surprised when Nanny scolded her for this sensible adaptation.

The only trouble was that they always had to leave this haven again for miserable Southwold. They went by car and that made her sick. Travelling did not suit her. Her mother, whom she seldom saw, continued to look gloomy, and Nanny was irritable most of the time. She pushed the big baby carriage, containing passive little Georgy, along the pavement, with Patricia walking alongside. She was seldom allowed in the pram now. They went past small houses, all alike, with tiny garden patches in front. Sometimes they went on to the shops, sometimes to a muddy country lane where tall posts by the roadside, linked by wires, sang a strange song of their own in the wind.

Patricia already knew that her mother was right about everything, and that she herself was wrong. What mother said was so, and no backchat. It was just Patricia's naughty nature that made her disagree with mother so often. Sometimes she stood in front of the hall mirror, gazing at her reflection with a stern expression on her face, and repeated over and over again, 'You mustn't do that.' It made no difference, for she went on doing the wrong things. With Nanny it was different. Although mother taught her that grown-ups were always right, Patricia could see for herself that she did not really apply this principle to Nanny. Perhaps Nanny was not a proper grown-up. She had certainly done one very peculiar thing. Patricia knew that she must not take what did not belong to her (although Georgy often took her things and no one stopped him). She knew, too, that one must not enter another person's garden uninvited, let alone pick their flowers without permission. Yet one fine morning Nanny made Patricia break both these rules. They were walking past a house whose front garden was full of blue, pink and white hyacinths. Nanny stopped the pram at the open gateway and told Patricia to enter the garden of this unknown house and pick a bunch of the heavily-scented beauties. Fearful, but not daring to disobey, she crept in, hurriedly picked a few, and ran back to Nanny, who hid them under the pram cover. Then they continued their walk, Patricia anxious to get away as quickly as possible, lest an angry garden-owner come chasing after her. She hoped such a misdeed would never be required of her again. She felt sure that Mother never knew of the crime. She kept quiet about it, for grown-ups sided with grown-ups, and children ended up confounded.

Georgy, who in the lost land of the sun had been a bald, white little creature, was changing. His head was now covered with silky brown hair, and his blue eyes gazed gently upon the world. He could say a few words. Syria and Nanny were united in their adoring preference for him. He gave them very little trouble. But Patricia did not find him as easy to be with as in the days at the Farm when she broke through her playpen to share a toy with him. Now he could move from place to place and steal her toys, and worse, he could break them. She was enraged when he got hold of her set of red wooden bowls that fitted neatly into each other in graded sizes. She loved their smooth scarlet shapes. He took them secretly and she did not discover the theft until he had broken all of them except one. Her cherished set of bowls was ruined. He had not even played with them, for she found him simply sitting there, breaking the thin wooden sides by banging them against the floor. It was very wrong of him, and he was a stupid creature. She rushed at him with a roar, seized one destructive little hand, thrust the whole of it into her mouth and bit it hard. He shrieked, Nanny burst into the room, and Patricia expected her to turn on him too, but to her amazement, it was she whom Nanny attacked, smacked, and shut away in a room by herself, while Georgy was petted and fussed over.

The one remaining bowl, the largest, was not restored to her. Mother confiscated it for good and put it out of reach on her bedroom mantelpiece, whence the middle-aged Patricia surprised herself by retrieving it on her mother's death, with a ridiculous feeling of justice having at last been done.

The bad times went on. Georgy grizzled, Nanny scolded, and mother was aloof and sad. Grey clouds raced over dark skies. Lights shone in the afternoon shops, but gave no warmth. They often shivered in their chilly house, heated for the most part by tall black oil stoves. The bedroom ceiling still leaked. Patricia felt sick and was dosed with castor oil which made her sicker still. She overheard snatches of cross conversations between her mother and Nanny. It seemed that just as children mattered less than grown-ups, so some grown-ups mattered less than others, and if they argued, they were being rude, just like children. Nanny, it was clear, was much less important than Mother, who sometimes treated her like a very rude child indeed, and then went about silent and grim-lipped. The children were often left alone while Nanny was busy about various household tasks. Still feeling angry with Georgy, Patricia decided to give him coal to eat one morning when they were alone together. To her surprise, Georgy told her he liked it, so her little act of revenge misfired.

CHAPTER 15

One spring day they left the Southwold house and never went back. They moved to a roomier place, in better repair, in the little town of Leiston, a few miles away. It was a semi-detached late Victorian house, one of a row on the edge of the country, opposite the doctor's house. There was a tiny front garden, entirely filled up by an enormous clump of feathery pampas grass. On the front gate, Syria had set a board which named the house Gaveston, after the Farm in Rhodesia. There was a French window at the back, leading into a garden which was nearly all lawn, with a flower bed on the left and a few fruit trees on the right. The end of the garden was cut off from the rest of the world by a high red brick wall, and just in front of this Syria had set up a pleasant wooden summerhouse. This was to be much used for summer lessons and for afternoon tea. It faced south and received the sun.

Indoors, there was a dark dining room in front, where the pampas grass permanently obscured the light. A shadowy staircase led to the bedrooms and Syria's drawing room, which had two big sash windows through which Patricia watched a man on a ladder lighting the street lamps as dusk. The room housed an ebony upright piano with three pedals. It had had to be hoisted piecemeal through the window from the garden below because it proved too big for the narrow staircase.

As was her custom, Syria recruited an army of part-time helpers to keep the establishment going. There was a weekly gardener, a washerwoman, and cleaning girls who came and went. There was one daily regular, Winnie, who did most of the cooking and had a talent for sketching small, neat heads which she copied off postage stamps. There was an amiable retired district nurse call Hughie, who contributed occasional services on Nanny's half-day off. Patricia shared her mother's liking for Hughie, a kindly woman of even temperament, the sort of person Syria seldom felt a need to scold. Her own sister Edie and husband Ayscough had been assiduous in helping her to set up house and introducing local friends, but Syria noticed that they always seemed anxious to get away as soon as possible. Ayscough would never stay to tea. She was aggrieved, but decided not to make an issue of it.

Numerous ladies called and left visiting cards, among them the doctor's wife from across the road and the vicar's wife from the church which Syria had begun to attend. She went to the eleven o'clock Sunday Mattins, and in school holidays she took with her Grey, who dragged his feet, and Peter, who was willing to accompany her anywhere. In term time she occasionally took Patricia who felt favoured but did not follow anything, and did not like the darkness of the church. They left before the sermon.

The leaving of a visiting card had to be reciprocated within a few days, so to begin with, Syria was kept fairly busy with this social duty. It provided some relief from a timetable of tasks, which included practising her piano pieces, and mending and writing letters. Syria was a meticulous correspondent, both in business matters and with her children and everyone else she knew, and by old age had covered thousands of sheets of paper with her firm, clear hand, which never faltered into feebleness until her final frail year. Even then, during convalescence after a major operation, she managed to drag it back into something approaching its former strength. She exacted twice-weekly letters from her children, not only during school years, but for as long after that as they would stand for it. When Patricia finally flagged, Syria produced such a powerful combination of displeasure and pathos that she found herself continuing to write once a fortnight almost to the end of her mother's days. Then, just when they should least have done so, her timings became erratic, and her last letter to her mother arrived, too late to be read, the day after her sudden death. Telephone calls were not accepted as a substitute for a properly composed letter, with its family news and reassuring, if ritualistic affirmations of affection. And letters flowed back in return, and Patricia had to admit that Syria was capable of an entertaining turn of phrase, as well as an exquisitely tuned ability to provoke. Correspondence could become acerbic, but there was always the obligatory loving ending and the row of kisses. It was hard to take in, after she died at the age of eighty three, that not one more letter would be coming, and not one more need be written.

Syria derived much pleasure from Peter's adoration. 'He is such a dear,' she wrote in her diary after meeting his train from school, 'and seemed so glad to be with me.' Every evening after supper she had Grey and Peter join her in the drawing room for half an hour. Sometimes she took them for walks along country lanes. She remained frustrated at her failure to make a firm conquest of Grey. She was still struggling to keep grief at bay, and though she held out in the day, too proud to let anyone see her cry, her diary tells of how she often broke down at night. But despite the difficulties with Grey, the children could be unexpectedly cheering. The boys had been invited out for a motor car picnic by one of the local ladies and her young son. Syria had not expected to accompany them, but at the last moment was invited to join them. 'How nice!' exclaimed Peter. 'It will be twice as nice if you come.' That evening, as he was about to recite his prayers, Peter said, 'You're a real Mummie, not a doll!' And Syria noted: 'He says such quaint things. He seems so fond of me, and it seems almost too good to be true.'

Georgy, too, was proving an asset. 'When I was bathing Baby, the church bells started ringing, and I made him listen. It made me feel insufferably sad and yearning for my husband (who loved bells too) and it seemed exactly as though Georgy understood, for simultaneously with my sudden hugging of him to me, he threw his dear head on my breast and clung to me. He just wouldn't let me go, but stayed like that for some minutes, and I think it was the only thing in the world that could have comforted the keen agony of my soul. I wonder if Arthur was the force that made him do it. I love to think so. The habit of loneliness will never become easy.'

Grey made sporadic efforts to break through into the natural ways of a boy of his age. They had unfortunate effects. Returning home after a day in Ipswich, Syria was depressed and worried to discover that he had been out for three hours in the cold without permission, after a hot bath, and with wet hair.' I was very angry,' Syria's anger was expressed with an arctic coldness, so that the recipient felt effectively banished from the human race. The next day she cut Grey's hair and gave him what she called a talking to. He told her that he believed she loved Patricia more than him. He was wrong. The true object of jealousy should have been Georgy. Subsequently he became quite clear about this, and told Patricia that he had had a dream of dancing on a pile of skulls, all of them Georgy's.

There were few things that Syria liked doing more than making out neat timetables for her employees and children. Prior consultation seems never to have been undertaken, and, once defined on paper, a timetable had the force of law. Arrival in the Leiston house gave occasion for new programmes. Nurse was called in to go over hers in detail.

'I told her about having to do the day nursery fire now, preparing it at night. She flatly refused, and said she wasn't going to do any more work at night, that she got no time to herself, not even to write her letters. I said that this was the usual way a nurse had to do, and I could run my house in no other way.' But Syria had been discovering compromise was sometimes necessary with Nurse. 'I advised her to think it over, trying it out for a week. She was very obstinate and inclined to be rude, so I said I wanted no words between us and hoped she would do her best to carry out the rules for a week at least and then talk to me again.' Nurse continued to object to the rules, so that Syria had to give in and pay Winnie the maid for an extra hour's work instead.

Leiston social life was gathering pace. One contact led to another. More calls were made and returned. Syria made critical comments in her diary about most of the ladies, but she needed them to go on coming. She invited them to afternoon tea, followed by card games. The visitors left at six. Syria did not encourage anyone to stay longer. But her depression was lifting. One day in April, about two years after Arthur's death, she recorded 'Lazed, smoked and read a book this afternoon for the first time since I was in Bulawayo hospital.'

Two days later, Mrs Starling, mother-in-law of a local widower, the retired Royal Naval officer, Captain Hugh Thring, called with his three motherless children, and invited Grey and Peter to tea. Syria resented grandmother Starling's searching questions to the two boys as to what had happened to their father and how he had died, betraying what she regarded as bad taste. When she grew older, Patricia was to ponder over her mother's sensitivities regarding what seemed quite inoffensive questions about herself. Syria had no qualms about probing into every corner of her children's lives.

She found the two older Thring children well-mannered and acceptable. They were near in age to her two boys. No comment was made about the youngest, a girl of ten. Shortly after this visit, Peter sought to reassure himself that Syria would never remarry. She asked him if he would mind much if she did, and he said he would hate it, for it would make him forget his own father. He went on to enquire how you got a woman to marry you. Perhaps he wondered if an earlier childhood vision of walking down the aisle with his mother might even now rescue him from a new and unknown father.

It was very different with Grey. Although there had been moments when he had seemed almost as pleasingly devoted to her as Peter, a chronic state of unease existed between them. He started wandering about the house at night, and Syria had to be what she described as rather firm with him, and he cried. She had a knack of extracting tears from him. Despite her firmness, Grey's night wanderings continued until the time came for him to return to Berkhamsted School. This time the tribute of tears came as routine. 'Grey cried over his prayers – is very sad at leaving me – says he feels it much more that he did going to his Rhodesian school as he loves me more than he did then.' Peter, as was to be expected, cried too. Next morning the reluctant pair were taken to London and seen off, each on his respective train. Syria spent the night at a hotel to avoid the unpleasantness of staying with her Ealing in-laws. More frosty letters had been exchanged, and Ealing was for the present a no-man's-land. Next day she had lunch at D.H. Evans, a large store in Oxford Street. It was a popular rendezvous for shopping ladies and had a big restaurant with uniformed waitresses. Here she fell into conversation with a well-dressed woman of young middle age.

'We discussed women's morals, morals generally, boys' schools, present-day woman, the Secret Service, Roman Catholicism and the power of their priests even in politics, the decadence of Winchester School, Winston Churchill, and I don't know what not. Disappointingly, she did not give me her card, but left, thanking me for the delightful conversation. She gave me the impression that her husband is in the Army, and that she moves in high circles.' What might have been a valuable catch, had eluded Syria.

The next day she met with what she felt was a direct snub from an unexpected quarter. Although her brother-in-law Harry John shared a home with the alienated Ealing women, it had never occurred to her that he might also share their views about her. He must have taken care to steer clear of the squabbles. But when she called uninvited at his Whitehall office, he was not welcoming. He did not even ask her to sit down and, making no convincing excuse, left immediately. She felt a wet sponge had been thrown in her face.

Disappointed, she travelled back to Ipswich, and spent the night at The Girls' Friendly Society, to economise after staying at the London hotel. She hated it there, and hurried home to Leiston next day in low spirits. Tea at the Rectory that afternoon made a happy change, and they gave her a bunch of cowslips from their garden. She was comforted too, by the presence of the "Babies," although Nurse seemed to have something on her mind.

During that May, Syria suffered from neuralgia, and from attacks of intense irritability which she could not account for. One morning it was the yelling of both her babies, which tore her nerves to shreds. She dealt with it by sticking to a stiff routine, which seemed endlessly overcrowded despite all the help she had in the house. But relief came at the end of May. All the pains and irritability cleared up instantly when she had a visit from old African friends, Mr and Mrs Moore. Syria would have preferred to have him all to herself, but she made the best of his wife, who enjoyed, not only her food but her drink as well. Syria did not approve of women who indulged in alcohol. She noted in her diary that Mrs Moore now weighed eleven stone. Syria prided herself on being only nine. However, she was a necessary condition of his visit, and Syria's spirits soared on that one happy day. They left, planning to return next year.

Meantime, Syria had to undergo an experience she dreaded. Her feet were still distorted by ill-fitting shoes handed down in childhood, and they had continued to trouble her despite an operation in Bulawayo. She made arrangements to go into Guy's, Arthur's old teaching hospital in London, to have her two hammer toes operated on. She had to go into a large public ward in the days well before the

National Health Service. There was a heavy institutional air about this long ward, with its double row of beds facing each other. As soon as she saw it, she felt like running straight home. It was, she commented, an indescribable experience, and no doubt good for one to have to go through. It was one way of seeing life. Her bed, next to the door, was Number 20. Next to her was an old woman who had badly injured her nose on Whit Monday, and next to this patient was a seriously ill, scalded baby of fifteen months. Another patient, a young woman, was brought in drunk on Whit Monday, but soon after Syria's arrival, she had to have a gangrenous leg amputated, and died shortly afterwards.

Syria's toes continued to be very painful after the operation, and the baby screamed incessantly. Suddenly her nerve snapped, and she had what she described as a most undignified fit of sobbing, through which she was steered by the unexpected kindness of one of the nurses. She had several visitors, including a visit of conscience by the two Ealing women. There was a determination on both sides not to be seen at fault, and this necessitated a hospital visit, which Syria could well have dispensed with.

Open warfare between Syria and her surgeon broke out a day or so later when he inspected her feet and gave instructions about dressings over the next four weeks. For these she would have to return to the foot clinic.

'He was very upset with me because I asked him when I could leave hospital. He said, 'Why do you want to leave hospital?' I counterattacked by asking him if he would like to be in hospital. He just went off the deep end at me before the whole ward. He had started the interview by being rather discourteous, I thought, asking Nurse whether I always looked depressed, and whether I was ever cheerful. His own face rather resembles the Black Sea during a thunderstorm.'

It was a shock to Syria to encounter a doctor who did not live up to her idealistic view of the profession. The unpleasantness was offset by a visit next day from Sir Alfred Fripp, a top member of the hierarchy.

'He came to see me and stayed twenty minutes, and was most kind and charming, called me 'my dear' twice, in such a nice, fatherly way. I was most attracted to him. He wished for my address, saying he thought it quite possible he might hear of someone who would buy my Farm. He asked me the manner of Arthur's death. I asked him to let me write it to him as I could not bear to speak of it.' His opening remark was, 'So you married my dear old Arthur Pearson, my house surgeon.'

Fellow patients continued to be objects of curiosity and some disapproval. One woman, coming round from chloroform, made, 'a hysterical fuss,' and the occupants of some of the beds were "coarse" in their conversation. The talk, that particular evening, was very vivid, and "distinctly recherché," as Syria put it, and all the ward received a detailed account of one patient's love life.

Sir Alfred paid another friendly visit, in which he described his own early struggles to qualify and support his family. He had no sooner qualified than both parents and his brother died within ten days of each other. Despite this blow, he had, he said, retained a faith in the existence of an all-powerful and wise Being, and he had no doubts about a future life. This was just what Syria needed to hear. He held her hand a minute before going and said they must keep in touch.

A day or two later, she left, with a special farewell to the nurse who had seen her through her lowest moments. By an extraordinary coincidence, it turned out that she was the sister-in-law of motherly Sister Marcus in Rhodesia, who had looked after Syria during Georgy's birth at the Farm, 'I could get very fond of this woman,' wrote Syria, summing her up in terms of unusual praise: 'She is faithful, sympathetic, unselfish and warm-hearted.'

Two of the other nurses received good reports for qualifying as "ladies." A fourth was written off. She suffered from a swollen head, and was too fond of men. Syria was surprised and gratified to receive many friendly parting wishes from the other patients, hysterical and coarse though she might have judged some of them to be, and she was pleased when one of them told her that she looked much too young to be the mother of four children.

She now set out to visit each of her sons in turn at their boarding schools. The visit to Peter at Christ's Hospital went off smoothly, as events involving Peter nearly always did. The same could not said of her visit to Grey at Berkhamsted School. She was spending a few days with Arthur's stockbroker brother and his glamorous wife at their house on the edge of Ashridge golf course, and she went from there to take Grey out to tea. They had not been together long before Syria began to suffer from the usual irritation. His appearance was all wrong. He had lost his white cricket sweater and his handkerchief was inky. He made one or two of his confessions to her, which put his account even more deeply into the red. Had he, she enquired, written to thank Aunt Edie for the cakes she had sent him? Yes, he said, and had posted the letter. A few minutes later he was moved to confess that it was still lying in his locker. She passed over this aberration fairly lightly, but he came out with another confession shortly after. He had been talking in the dormitory after lights-out, until eleven o'clock. She could not take pride in this slovenly, untruthful schoolboy, so unlike the upright fellow his father had been. It seemed to make it worse that he looked so like Arthur. She did her best to say goodbye to him without showing her annoyance too openly.

On her return to Leiston, she received an impressive welcome from Patricia and Georgy. 'They look and behave splendidly,' she wrote. 'And are so happy. The improvement in them is most marked in every way.' Syria had been absent from home for about six weeks.

Next day the vicar's wife called and took her out in the car for tea, sending her home with a huge bunch of roses from the Vicarage garden. But acute attacks of inner loneliness were never far away. She kept up her piano practice, remembering how Arthur used to enjoy listening to her playing when he came back to the Farm in the evening. Now young children were her only audience, though an appreciative one. The piano tuner came, and she invited him to lunch for company, needing above all at that moment to have someone to talk to. Such events were only palliative. She wrote poignantly: 'Had a desperate evening, felt hopeless with loneliness and the silence, when I was craving companionship. Read a book, but nothing reduced it. Slept splendidly, and woke up at 5.45 in the morning, and thanked God for the seven hours oblivion he had granted me.'

Patricia was yelling again a good deal these days. However hard Nurse tried not show it, she felt an antipathy for her. Georgy, by contrast, was so easy to like. Patricia was irritable and unbiddable.

At the Farm, Syria had felt driven to intervene sometimes when Nurse had shown obvious unkindness, and she did so again now. 'Was annoyed because Nurse deliberately left Patricia screaming in her room, and I had to go to her. She left Patricia screaming again when she brought Baby to breakfast yesterday because she couldn't manage her. When I told her she must not leave her like that, Nurse said she couldn't always humour her.' Patricia's yells upset Syria, but Nurse seemed to have quite a tolerance for them.

At the end of July, Syria went to London and met again her great support Mr Moore and his wife, due to return soon to their home in Northern Rhodesia. 'I loved being with him, and thank God for such a dear, true friend. Then an afterthought, 'She was also nice.'

Syria went to London to meet the two boys off their trains for the summer holidays. She met Grey at Euston and felt the familiar distaste. 'He had his macintosh on,' she wrote. 'He held his straw hat, his rug, his despatch case, and a disgracefully kicked and rubbed pair of slippers, tied together with string. He had no tie on, collar and vest undone, a horrid outbreak on his face. In his pockets, which were bulging, were six large handkerchiefs, two ties, two boxes, and a cap. I had to take him to a waiting room before I could be seen out with him. His face and neck were very dirty. His toothpowder, sent to him on June 26th, hadn't been touched. He really is a trying child. I felt like chucking his untidy shoes to the winds and going off to the South Sea Islands. One gets so weary of scolding. He says the boys in his dormitory are allowed to take books to bed with them to read.' That was something never allowed in Syria's household.

Next, she met Peter off the train from Horsham, neatly turned out in his Christ's Hospital uniform, with long navy coat, bright gilt buttons and yellow knee-length stockings. His appearance never let her down. They all returned to Leiston together, and for Syria the gloom seems to have intensified. She cried every night in bed and was sleeping badly. She felt she could not stand much more. She gave two-year old Georgy his first whipping because, for the fourth time (Syria was always accurate with numbers) he was tearing wallpaper off the wall. 'Had to whip Patricia too,' she continued, though why was not disclosed. Whipping did not mean mere smacking. It was a ritualised, pants-down affair, which went on long enough to give rise to a good deal of bellowing, compounded of pain and outrage.

Grey continued to annoy. Syria set about doctoring the spots on his face and she administered hot fomentations to a festering toenail. On the first day of the holiday she fomented it five times. Fomentation was an excellent training in stoicism. She slapped the lint straight out of boiling water onto the shrinking, often bleeding wound, and firmly pressed a piece of green, waterproof cloth on top to keep the heat in, securing all with a bandage. Grey's foot continued to give trouble.

'He became unhappy because I have no further birthday present for him, having given him one last May in advance. He said didn't I promise him something else. I sat on him. That sort of thing annoys me so.' Why, reasoned Syria, should a boy whose birthday falls in the last week of August, expect anything else if he had a present in May?

Grey had not finished with his complaints. He grumbled again about his name, mentioning that Aunt Ethel had a surname for a Christian name, but did not use it. 'When he began to get argumentative I sat on him again. He gets very sulky-tempered over these situations. I feel I ought to be able to avoid them, but don't know how. It ends in it getting on my nerves after two or three weeks of it. There had been only five days of the holiday so far.

But at bedtime Grey could be counted upon to make the required gesture. 'He apologised so sweetly to me after saying his prayers tonight.' She had the grace to add, 'I just felt ashamed of my sharp temper. He also begged to be allowed to come up earlier to sit with me after supper, or he'd see nothing of me, and I do feel surprised that he wants to, for I'm generally too busy and too tired to be the attractive person that I ought to be to him.'

Soon they had a short rest from each other. Syria had been invited to visit former friends from Africa at their house in Dorset. They had settled in Rhodesia years earlier and had made a financial success of farming, acquiring 95,000 acres on two separate farms. Leaving these farms with managers until such time as they would fetch a good price, they had returned to England and bought a country estate near Blandford Forum. During her stay with them, Syria met many county folk. Some were relatives of James and Diana Thompson-Perry her hosts, and all were connected by networks of marriage or long friendship. Syria filled several closely written pages of her diary with details of their histories. She went for walks with her hostess, did jigsaws, played bridge, and discussed African prospects. Diana Thompson-Perry thought she knew someone who might be interested in Gaveston. Trouble was looming for Syria. She had to continue paying the mortgage, and the present lessee had intimated that he did not wish to stay on for another year.

Relations with her hostess remained harmonious, and Syria left this pleasant place reluctantly. Invitations for the future had been forthcoming from some of the guests. It was a big contrast to Leiston. There was another rather grand social event soon after she got home. She was invited to a party with the people who lived at Sizewell Hall, which introduced her to another promising network. Syria made further notes of anyone with connections, and even allowed herself a fleeting hope that one day she might use them to present Patricia at Court.

A less satisfactory event was a visit from her own brother, a retired civil engineer, who arrived in his Morris Cowley with a young son of nine years old. Syria did not enjoy this visit. Her brother seemed to her sadly altered, and the child spoilt and rude. Patricia herself retained a faint memory of the event. The boy who was several years older than she was seemed very distant and grown up. On departure he refused to say goodbye to Syria, who dismissed him altogether as a very rude child. No further contacts were ever made, so far as Patricia knew, with this branch of her mother's family.

Patricia's fourth birthday on August 22nd passed unrecorded by Syria, but not in Patricia's memory. She recalled it as the day of the biggest row to date with her mother. Syria demanded instant obedience, and Patricia could not supply it. Her disobediences were usually due to inattention. Something more interesting was distracting her. And then Syria's sharp orders, breaking through, simply invited defiance. She was discovering that her will was as strong as Syria's and that once matters had reached collision point, she had no choice but to dig her heels in. So it was that a major encounter took place on her fourth birthday. Instead of Nanny, her mother was taking her out for a walk. They went across the heath. Patricia ran ahead of Syria, happy in the privilege of being out alone with mother, and enjoying this sunny place with its big open spaces which reminded her of Africa. She picked up a stick. It was a perfectly ordinary little stick, and she did not know why she picked it up. She was probably on the point of putting it down again, when the order came rapping out sharply behind her, 'Put that stick down!' The outcome was inevitable. A second order, 'Put that stick down *at once*!' was naturally ignored. The happy mood of the walk vanished. Syria did not stoop to wrestling the stick away by force, but such disobedience had to be punished. She sentenced Patricia there and then to banishment from that day's lunch table. Patricia had been banished from meals before, and she did not like it, but she walked home silently, continuing to hold onto the stick.

At home, the excitement of the birthday blotted out all memory of the penalty. One of the Ealing aunts had given her a set of tablemats for a present, and she ran around the dining room, excitedly laying them in each place. In walked Syria. 'You may leave the mats there,' she said. 'But remember, you are not allowed in for lunch!' Patricia remembered, and then she felt a shock of fury that her mother could do this to her on her day of days. Her noisy rage in the room next door must have spoiled lunch for everyone. The mats were never seen again.

Punishments were coming thick and fast. On one occasion Syria locked Patricia, who was screaming her head off over their latest disagreement, into her bedroom. Patricia pulled hard at the garments hanging on the back of Syria's door, and tore the loops off them all.

She was fearfully ashamed of her outbursts. No one else made such a spectacle of themselves. Everyone could see how naughty and bad tempered she was. She was indeed a disgrace. No wonder everyone liked Georgy better.

Grey's birthday came the day after Patricia's. This year he had to make the best of not having anything more from Syria since he had been given a present last May, but she relented to the extent of giving him a birthday cake. She bought a marzipan-covered Balmoral Roll, the precedent for all future birthday cakes. It was unlike anyone else's birthday cakes, which were many-layered with cream and icing, and had candles and names on them. Patricia got used to the way Syria did things differently from other people, either because she somehow did not know how they did them, or because she knew, but considered it a waste of money.

Peter had begun to practise the piano every morning, which pleased his mother. He probably did it for that reason. Grey had no interest in the piano. Patricia sometimes stood close and listened to Peter practising. In the evenings Syria played. They seemed the most wonderfully difficult pieces, full of rich chords and fast runs and glorious snatches of tune.

Grey persevered in his obstreperousness. He failed to keep his cupboard tidy, and when scolded, wrote Syria, 'He wouldn't get over it healthily but it ended in his coming to the sitting room at ten fifteen because he couldn't sleep.' She offered him no comfort. He had become a real nuisance. This latest habit of his exasperated her and she let him know it, often driving him to tears. After one such stressful night, Syria was in cantankerous mood. 'Patricia was very tiresome and rude at lunch so I took her out and whipped her.' Meals were trouble times. Everything dished out had to be finished and a clean plate left, and there were several things that Patricia could hardly bear to touch, such as fatty meat and stewed prunes and figs. Syria allowed no quarter, made no compromises.

But the food that Patricia did like she enjoyed greedily, such delicacies as runny boiled eggs, spinach, and steamed suet pudding.

Nursery routine scarcely varied. Nanny, Georgy and Patricia shared a bedroom grandiosely called the night nursery, an arrangement Patricia much preferred to sleeping by herself. In the morning, Winnie the maid, who arrived early at the house and lit the fires, brought up an enamel jug of hot water, and Nanny washed herself in the china basin on the washstand. Having dressed, she then dressed Patricia and Georgy. He wore tiny suits in velvet or knitted wool, trimmed with lace or crocheted collars, pure Victoriana. Blue particularly suited his milky blue eyes, set in that pale face, framed in a fringe of soft straight brown hair. It was a gentle face, never disfigured by rage, so different from Patricia's. Syria still regarded Georgy as delicate. She could never convince herself that this precious legacy of Arthur's had fully recovered from his birth sickliness. It gave her and Nanny an excellent pretext for special cosseting. "He's like a little angel," Nanny said, and Patricia agreed with her. "One of these days," she added, "he's going to be a Bishop."

Patricia was dressed, too often for her liking, in a brown tweed skirt the colour of mud, and a matching jumper. She hated brown. The skirt had been fashioned out of one of Syria's old garments. If it was warm, she often wore a dress of stiff, coarse white cotton, more than one layer thick in places, densely encrusted with machine-made broderie anglaise. The material came from Syria's pre-war Edwardian wardrobe. She never threw anything away, but had adult garments remade into child ones, until the residue finally fell to bits. There were just two dresses which Patricia liked, and they had both been made for her by her Ealing Aunt Madge.

After being dressed, the children went down to the nursery, and when Syria had formally said grace, they had breakfast. They were not given tea to drink until they were six. Immediately after breakfast came prayers. Syria cleared a space at the table for her brown leather Bible and matching prayerbook, and everyone pulled back their chairs. They sat upright with hands on laps. Winnie the maid joined them from the kitchen and sat on the chair nearest the passage. Then Syria carefully opened the Bible, fingering her way fastidiously through the fine pages, whose aery hesitations fascinated Patricia, until she came to the "portion." The silk marker was drawn firmly across the page, and she began to read. It was usually a Chapter from the Gospels or one of the Epistles. Patricia loved the story of how Jesus healed Jairus's daughter, and of how he stuck up for children.

The portion over, they all turned round, buried their faces in the chair seats, and recited the ARFATHER. Finally, Syria read in a precise, cool voice that never word-stumbled, the Collect for the week. Day after day, until she was ten years old and was sent to boarding school, the daily ritual of an English spoken centuries ago poured through her ears. She knew it was different from the English she spoke now, but she never stopped to wonder at that. She simply accepted it. The fact that she did not understand quite all of it did not bother her. It was just religious language. It came in books bound in fine-smelling leather, and the pages were edged with gold.

CHAPTER 17

Patricia was becoming more aware of Grey. She was interested and she was sometimes alarmed. Here was a big, energetic person, strong and noisy, and what was more, she soon discovered, none too pleased with her. He seemed almost grown up. He was six feet tall already, and Syria must have had quite a job by now to put him to bed. Patricia realised, from photographs all over the house, that he looked very like her missing father. She could not be sure whether the young man gazing earnestly out from his position as Captain of the School Football team was her father or Grey. She admired him tremendously and tried to win his attention by simple devices, such as prodding him suddenly in the rear with one finger, or pleading with him to play with her. He did not want to play with her, and he hated being prodded. He did not enjoy being shut up in a nursery with a silly little girl, and he punished her by telling her that he preferred Georgy, who left him in peace. For a while Syria insisted that Grey and Peter accompany Nanny and the little ones on routine country walks. They came, scowling, wielding butterfly nets, and putting as much distance as they could between themselves and the others. This was not the life that Grey, fresh from public school, deemed suitable. What would the fellows say if they could see him now, in tow of a Nurse, a pram and two babies?

Once Syria had ordained what she termed a rule, others had to fall in with it and it is unlikely that she would have heeded the boys' protests, but Nanny objected that she had not been engaged to look after two great boys as well as Patricia and Georgy, and Syria had become wary of upsetting Nanny who, when pushed, could fight back. So Grey and Peter were liberated. They roamed the Suffolk lanes together on bicycles, following their favourite pursuits of butterfly netting, bird nesting and exploring. There were few motorists about; all heavy farmwork was done by men and horses; manure was richly and smellily organic; the hedges and grassy verges were strewn with flowers. Hedges were pruned only in winter by a man with a hand scythe and many were left several years to grow tall and dense. People ignored the butterflies; they were so common.

When Grey was not forced into Patricia's company, he could be friendly, and show off his butterfly collection to her. He had two or three big flat wooden boxes filled with the lovely dead creatures, pinned out in glowing rows. The more exotic ones he had not caught himself but had bought from a dealer. One box housed some magnificent moths with thick, furry bodies and widely outspread wings, coarser than butterflies, Grcy had a sinister dark green "killing bottle" filled with laurel leaves, in whose dim poisonous depths a poor captive moved weakly. Patricia pitied the prisoner in the bottle; she hated the sight of the sharp pins impaling the slender bodies in boxes, but she could not help admiring the loveliness of that brilliant mortuary. She never sought to capture a butterfly herself. It was something done by big boys, in their world so different from hers, and she was flattered when Grey condescended to show her his treasures. She had to keep to the right side of him, for he was capable of terrifying actions directed at herself. For her fifth birthday, Grey and Peter had given her a china dolls' tea service. It was white, covered in a dense coral, blue and terracotta flower pattern. She treasured it so highly that as soon as she was left alone with it for a few moments, she buried it in a flowerbed, safe from Georgy's destructive little hands.

On returning later from her morning walk, she was met by a couple of outraged brothers. Grey had stumbled on the thin layer of earth covering the teaset and had dug up the fragments. Only two pieces were left intact. He was beside himself with indignation. So this was how she valued their gift! Seizing the two survivors, he marched over to the bewildered Georgy. 'I'm giving these to him now!' he shouted. 'They're too good for you!' Then he advanced upon Patricia, seized her by both feet, and swung her about upside down in the air. To be upside down was worse than having to eat figs or caster oil. For some time after that she studied to avoid Grey. Peter was far less frightening. He had faintly echoed Grey over the teaset disaster, but he was never violent towards her. For years Patricia mourned her beautiful teaset, possessed for so short a time.

In later years, Patricia and Grey grew close to each other. There were affinities of temperament which differentiated them from the other two, and both were like their father to look at. But at this stage, Grey was jealous of Syria's imagined preference for Patricia, and Patricia feared Grey's upending powers and cutting remarks. One winter evening after tea, Grey's teasing led her into a world of night terrors, which persisted for years. They were gathered in the living room, or day nursery as Syria chose to call it. It was lit rather dimly by oil lamps with reflectors. Oil was cheap, and it saved the gas bill. Grey and Peter had been huddled for some time over a thick book bound in brown wrapping paper to hold it together. It was a child's storybook, inherited from some uncle or aunt's childhood, and its pages were luridly illustrated by black and white drawings, depicting unpleasant things happening to children. The boys had already read some of them to her and showed her pictures. There was the tale of *Harriet and the Matches*, in which Harriet, who has been warned not to play with matches, does so, and is burned to death. There was another about a sinister-looking man looming over some little boys, entitled *Agrippa and the Inky Boys*. Even worse was the one about a small boy and girl, it might have been Patricia and Georgy, who had got lost in the woods and were trapped in a baby cage baited with sugar bread. This trap had been set by a hideous old couple who dragged their two captives into their house, and then, as the story recounted:

'The bloated ruffian at the table sits,
Longing to chop his relish into bits;
While the bad wife, with just the same desire,
To boil the babes, makes up a roaring fire.'

After a life-or-death chase, the babes trap the bloated ruffian in his own baby cage as he comes to grab them for the pot. Then seizing the unaware wife by the heels, they heave her into her own boiling cauldron. The illustrations were the work of a maleficent genius. They fascinated and terrified. Nothing good could come out of that book, and now her brothers were plotting to show her something worse than anything she had yet seen in it. It turned out to be the legend of Beowulf and the ogre Grendel and Grendel's witch-mother.

'Come and look at this, Patricia!' ordered Grey.

'No, no, I don't want to.'

'You've got to. Come over here!'

'I won't!'

Grey came over, dragged her to the book, and pulled her hands away from her eyes. She had to see the full-length picture of Grendel's mother, looming over the sleeping warrior whom she was about to strangle. She had long straggling plaits, staring eyeballs, pointed vampire teeth, and a long scrawny neck. There was a look of hatred on her face, and her skinny arms, with their talon fingers, reached murderously towards her unaware victim.

Laughing, Grey turned the page, and there were more pictures of this female monster. One showed her descending to the floor of her underwater lair in the great mere, clutching the hero Beowulf in her arms. She had the same leer of loathing which was to haunt Patricia's night-time hours for years, and it did not much help that the final picture showed Beowulf triumphantly holding up her decapitated head, the neck dripping with gore.

Patricia protested vigorously and tried to push the book away, shouting with unusual prescience, 'I won't be able to sleep!' Grey found it very amusing, but Patricia was making so much noise that Nanny came running into the room and put an end to his teasing. Patricia could never remember the happenings of that night, but Nanny told her that she had had to get up to her because she had been screaming so much in her sleep.

Patricia was becoming ever more expert at annoying everyone except Georgy and Winnie the maid. She did it every day. She longed not to, and especially she longed not to upset her mother. She was grateful to Georgy for remaining kind. She knew she could rely on him never to turn on her and add his scoldings to the general chorus.

She did not particularly mind Nanny's frequent displeasure. She had always looked after her somewhat wearily. Her preference for Georgy was annoying but there was nothing she could do about it since he was obviously the nicer child. Patricia loved him too, but Syria was the pivot of her existence. Everything revolved around her. She walked with a very upright gait, and she had calm, green eyes that could dispense either love or a cold anger. She had a low, distinct voice that could caress or threaten. Patricia thought she was perfectly beautiful. She admired her mother's pretty clothes. At some point

Syria had made the acquaintance of a Court dressmaker, who was the source of scarcely worn, hand-made model garments and elegant kid gloves. Somewhere Syria had acquired an air of aloof authority. Her manner with most women and all social "inferiors" throughout her life was arrogant, and a frequent source of embarrassment to Patricia as she grew up. She had a simple conviction of superiority.

Ironically, it seemed that in her own daughter, Syria had landed herself with a female creature who annoyed her more than most. She knew of only one way to deal with Patricia's stubbornness and that was, if necessary, to break her will. They clashed headlong, and on the face of it, the outcome was always defeat for Patricia. But she went down fighting, and the house often resounded to her angry roars. She was dreadfully ashamed of her swollen eyes and hideously reddened face, which told everyone she was at it again. But so it had to be. Sometimes her rages reached orgiastic pitch when she would strike out at her mother and kick the furniture. Then Syria would seize her with strong hands, force her struggling across her knee, tear off her knickers and whip her on the bottom. This was excessively shaming. Even the way she pronounced the words, 'I am going to *whip* you,' carried a special charge, for she seemed to savour each word, whistling slightly on the 'H' in whip. This ritual emphasised how low Patricia had fallen, so low that she was having to lay bare that part of her anatomy of which Syria had taught her to be ashamed.

The one time Syria could be relied upon to be in gentler mood was after tea, when Patricia and Georgy spent an hour alone with her in her drawing room upstairs. Every evening Syria gave a short recital of the pieces and studies she had played since girlhood. She had a repertoire that she could play without the music sheets. They included Mendelssohn's *Songs Without Words*, Dvorak's *Humoresque*, some fast studies by Czerny, and a haunting air from a book of Victorian drawing room pieces called *The Shepherd Boy*. Patricia never heard it anywhere else. Syria also played hymn tunes from Mrs. Alexander's 'Hymnal' and 'Hymns Ancient and Modern'. Patricia came to know the tunes of *Abide with me*, *Rock of Ages*, and many others, imbued with the very essence of Victorian religiosity. She enjoyed them as much as any of Nanny's nursery rhymes and sentimental songs.

There was a strange, sad pleasure in hearing Syria play. It stirred thoughts of her father and her lost home in Africa. She was careful to cherish and preserve memories of that home. Of her father there were no memories to cherish. The amnesia of early childhood had cut off all, except perhaps some wisps of feeling, that precursor of memory.

Syria's grieving for him went on and on. In these softer moods, she seemed clothed in sadness. It made her more approachable, but it was also pitiful. Syria talked to them of the walks she and Arthur had taken together in the wilds. She often spoke to them of his hunting expeditions and read his accounts of them in old copies of *The Empire Review*. Patricia was thrilled by these adventures. She also liked hearing about the villages he stayed in on his journeys. He described a harmony which is no longer associated with those regions of Central Africa.

'A village scene rises up before me at eventide, the women pounding corn to the time of their singing, the children playing around, with their pretty gestures and unconscious grace, as children will all the world over. The "boys" are coming in from the forest carrying their contribution to my fire in the shape of a great log apiece; scattered around are the tiny circular huts of the villagers, each with its column of thin blue smoke curling and wreathing through the thatch up into the still evening air; and baskets of native flour and potatoes, presents from the chief who has just left me, are placed on the ground by my chair. As I sit and smoke and watch, there comes to my ears the calling of partridges away in the woods and the swift rush of pigeons as they fly homewards from their feast in the gardens. To me a scene of this kind is life. It is a poem, one tuneful harmonious whole in which my soul joins and feels that here, away from the smoke of great cities, here in the vast silent forests of Central Africa, it can feel content and be at rest.'

Such passages helped to bring her father to life for Patricia.

Syria gave Patricia and Georgy glossy copies of the *Rhodesian Annual* to look at. Boomerang, Patricia's godfather, sent them to her every Christmas from Bulawayo. Patricia studied the photographs of families in beautiful gardens. She gazed at pictures of the gold veldt, with its boulder-strewn hilltops, and she greatly envied those children who were living the life she might have lived.

Syria talked much, too, of Father's prowess as a doctor, his skill in curing all manner of diseases. She claimed that he had been the first to cure a case of sleeping sickness in a white man. Above all, he was a hero, almost a saint; a man who had laid down his life (albeit accidentally, but Patricia did not learn this till years later) for another man. In Syria's memory, Arthur was canonised. She was consoled to some extent by sharing with her children her vision of him. She had been brought up in the bourgeois Edwardian ideal of the perfect romantic marriage - never a cross word, never a selfish motive, aims all of the highest. Now no one could disprove any of it.

Patricia was proud of having had such a father. He was on a green hill, far away, like Jesus, and like Jesus he had healed the sick and sacrificed himself for another. But Patricia wished very much that he hadn't been quite so good.

One dreadful evening, when Patricia was alone with Syria after tea, she burst out, 'Oh, I wish I was dead!' Patricia was smitten. How could her mother wish such a thing? She couldn't manage without Syria, but obviously, she did not mean nearly so much to her mother, who realised at once that she should not have said what she had, and tried to reassure Patricia that of course she didn't really mean it. But if she hadn't meant it, why had she said it? They were both miserable together that evening. Patricia had had proof of what she had known all along; that she was nowhere near being the little comfort that her father had promised her mother she would be. She felt despairing about her failure to be loveable. She would have to try harder.

Her dread of losing her mother intensified. People they met in the street remarked how pale she looked. She slept badly and Grendel's mother haunted her dreams. Sometimes Syria went away on a round of visits that lasted two or three weeks. It always seemed to be winter when she left, and at night the oil lamps flickered against their reflectors in dark rooms, shadows threatened, and the wind moaned outside curtained windows.

'You will promise me to come back, won't you,' Patricia pleaded. She pictured her mother ill, lost, run over by a car. She felt panic at the merest thought of her loss. She was obsessed by fear of it. Syria must have been gratified that Patricia was showing such signs of devotion. She kissed her little daughter and promised to return.

After Syria's departure, Patricia settled down better. No floating afternoon dresses, no perfume, no Mendelssohn after tea, no gently mournful reminiscences. But also, no rapped-out orders, no prohibitions on sweets or dinners, no banishments, no whippings. But then she would hear the wind sighing down the chimney at night, and it seemed to be saying, 'She has gone, she has gone, she will never come back.' Surges of anxiety disturbed her again, and Syria's return was greeted with relief.

Once more, the golden light of the oil lamp bathed them in its soft glow after tea, and for a little while the harmony would hold between them, as they sat close in the familiar atmosphere of melancholy. Patricia was undoubtedly sorry for herself at not having a father, but she was even sorrier for her mother. She seemed so alone, this mistress of their kingdom. 'Do you love me or Daddy best?' she asked her. The answer was fair, but not the one she wanted. 'I love you both, but it's different.'

Grey and Peter had returned to their boarding schools, and early in November, Syria set off to visit them for half term. The visit to Christ's Hospital went off uneventfully as usual. There was a lunch out in Horsham, followed by the predictable choked down tears at parting.

The visit to Grey at Berkhamsted did not go so satisfactorily. She had a talk with Mr. Greene, bringing up the matter of Grey's Confirmation. Grey was barely fifteen, and the Head advised waiting. She then asked for a candid opinion of Grey's progress, and received the usual schoolmaster's comment that he could do better if he tried. He was, said Mr. Greene, inclined to let things slide and not pay enough attention, but he added that his early education might have put him to some disadvantage. Scrappy and disrupted as it had been, this seems a fair assessment. Unfortunately he used the word 'careless,' which was seized upon by Syria who regarded carelessness as near-criminal. She told the Head she was glad he was being strict with Grey, although his comments could equally well have implied that he had quite a sympathetic understanding of him. Later that day, Syria took her boy out of school for a walk in Ashridge Park. He kept her waiting, having been kept in late for Latin. She reported the contents of her discussion with the Head, and extracted from him a promise to try to do better. They then had what she described as a jolly tea, but Grey was not yet clear of trouble.

'I took him to my room and sorted out a heterogeneous mass of papers and rubbish in his best coat pocket (which I fear he has been absent-mindedly wearing ever since his return to school), and came across a foolscap sheet of lines - a queer wording for which I asked an explanation. His replies were hopelessly elusive and stupid, but I at last brought to light that they had been written as a punishment for going to visit his uncle and aunt here on Saturday instead of doing a punishment task, and he had told Mr. Hudson 'he forgot'. He confessed to me that he had not forgotten really. I told him to go and confess this to Mr. Hudson the first thing tomorrow and he promised. He cried very much. I am very glad I visited Grey. He seems to go to bits at half-term. Last term it was the case of a lie too.' Syria's half-term visits do seem to have turned into disaster times for Grey. By now he had acquired a compulsion for "confessions." At the end of term he felt impelled to confess that, despite his promises to her, he had not, after all, confessed his half-term sin to Mr. Hudson. Perhaps that pointed to some survival instinct, as well as sparing Mr. Hudson the problem of knowing how to handle such unnatural self-incrimination. On hearing of this ultimate failure to confess, Syria felt worried and slept badly.

The next day she wrote eighteen letters, and had a serious talk with Grey and Peter about accounts, a subject with which she had an obsession. Patricia herself was later required to keep detailed accounts at boarding school between the ages of ten to eighteen. Every penny of the eighteen shillings pocket money which she was given to last over the twelve weeks of term had to be accounted for to Syria. Patricia was not account-minded and this led to complications when she got home for the holidays. Her mother went through every single item of expenditure with her, not forgetting stamps or the penny for the school chapel collection, to which was later added the silver threepenny piece for Holy Communion. There were numerous gaps and sums which did not add up. Patricia found it necessary to devise a life-saving system for herself. It was not that she had spent much. The sum allowed for the term was not sufficient to allow her to lay out the sixpence per week permitted by the school for sweets. She had to accustom herself to buying no sweets at all. This meant that she could not accept sweets from friends, for if you did that, you had to be able to offer some back. But nonetheless, what with stamps, toothpaste, birthday presents for other girls, and various unavoidable items of expenditure, her accounts looked a mess, and at the end of Syria's meticulous inspections, reproaches and scoldings ensued.

She hit on the perfect solution to all this trouble. She did no accounts whatever until the last week of term, and then, with diary in hand, cooked them to match the few pence left. Syria never noticed.

CHAPTER 18

One morning, soon after Patricia's fifth birthday, Nanny left. She did not say goodbye. 'Where is Nanny?' Patricia asked.

'She has left,' replied Syria. And that was all.

Patricia could not properly take it in for a while. She did not particularly mind, but it seemed strange. At the same time, the big black perambulator in which Nanny had pushed Georgy around, disappeared for ever.

Patricia did not grieve for Nanny. There had been some blistering rows in which Nanny always came off best. One of them had left a lifelong scar under Patricia's chin. During one of Syria's absences from home, Nanny had ordered Patricia to go upstairs at a moment when Patricia did not wish to go. She remembered Nanny seizing her by the hand and dragging her roughly up the stairs, strongly opposed by Patricia who pulled in the opposite direction. She stumbled and fell on the harsh edge of the stair and suffered a deep cut under the chin. It bled like a river and Nanny's mood changed. Frightened, she hurried Patricia to the bathroom, and turning the cold tap on full, bathed the streaming chin. Blood and water poured into the bath and Patricia screamed at the sight. Nanny then hastened her across the road to their doctor's surgery, and stitches were put in. It must have been an alarming episode for the poor woman, who was doing no more than the kind of thing she had seen her employer do. When Patricia did not meekly obey, it was customary to use force on her.

But when Nanny left without any warning, Patricia was taken aback by the suddenness of the change. Nanny had been with her for ever, and much more present than her mother had been. There had been some interesting conversations, and there had been songs when that over-worked woman was in a good mood.

An interregnum followed. Two short-term Nannies came. They were retired district nurses whose job had been general nursing in the community. One of them Patricia liked. She was kind and soft-spoken, and she came in daily from her own home nearby. During her reign she was detailed by Syria to carry out a curious ritual every afternoon on Patricia who had a protuberant umbilicus, and Nurse

Ryland's job was to massage it with olive oil. Patricia liked the smell of olive oil and did not object to Nurse Ryland's ministrations, but apart from realising that there must be something wrong with her stomach, she had no idea what it was. She rather wondered if it stuck out too much. Perhaps there were lurking recollections of Syria's pregnancy with Georgy. The last two months of that pregnancy following Arthur's death, she had slept in Patricia's bedroom.

Nurse Ryland came to her rescue several times when she awoke from her after-lunch rest, crying, she did not know what about. Then one afternoon she had her first remembered nightmare.

The dream was brief. It concerned some impossibly difficult task she had to perform. There was no choice in the matter. But in fact she was unable to do it, try as she might, and she knew she never would be able to do it. The dilemma was awful. She awoke crying and was again rescued by the kindly Nurse.

Patricia and Georgy wanted Nurse Ryland to stay, but she left, and in her place came a woman they both detested. She had a stern bespectacled face, hair scraped back in a small bun, and she never smiled. Nurse Grove was adept at subduing her charges. She had no conversations with them. To Patricia's alarm, Syria seemed to like her. But strangely, this dried-up woman knitted for Georgy a shapeless navy blue teddy bear which both the children adored. It was stuffed with cotton wool, a travesty of the species teddy bear, and it was cuddlesome and appealing, everything that its creator was not, and it accompanied them throughout the years of their childhood, a dearly loved object. Perhaps Nurse Grove had knitted her own frustrated impulses of affection into the creature.

To the children's relief, Nurse Grove left after a few weeks, and for some days there was no one.

Then Miss Glover arrived. Patricia and Georgy observed her critically. The nice ones disappeared, the bad ones stayed too long. Which was this one going to be? This specimen was elderly, small, with long straight grey hair fastened behind in a tumbling bun. Her skin was finely wrinkled and slightly sallow, and her eyes were greeny brown. Her mouth was very slightly crooked, which meant that it did not set in a straight hard line. She had a quiet, conversational voice.

She did not wear uniform as the others had done. She called both of them 'darling' straight away. On the second day of her arrival in their lives, she announced that she was going to make herself a new dress, and she took them with her to the draper's shop in the town. They had never seen a dress made out of new material before. At the little shop, with its dark mahogany counters and its shelves full of rolls of all kinds of cloth, she bought some multi-coloured, striped, silky material that looked like a rainbow. The length she asked for was measured out on a brass yard measure set into the side of the counter. Amiable chat went on meanwhile between Miss Glover and the shop assistant. Syria never chatted with shop assistants.

Patricia and Georgy watched closely for the next few days as she worked away on the old household sewing machine, transforming the fluid yards into a neat, long-sleeved dress. They thought it was beautiful. There was enough material left over to trim a straw hat. The outfit glowed on her small form. Patricia found herself wanting to sew too, so Miss Glover bought some canvas and wool and taught her how to make a kettleholder with cross-stitch. Officially, it was Patricia who achieved this, though Miss Glover did most of the work herself. It is indeed a very faded and ancient little object that Patricia still keeps in a drawer among her own children's first garments. The predominant colour was pale yellow, like sunshine.

After this, Miss Glover unpicked the silky knitted pink jacket that Patricia had worn on the voyage back from South Africa while sitting on the cold deck with her mother and pretending to feel sick. She washed the crinkled thread in warm soapsuds. It was the first time Patricia had handled the slithery white flakes or run her fingers through the feathery suds. Then Miss Glover rewound the yarn and knitted it into a broad scarf in a pattern of knit - purl squares, specially for Patricia herself. This meant she had to teach Patricia knitting too, and she got going on a narrow uneven scarf in bright green wool, which was somehow never finished.

Miss Glover did not want the children to call her Nanny. 'I'm not a Nanny,' she said, 'and I don't want to sail under false colours.' It was thus she discreetly safeguarded the middle-class status that was so precious to her in her precarious position half above stairs and half below them.

'You can call me "Glovie",' she said. So they called her Glovie, and they invented other names for her too. The one that stuck the longest, and was used only by Patricia and Georgy, was Meekie. They found that she did not mind them being very frank in their observations on her appearance. A form of affectionate ritual chant developed: 'Funny little browny creasy Glovie.'

'Of course I've got creases,' she said. 'So will you have when you've lived as long as me.'

'How old are you?'

'One hundred years.'

'Will you be a hundred and one next birthday?'

'That's what it looks like!'

From the very start of her life with them, which was to last twelve years, Glovie never stopped making or mending. When she was not mending for Syria, a perpetual task from which respites were rare, she was making her own clothes, and some of Patricia's too. She taught Patricia to sew, first in cross stitch on canvas, then in woollen stitches which outlined pictures on pieces of cardboard.

Next came the foundation stitches of needlework; hemming, oversewing, running and felling. Patricia never took much to sewing, but she applied herself as industriously as she could to hemming handkerchiefs and dusters in big clumsy stitches which never matched Glovie's neat work. She watched Glovie darning socks, and learned to darn herself, carefully squared-off criss-cross patterns, sometimes in two colours, which made a form of embroidery. She learned to knit, plain and purl, though Patricia's competence never rose above the level of a long uneven muffler. Glovie unpicked the most despairing sections after Patricia had gone to bed, reknitting them rapidly so that next morning both were able to pretend that it was all her own work.

Quite soon Patricia realised that here was someone different; someone who actually seemed to love her just as much as her untroublesome brother. She might even, Patricia suspected, love her a little bit more, though nothing was ever said.

Her formal education now began, and she was to continue under

Glovie's sole tutelage until boarding school disrupted her world at the age of ten. No one ever enquired, to the best of her knowledge, why she was not attending school. Private governesses were still employed by some families, especially where money was tight, and all that was available had to be spent on sending the boys to school.

Girls could be economised on, as they always had been. But this did not fall out to Patricia's disadvantage.

The early stages of learning anything were always fascinating. Glovie opened a new exercise book, revealing a clean white sheet, and carefully ruled a series of lines with a pencil. The first pair was ruled close together, then a broad space was left, followed by another close pair and broad space, and so on, all the way down the page. The body of each letter had to be contained within the narrow pair of lines, while loops and tall strokes; roamed generously in the broad spaces above and below. Capital letters, too, soared above the modest corridor assigned to ordinary letters. This must have been the system used by the Victorians and even earlier, for the teaching of copperplate writing. Glovie was born in 1867 and was a mid-Victorian.

Copying the sample letters written in by Glovie at the beginning of each line, Patricia soon mastered writing and reading. She wanted very much to learn to read for she loved being read to, and at last she was able to work her own way through the story of *Snow White*. The beautiful wicked stepmother fascinated her in particular, and she was soon off on the track of witches wherever she could find them. She discovered that Grey had a talent for drawing them. They were not terrifying Grendel-mother figures, but almost funny caricatures, with pointed chins, hooked noses, hairy warts and peaked caps. If in a good mood, he sometimes drew one or two for her. His witches were often depicted with a knife and fork, eating babies off a large plate.

Patricia was, she knew quite well, a difficult pupil. When her hand would not obey her intention in writing, or when she was unable to spell out the sense of a word, she was liable to fly into a rage. Glovie remained impervious. It was almost impossible to make her angry. Patricia's tantrums beat upon the rock of Glovie's good nature and receded harmlessly. She never punished. The worst that could be expected was a mild reproach. Only once in all their years together did her marvellous forbearance collapse. Patricia must have goaded her too hard and too long, or perhaps that day she did not feel well, for suddenly Glovie seized her head in both hands and banged it quite fiercely against the wall. Patricia was startled and her head rang, but it seemed only just, and she felt sorry to have forced such uncharacteristic behaviour out of her dear old friend. She understood about sudden rages. They forgave each other without further explanation.

The daily battles with Syria continued. She had hit upon a new provocation. 'I am your Mother,' she would say. 'You are only a little girl.' This was clear already. Its effect was to infuriate Patricia further. She hit out until physically restrained. Syria had very hard hands. Georgy sat and watched and caused no one any trouble.

It was not long before Patricia made an even more surprising discovery about Glovie. She was a discreet sympathiser. The realisation came about through a big lunchtime row. There had been treacle sponge pudding, Patricia's favourite. After finishing the first plateful, she had cheerfully asked for more. Instead of responding as expected, her mother said:

'What did I tell you, Patricia, I would do if you asked for a second helping without waiting to be asked?'

Patricia could not recall that the subject had ever come up. 'I see that you did not pay attention to me. I told you that you would be sent out of the room. Leave the room, Patricia!'

Patricia was dumbfounded. She had been innocently unaware of having committed an offence. The prospect of more pudding vanished. She had to be forcibly thrown out of the room by Syria, and deposited, bellowing, on the nursery sofa. She went on making plenty of noise. After a while, the door opened and Glovie entered, and closed the door behind her. She sat down beside Patricia on the couch and put her arms round her. 'There, there, darling, never mind,' she said. Gradually Patricia calmed down. If she had failed to grasp it before, this episode certainly taught her never to ask for a second helping. It also rammed home the lesson that girls who wanted to keep out of trouble had better have a good memory. There was no room for forgetting in Syria's kingdom.

When Grey heard about it, he said something which Patricia pondered long: 'Don't ask, don't want. Ask, don't get.' It was a riddle to which there was no answer.

CHAPTER 19

Syria was still in very low spirits. In spite of all her efforts to engage in the social life of Leiston, and her visits to friends of former years across the country; despite the many activities with which she crammed her day at home, she grieved much in secret. Some days and nights were worse than others. It was still not much more than two years since Arthur's death.

'Have a bad fit of depression,' she wrote in her diary. 'I dreamed delightfully of Arthur, and it woke me up and made me dreadfully restless.' Next night, not surprisingly: 'Had a rotten time getting to sleep. I felt desperately lonely and sad.'

Syria never cried in public or before her children, but there were many uncomforted tears at night. She was becoming quite desperate. 'This simply won't do. I feel I cannot go on like this.'

Her taut nerves made her more intolerant with her children. The mood infected them all, though for Patricia and Georgy there was the refuge of Glovie's calming company. Grey was, as usual, the main magnet for her irritability. He seemed unable to please her, and was frequently manoeuvred into humiliating apologies. It was a pyhrric victory. The long-term consequences for Syria were not good.

It was about this time that Patricia decided that what her mother needed to make her happy was another husband. This would also have the advantage of providing Patricia with a live father. What she did not know was that significant contacts with the Thring family were afoot. The retired naval Captain Hugh Thring ran a small private school for his three motherless children at his home on the fringe of Leiston, and Grey and Peter were frequently invited to play with them in their large, rambling garden. Life there ran on relaxed lines, under the eye of a housekeeper, and their maternal grandmother, who, in Syria's opinion, did not discipline the children properly. But Captain Thring sought a more permanent replacement mother for his children, and he and Syria were by now eyeing each other.

One spring evening, as Syria was drying Patricia after her bath, she made a suggestion.

'I think you ought to have another Daddy.' Syria had almost

certainly already been more than interested in winning Commander Porter for this role, but of late he had been less attentive. There had been shorter letters and last minute cancellations. It was no advantage that he spent most of his life crossing and recrossing the oceans, and perhaps Syria found this not entirely suitable. She appeared to consider Patricia's suggestion that evening and the very next day told her that she had decided to marry again. Patricia was convinced that this was the direct consequence of their talk the day before, and was pleased with herself for having at last managed to be really helpful.

Glovie already knew about it. She had met Captain Thring a few days earlier and was non-committal. Grey and Peter were very excited.

'We're going to move from here soon,' they told her. 'We're going to live in a big house with a proper garden.' By now they had played several times with the Thrings, and they told Patricia in a rather secretive manner that on their last visit to the Thring house, things had gone strangely there. It seemed that the youngest child, an amazing tomboy, had in the course of a roughish game among the outhouses, nearly brained them, deliberately they suspected, by slamming a trapdoor down upon their heads as they climbed up a ladder towards her. The other children had shouted a warning only just in time. Jane's reputation for unpredictable ways was established early.

Within days, Patricia and Georgy were taken over to Chase Lodge to meet their future stepfather and his family. The house was a big contrast to theirs. It was a sprawling Edwardian place in mellow red brick, set amid flower and vegetable gardens, lawns and orchards, on the far edge of town. Patricia gathered from Glovie, who chatted with Chase Lodge staff, that the Thring children had been allowed to run fairly wild and free since the death of their young mother a few years previously. They were fond of their grandmother and the housekeeper. Their father, retired early from the Royal Navy and in his fifties, had tried to run the place as a small school for his children and those of a few neighbours. He thought now that it was time for them to have more formal teaching, and in any case, he realised that he did not have the patience for this type of work. He decided to give up his educational venture and to send his children off to boarding school in the autumn.

He and Syria became engaged for mutual convenience, without any romantic feeling, at least so far as Syria was concerned. Towards the end of her life, she confessed in a rare moment of self-revelation to Patricia that she had never been in love with him but had married him out of fear of loneliness. Once married, they shared a bedroom for a few weeks only.

The only person who made an impression on Patricia at this first meeting with her future step family, was the eldest girl, Bryn. At fourteen years of age, she seemed already a young woman, tall, sturdily built, with long blonde hair such as Patricia would have liked to have herself. She had blue eyes in a small oval face, and Patricia thought her beautiful. She was pleased when Bryn showed a special interest in her. Soon they were going round the garden alone together. They settled down behind some gooseberry bushes, where Bryn gave her home-made fudge and told her stories of children doing adventurous things. The afternoon wore on. Patricia was under a spell and completely forgot about the others until it dawned upon her that her name was being called out again and again. She emerged from the gooseberry bushes with her big new friend. Her mother was angry with her for disappearing and forbade sweets next day as a punishment. Patricia did not mind much. She knew it had been worth it.

Syria's engagement to Captain Hugh Thring marked a rescue from the miserably insecure position in which Arthur's sudden death had landed her. In Africa, as his wife, and mistress of the Farm Gaveston, she had had a definite role. She had also nursed high hopes for him. When he died, these were summed up in a letter from a Rhodesian friend, who wrote, 'I had hoped that Arthur might be the man to lead his country on to the emergence of Dominion Status.' However that might be, he was a man with a presence and a long experience of Africa. Syria idealised him as a big man in every way, and it was her proper destiny to be his helpmeet. When he was taken so suddenly, she was not only personally bereft, but the whole edifice of a full life shared with him collapsed overnight.

Patricia and Georgy cherished this paragon, their father. The only trouble was that he was never there. Patricia saw other children's fathers and envied them the closeness, the touch, the reassuring strength of male arms, the rough and tumble of male play. She was to know scarcely any of this. She made the best of it she could. Her father, though hopelessly out of sight, was perfect, unlike other fathers. She constructed a secret legend around him and herself which she played out in serial form night after night, well into her teens. In fantasy, she brought him as alive as she could.

Because of her engagement, Syria was able to feel better about her position in local hierarchies. This was a thing that mattered to her, as it mattered, unashamedly, to a great many people in that period, especially middle class people in shaky financial situations. Her loneliness had been compounded by the humiliation she felt at being a widow of small income, living in an unprestigious house with, for those days, a very modest amount of domestic help. The self-respect earned through professional achievement was not open to her; like most intelligent girls of her generation her education had never been taken seriously, as had that of her brothers. The past few years had been a painful interregnum, but now she was to be reinstated.

Patricia accepted her mother completely at her own valuation. She was in awe of her style. Syria was dignified in her manner. She gave nothing away about herself. Small gossip was not her affair. It would have been in bad taste. The most she would descend to were remote hints that so and so had rendered herself (it was usually a woman) unworthy of further notice. She disliked people who were 'forward' 'made themselves cheap,' or became emotional. She disapproved of those who made their meaning too explicit, and understatement was an important part of her style. The impulsive expression of enthusiasm was anathema to her, a characteristic she would share with her second husband. It was bad form. She expressed herself succinctly in a clear, low voice, using the approved verbal affectations of her time, such as the distortion of "girl" into "gel" or "golf" into "goff." Her children were instructed never to say serviette but always table napkin, and to understand that only very ordinary people said toilet instead of lavatory. If any vowel was not accorded its pure Oxford English pronunciation, the speaker was cut short and the offending word had to be repeated until he or she got it right. Grey resisted this conditioning and lived up to his awkward reputation with Syria by developing a finely-tuned Cockney accent which he stubbornly refused to do anything about.

The weeks before the wedding were among the happiest of Patricia's childhood. The sunny summer weather seemed perpetual, that year of 1927. She and Georgy were despatched with Glovie to Tunstall Rectory. Much reduced in stateliness from the Queen Anne Rectory where Patricia was born, it was a more comfortable size and a very pleasant rural place, set on a slight rise amid miles of fields, woods and heathland, not far from the site where, a decade later, the splendid Saxon burial ship, full of gold treasures, was unearthed at Sutton Hoo. A short drive led off the narrow Tunstall lane, not then metalled, and dusty or muddy according to the season. Approaching the house, there was a line of tall field trees on the left, and a lawn for flowerbeds on the right. Patricia knew the back garden better. The two children were let out on their own for hours to play. It was there that she was initiated into the incomparable scents and smells of an enclosed vegetable and fruit garden. Small white carnations, which Glovie called 'Mrs Simpkins' and which she pronounced her favourite flowers, grew fragrantly along the path borders, alternating with areas of low box hedge which released its aroma in the sunshine. There were broad beans and peas; the tall runner bean plants already carried their scarlet flowers on sticks; there were screens of multi-coloured richly scented sweet peas; there were lavender and rosemary bushes; and there were gooseberry, raspberry and sharp-scented blackcurrant bushes. All grew in order among rows of neatly-tended vegetables.

The children could pick and sniff and wander at will. To one side of this little paradise was a small wicket gate, whence a grassy path led down a slight slope into a little dell where Uncle Ayscough kept pigs in a muddy enclosure which combined pigsty and exercise yard.

She met again the elderly gardener Alfred, whom she remembered from her first visit to Tunstall soon after her return from Africa. She enjoyed keeping him company and singing him some more songs. Glovie was teaching her new ones all the time.

For the first time, Patricia felt no grief on separation from her mother. That first night in the Rectory, when Glovie was bathing her, and she was splashing about in the warm water, she confided, 'I love you better than Mummie.'

'Hush,' Glovie replied. 'You must never say that.' Patricia understood at once what she meant. It was dangerous to put such thoughts into words. She had not quite realised the enormity of her confession, but Glovie's warning response brought it home to her. Mother must never discover this truth. She would send Glovie away. So Patricia never referred to the subject again, but she never forgot it, and she was sure that Glovie had not forgotten it either, She was always glad to have said it this once.

The happy days ran on, carefree, in that hospitable rectory, presided over by the aunt who was so unlike Syria and by the kindly uncle. Patricia loved him simply for being a man, and a big one at that. It was now over four years since her father had sat her on his knee at breakfast, and then gone out of her life. Uncle Ayscough smelled good, he was easy-going, and he liked picking Patricia up in his great big arms and kissing her through his bushy moustaches.

The morning came when Patricia and Georgy were dressed in their best Sunday clothes although it was not Sunday. This meant a pale blue velvet Little Lord Fauntleroy suit trimmed with lace collar and cuffs for Georgy, and her cream silk smocked frock, made for her by Aunt Madge, for Patricia. Georgy's outfits, though the children had no idea of it, were a full decade or so out of date. They had been handed down from Grey and Peter who had worn them during the years of World War One, and had frequently been photographed in them, so that their absentee parents on the far side of the equator could keep themselves up to date on their appearance. Little boys of Georgy's age, nearly four, would have been dressed for a formal occasion in something less theatrical, such as a navy and white sailor suit. But where her children were concerned, being twenty or so years out of date never worried Syria. It is unlikely she registered that children's fashions did change, albeit slowly, and had moved on quite noticeably from the period of her own childhood. The garments were often charming in themselves. They were carefully laundered and pressed, and before they reached school age, her children had no reason to object to most of them. Many of them had not been bought in shops at all but made at home out of Syria's old clothes. Material took a long time to wear out in those days.

Glovie dressed herself in her smartest outfit and carefully selected a ribbon-trimmed straw hat from her collection. Then they were driven by the aunt and uncle twenty or so miles through country lanes till they came to the sturdy parish church at Leiston. The bells were pealing and the churchyard was full of people. Glovie had told the children in the car that they were on their way to their mother's wedding. Patricia had already discovered that mothers did not have children if they were not married, and although she knew perfectly well that this was her mother's second wedding, she was puzzled as to what people might make of it if they found that she and Georgy were the children of the bride. Perhaps they would not believe it. How would it all fit together? Glovie clearly had no worries. She led them into the church where an usher, seeing a little old woman of meek aspect conducting two anonymous children, led them to dark, badly-placed seats at the back. Glovie, on seeing what was intended for them, was startled out of meekness, and snorted, 'I should have thought the bride's children deserved something better than this!' The usher changed direction promptly, and led the trio to a front pew. To be the bride's child was obviously all right.

The big dark parish church was full of people Patricia had never seen before. There were many flowers, and the organ played some rousing music. She had expected her mother to be in white, with a long veil, and was disappointed to see her advancing up the aisle wearing a coffee-coloured gown in dull satin, trimmed all the way down the front with matching coffee-coloured satin buttons that looked like sweets. Instead of a veil, she wore a close-fitting cloche hat made of coffee-coloured coils that hugged her face and hid nearly all her hair. Patricia accepted the dress, but she did not think the hat suited her. Syria had in fact chosen a charmingly fashionable outfit for a summer afternoon second wedding in 1927.

She must have acquired it, almost new, from her friend the court dressmaker. Patricia quite often saw her wearing it again, for from now on her mother took to "dressing" regularly for the evening. With it she always wore the high-heeled, pointed-toe, satin-covered strap shoes that completed the ensemble. Eventually the dress disintegrated, but her mother preserved a fragment of it for the rest of her life, hoarded away in one of several ageing cabin trunks. Together with it was preserved a fragment of the cream satin gown she had worn at her first wedding in her father's Church at Tunstall in January 1911. And in the same faded piece of tissue paper lay the tiny embroidered handkerchief of fine cambric that she had carried on that far off day. Finding it after her mother's death touched Patricia in a way that had surprised her.

On this occasion she disapproved of coffee-coloured satin. Brides ought to wear white.

The reception was held in the grounds of Chase Lodge, and when the children arrived there with Glovie, Patricia saw her mother standing a little apart with her new father. People were going up to them in a slow procession, shaking hands and moving on. It swept over Patricia that at last she had a father of her own. Breaking away from Glovie and Georgy she ran through the waiting knots of guests and up to him with her arms stretched out. He looked at her, and turned away as she reached him.

CHAPTER 20

After the wedding Patricia's parents went on honeymoon, occupying themselves with buying and setting up a new home, deep in the Norfolk countryside. Chase Lodge was sold to a pioneer in permissive education. His school was co-educational and the pupils assisted actively in its administration. Grey reported incredulously that they were also allowed to drive a car within the grounds. It was not, of course, the kind of school that the Pearson-Thring children were sent to. During the rest of the summer and early autumn, Patricia and Georgy, "the Little Ones" as they were to become so irritatingly known in this new family of seven children, remained with Glovie at Tunstall Rectory. Aunt Edie was much older than Syria. The one characteristic they had in common was a reserve in manner. She referred to herself in the third person as Auntie. 'Auntie would like you to go and rest now,' or 'Finish this up for Auntie,' It was never 'I' or 'me'. She was the eldest of ten children, born between 1869 and 1885. Three had died in infancy. The names and dates of all of them were recorded in a heavy family Bible. Edie had been obliged by her mother's encroaching invalidism to take over most of the family management from the age of sixteen. Their father, the Reverend Thomas, enjoyed vigorous health. He was an autocratic, heavily-bearded person, who was consigned for his uncompromising views to non-advancement in the Church of England, though he made a promising start as Rector of high-steepled Tetbury in the Cotswolds. Apparently a talented young man, he obtained the living without the usual benefit of patronage. But his career there was not a happy one. He was a man of stubborn convictions and very Low Church. He soon clashed headlong with his parishioners through his insistence on conducting his ministry in stern and unfamiliar ways. They turned hostile, and worked long and hard to get him removed from their midst. All charitable feeling between the parties seems to have evaporated. They manoeuvred him out eventually. Syria spent her earliest years at Tetbury, until they left for the small parish of Tunstall, tucked away between the heathery heaths of Suffolk, and the sea. There was very little money. Grandmother's childbearing years went on punishingly long until she was into her fifties. As Syria once remarked in a rare confidential moment, 'Perhaps she shouldn't have had me.' In a minor key, Grandmother echoed Grandfather's principles. They were both shocked when a young priest of their acquaintance said prayers for the dead. In their view, that was a Popish heresy. Even worse, the Bishop promoted him. They wrote to the Bishop in protest, which presumably did nothing to help advancement. They saw themselves answerable only to the God of the Thirty Nine Articles in the Book of Common Prayer, and could not condone theological malpractice.

The tale was proudly told of how the Bishop notified Thomas of an intended visit to the parish. The Rectory was next door to the church and linked to it by a private pathway. But Thomas had no intention of honouring, with an invitation to lunch, a Bishop of whose theology he could not approve. They met in the church at the appointed hour, and the Bishop officiated at a service. Afterwards Thomas handed him a plate of sandwiches and left him to eat them in the vestry.

Despite the whippings and stern discipline, Syria loved her father. She liked to relate the story of how he had cared for a child of two who would have been her eldest brother had he lived. The little boy died of whooping cough on his second birthday, despite her father's desperate efforts to save his life. In the final stages, he had stayed up all night walking about the house with the child in his arms.

Syria claimed that her family had some connection with the prison reformer Elizabeth Fry. Patricia came to suspect that it was mythical. The more she tried to establish the facts, the vaguer Syria became, but the speculative relationship must have been important to her, for a link with Elizabeth Fry provided a claim to distinction.

Syria's mother had had to marry her second choice when she took on the Reverend Thomas. An unrequited love was rumoured to have been felt for the curate of a neighbouring village near Weston on Sea. Thomas's ancestors were a vigorous and fruitful lot, as testified to by local country churchyards. He went on to beget a large family on his unprotesting wife. Syria was the youngest, and was cared for mainly by her eldest sister and a succession of young maids. She idealised her mother fondly, and when she died, over eighty years of age, Syria sincerely mourned her. It was often she, who as a young girl, had administered the soothing handkerchief, moistened with eau de cologne, in the shaded room. The gentler side of Syria's nature always found expression in the tenderness with which she nursed a sick person.

The Reverend Thomas worked on to the end of his life, preaching morning and evening sermons to his rural congregation in their closed oak pews. Every Sunday, just before eleven o'clock Mattins, he swallowed a raw egg whole, to improve the quality of his voice. When she came to stay at Tunstall, Patricia was taken to church there by Glovie and sat in those same pews, each with its little door, listening to Uncle Ayscough who took over when Thomas died.

Summer merged peacefully into a golden autumn at Tunstall. Patricia looked back on that time as upon some eternal balmy afternoon. She still had to rest in bed for an hour after lunch, an institution which she hated then and forever after, but its boredom was mitigated to some extent by a big framed case of multi-coloured cotton reels set into the wall near her bed. The rainbow display of graded, softly glowing colours fascinated her. She lay there, slightly afraid, as always, of the shadowy, curtained light, but diverted by those lovely playthings, immobilised behind glass. Uncle had brought them back with him from South America. They had been made for use, but would never be used.

Aunt Edie was very sedate, and though Patricia knew her to be benevolent, her reserve was awe-inspiring. Tapioca milk pudding drove Patricia at last to trespass across bounds. She made a desperate attempt to eat the slimy jelly globules, having been conditioned not to refuse what she had been given. She could not bring herself to swallow this; it seemed half alive; it was like the frog spawn that had once been pointed out to her on a walk. She would have to run the awful risk. 'Auntie,' she said timidly. 'I like everything in your house. Very much indeed. Except this pudding.'

Her aunt turned a long gaze on her. Patricia stared back, gripped by the horror of having spoken the unspeakable, and trembling to think what would follow. Her mother would certainly have sent her out of the room, for a start, and would then have refused to have any more to do with her until she had eaten up the pudding. As she would never have been able to do that, things would have gone on to a whipping and roars of rage. An apology at bedtime would be the very least she could get away with.

Aunt Edie said nothing, but with a severe expression on her face, slowly removed the plate. Tapioca pudding did not appear again. It would have been different with Syria, who simply did not accept food refusal, and always made sure that the offending stuff was presented to the culprit rather more often than before, until protests were worn down. As she liked to say, 'I will be mistress in my own house.'

Glovie and the children continued their uneventful and peaceful existence at the Rectory until late October. Sometimes they went for a walk together down the deep lane, rutted by farmcart wheels, to the tiny village. Sometimes they walked to the heath, with its carpet of late bracken and its vistas of woodland. The wide spaces recalled to Patricia her lost Rhodesian world. Most often, the children spent all day in the garden, playing with the kittens of Aunt Edie's black and white cat. The housemaid and the cook made a fuss of them. The kittens became dearer. Glovie helped Patricia to write a letter to her mother asking to be allowed to keep one of them. Aunt Edie was willing, and Glovie enclosed her own plea. But Syria wrote back to say that on no account was Patricia to keep a kitten. Patricia could hardly believe that she and it were going to have to part. She was bitterly disappointed and she was angry. The day of departure from this happy place and these kindly, people came at last. Somehow Patricia took her farewell of the kitten, which she felt convinced would miss her as much as she would miss it.

The journey from Tunstall in Suffolk to Coltishall in Norfolk was about fifty miles, but to Patricia it seemed an endless distance. At Ipswich they boarded a train which stopped at every station. Glovie and Georgy sat back to the engine and Patricia occupied the opposite corner. They had the compartment to themselves until a middle-aged man entered and sat down next to Patricia. He was a big, comfortable, tweedy person, and immediately he spoke to her she fell in love with him. They talked together continuously as the train puffed and rumbled on its way. They belonged together. It was a blow, and one over which she brooded for years afterwards, when the train stopped at a small country station, and he rose.

'I have to get out here, my dear,' he said, looking kindly down at her. He patted her cheek. 'To think I'll never see your pretty little face again.'

He was gone, and the train moved on. They would, as he said, never see each other again, although she could not think how she was going to manage without him. And he had called her pretty! No one else had ever done so. She clung to that solitary compliment for many a year. He was the one she wanted for her father instead of that frosty little man with cold eyes whom she had met at her mother's wedding. But as Glovie often said, 'If wishes were horses, beggars would ride.'

MISTRESS IN HER OWN HOUSE

PART III
Norfolk

CHAPTER 21

After their wedding in the summer, Captain Hugh Thring and Syria went house-hunting. They decided on a pleasant house, one mile from the village of Coltishall, with seven acres of garden and land, set among the fields and woods. It was close to the River Bure, and large enough to accommodate themselves and the seven assorted children of their two widowed marriages, as well as Glovie and two resident servants. The time had come for another move in Patricia's life since she had left the Gaveston Farm in Southern Rhodesia*, where her father lay buried on his lonely hill.

She awoke to a dull morning in an unfamiliar room, and looked out of the window. Already leaves were being hurried off the trees by a chilly October wind. She missed the mellow Tunstall Rectory, where the sun always shone. Her mother, Syria, now Thring, came in to supervise the recital of Patricia's morning prayer, and soon after she had dressed, the gong boomed out for breakfast. Afterwards she and Georgy were allowed out into the garden surrounding the house, but not for long. Time and place at Seven Acres were to be strictly regulated from the start, and the timetable devised for the two Little Ones did not allow for impromptu outbreaks from nursery to garden, or anywhere else. On this their first day they were conducted round the estate by Syria herself, and puzzlingly by a big golden-haired dog who romped alongside them. Patricia was pleased that they were now dog-owners, but it was soon made clear that they were not. 'He has been left behind by the people who lived here before,' said Syria. 'We shall not be keeping him.' Patricia liked the friendly creature but she never saw him again. Her Mother preferred cats to dogs because they were less demanding.

A grey pall hung over Norfolk all that day, and muted the autumn colours of field and wood. There were errands to be done in the village of Coltishall and that afternoon Glovie and the children made their way through narrow, unmade lanes. Puddles and cart tracks made it none too easy for Glovie to push Georgy's chair. Although now four years old, he was still considered too fragile to be trusted

* Now Zimbabwe.

with the use of his legs for any distance. At the end of the drive they turned left and over a railway bridge, then down a long, slight incline which in Norfolk is called a hill.

On this, the first of innumerable such walks, Glovie and Patricia ran down the hill together with the pram. At its foot, a small barking dog burst out through the garden gate of a bungalow. Glovie, always terrified of even the mildest dog, for she had once been nipped, began to chatter nervous nonsense, climaxing as the animal advanced towards her, with a rune-like repetition of 'Yes, yes, yes'. The dog danced noisily round Glovie, and she chanted 'Yes!' and Patricia cruelly asked her, 'Why are you saying yes?' though she understood why perfectly well. The two owners appeared and called the animal off. Soon they would make good friends with Cuddy's owners, a pair of elderly Irish sisters, and even Glovie would lose her terror of Cuddy.

A little further on, they came to a pair of high double gates, from behind which furious barking broke out again. Trying to pull herself together with salvoes of 'Yeses,' Glovie rushed her convoy past this new hazard, still fortunately invisible. It was produced by a posse of dogs, all small and aggressive, with sharp white teeth, like their cousin Cuddy, tough little sentries at the entries to Great Hautbois House. Soon their owners, another pair of amiable maiden ladies, were also to become the children's friends.

Their walk continued, past a wood of high elms, heavy in their top storeys with untidy rooks' nests. Then, passing the doctor's house, they entered the village. It turned out to be early closing day. All the shops had their blinds down and doors locked, and none of Syria's errands could be carried out.

The village doctor would become a familiar figure, for Syria was an anxious parent. He was a stout, bluff man who had a daughter called Daisy. She wore her long blonde hair in a bun and went for walks with her two goats down the country lanes, where they often came across her, pasturing her omnivorous pets on the lushest patches of hedgerow.

Near the doctor lived a retired admiral and his wife, a hawk-faced lady whose kindly smile softened somewhat fierce features. Glovie explained to Patricia that admiral status commanded more respect in the village than did the rank of her stepfather, who was a mere captain. Both these retired officers retained the formal use of their rank, and Glovie always referred to Patricia's stepfather as 'The Captain.'

After these bigger houses came an assortment of small red brick cottages with long front gardens, well cultivated for fruit, vegetables and flowers. Next came the butcher's shop, with its gaunt, hung-up shapes. Stumps of legs remained, and sometimes they dripped real blood onto the sawdust floor.

Severed heads and cloven feet were to be seen in the window.

The ironmonger's came next. It was a cave of treasures, in which Patricia would spend happy hours, exploring and in due course pilfering. It was ill lit, and assistants in dark overalls moved dimly in the background. The place was stuffed with bric-a-brac; every cranny was crammed with shovels, pokers, fenders, oil stoves, kettles, carpentry tools, boxes of nails, and gramophone needles. At the darkest end, a battered wooden staircase led up to a storeroom, overflowing round the sides and down a long central table with teasets, dinnersets, teapots, milk jugs, and miscellaneous plates and saucers. Sometimes they were lucky enough to be commissioned to buy a teapot or even a cup and saucer, for the nursery. Then Glovie and Patricia wandered round, critically surveying the objects on offer, holding them up to the light which barely penetrated through permanently smeared windows, appraising and comparing, until a choice could be made. But on this, their first visit to the village, all the shops were firmly closed.

Nearby at a road junction, stood a garage. The Captain owned a large, gaunt Austin, elderly even by 1927 standards. Patricia was not interested in cars. In fact, she hated them, and longed for the clock to be put back to that time, not so long ago, of which Glovie often spoke, when people travelled on horseback or in dogcarts or carriages. Glovie herself, on her father's farm in the Lincolnshire fens, had ridden the lanes sidesaddle. It was, she maintained, the most comfortable and the safest way.

On the opposite side of the street stood a grocery, a shoeshop, a drapery and a clothes shop. They were linked by a through corridor, and were proudly designated ROY'S - THE WORLD'S LARGEST VILLAGE STORE. Mr Roy had anticipated the supermarket system by about sixty years. The two children and Glovie were to spend many absorbing hours under his roofs, often attended in person by Mr Roy or his amiable maiden aunt, who enjoyed bestowing small gifts on Georgy and Patricia. Between this store and a little Cottage Hospital stood the village post office, which specialised in pens, pencils and stationery. Finally, Mr Roy's kingdom was supplemented by a handsome new Roy's the Bakery. Fronting this little parade were a few trees with iron rings driven into them, where people arriving in dogcarts from the country around could tether their ponies while they shopped. Only the rare motor car drove past on its way between Norwich and the coast, or perhaps Wroxham, where Mr Roy had raised another of his emporiums. On the green opposite the Cottage Hospital stood the village War Memorial, with its long list of the fallen, grouped in families. Armistice Day was solemnly celebrated on the anniversary of the ending of The Great War. Patricia was to feel rather impressed as her stepfather, in full dress naval uniform and wearing his ceremonial sword, read the Lesson in the church service held on that day. It was, when she first came to live in Coltishall, only nine years since the eleventh hour of the eleventh day of the eleventh month when the war had ended, and the dead still lived for many in the village.

On this, their first day in the village, Glovie and the children turned for home the way they had come. Across the hedge they glimpsed the green marshes, striated with narrow, rush-fringed dykes, and scattered with duck, geese and moorhens. Next spring they would be lit with golden flashes of giant marshmallow. Cattle grazed peacefully, and beyond them, a graceful white bridge curved across the River Bure. On the horizon, beyond the trees, rose the flinty grey tower of Horstead Church.

CHAPTER 22

The parental pair had seven youngsters to organise, three of the Captain's and four of Syria's, with an age range of four to fifteen, Syria set up her own control system. She monitored the whereabouts of every child in the house, and not one of the older ones was allowed to cross the threshold of the Little Ones' nursery upstairs without applying for her permission. For this pair she instituted an inflexible regime which had rare variations.

Most of the older ones were not a serious challenge to her. Grey Pearson, her eldest son, was, at fifteen, the tallest and strongest, with a gentle, vague manner, but untidy, and from Syria's point of view, uncouth. Where had he picked up that hint of Cockney accent which he refused to do anything about? She suspected him of looking for subtle ways of annoying her. But she could still manage him, and had faced up to the duty of formally instructing him about sex, a task which she balked at asking her new husband to do. She had emphasised to him, as she did to her other offspring, the sacredness of sex, and impressed on him that if he played with himself, his health would deteriorate, and he might even go mad. Grey, as he told Patricia years later, found himself unable to resist this popular schoolboy pastime, and became so desperate that he went at last to the Headmaster of Berkhamsted School, and confessed his weakness. Mr Greene, having had some experience of Syria, sized up the problem, and was able to put his mind at rest.

Peter, Syria's second son, wanted only to make her happy. He was painfully sensitive to her continual silent grieving for his father. He drew little animals for her, and charmed her with affectionate nicknames. He had not wanted her to remarry, for, he said, it might make him forget his own father. As it was, the Captain offered no competition.

Her stepson, Meredith, now nearly thirteen, showed outstanding intellectual promise. He was also something of an athlete. He avoided emotional scenes, and seldom provoked his stepmother.

Bryn, Patricia's favourite, was the oldest Thring at just fourteen. She remembered her own mother, and showed Patricia a snapshot of her, a pretty, fair-haired woman, rather like Bryn herself. Quiet in manner, she liked to be helpful. She was the only Thring whom Syria trusted with the Little Ones, and the only one who seemed to want to spend time with them. Jane, at ten, was a precociously intelligent, and highly-strung rebel. The antipathy between herself and Syria could not have been greater. When crossed by Syria, she lay on her bed, in the room she refused to keep tidy, and screamed. Syria had to send for Bryn to coax her out of these tantrums. 'She does it because she doesn't know how to stop,' Bryn told Patricia, who was awestruck and secretly delighted by Jane's powers of defiance.

There was a cook and a housemaid, both living in; a gardener who came daily from the village, and who suffered from difficult moods, having been shell-shocked in the Great War, and there was Glovie herself, whose many roles defied definition, although her official designation was governess. One subsidiary task was the washing through of the Little Ones' clothes in a big white basin in Patricia's bedroom, which had hot and cold running water. Patricia watched the feathery suds, fascinated, and sometimes helped to squeeze out a sock or two.

Syria was a fair cook herself, and often had to teach the cook, a local girl straight off a farm, her craft. There were frequent changes of staff due to clashes between the girls and their exacting employer. But in those hard-up days of the Depression, there were always more girls available to share a groundfloor bedroom adjoining the scullery, which, together with an outside lavatory, had been built on for them at the time of the family's arrival. The scullery had a bath, entirely covered by a large removable board. The weaker spirits were weeded out, until Syria ended up with a robust pair of friends called Maud and Mabel. Some sort of truce, amounting to mutual tolerance, was achieved between them and Syria.

With her straitened income, Syria had always avoided buying new clothes for her children, so there was plenty of mending to do. With the addition of the Captain and another three children, the amount increased. Glovie did a great deal of it, and so did Syria, whose pride it was never to allow any hole, however large and ragged, to defeat her. Her darns were works of art, and tended to outlive the garment round them. More mending was taken out to a woman in the village who lived opposite the church. She never opened her windows and achieved what Patricia described as a cottagey smell.

Glovie's other constant job was helping with the washing up, which when everyone was home for the school holidays, amounted to a great deal. It was a life of hard labour that she had entered upon at the age of sixty. It was broken by one or two brief holidays when she went to stay with her married brother on his farm in Cambridgeshire, or in her own tiny terrace cottage on the Grantchester Road in Cambridge. She was paid a small sum by Syria in addition to her keep, but later on, when Patricia was ten and she and Georgy were sent away to boarding school, Glovie continued to come for keep only during their school holidays. Syria explained to Patricia that she had offered to come for nothing because she was lonely and missing the children. 'We are doing her a kindness,' said Syria. To Patricia it seemed that it was Glovie who was doing them a kindness. She was uneasy. She knew that Glovie was very poor, and yet she was always giving the children little gifts, and never returned from her holiday visits without a special package for each of them. Her mother disapproved of this habit. It was not quite honest, she said to Patricia, to spend on others money you could not afford. It was a pleasant luxury to give presents, and one in which she herself could not indulge on a whim. Glovie never complained about her poverty to the children, and save for her little collection of hats and unwearable shoes, travelled light through life.

Syria, by contrast, was endlessly oppressed by her financial situation. It bore down on her spirit and deadened generous impulses. For her stepchildren, this trait reached its apogee one Christmas when she gave each of them a tablet of soap as a present. Her second marriage had not made her feel any more secure. She still had to pay the mortgage on her farm, Gaveston, in Southern Rhodesia, which she had left a year or so after her husband's accidental death there. The hope of raising enough money to pay it off by a good sale was fading. She retained a small investment income derived from a life insurance policy which Arthur, with lucky prescience, had taken out a month or so before the disaster of his death. The only alternative to a second marriage was for her to live as a poor relation of her husband's family, which would have been insufferable to her.

Marriage to the ascetic and abstinent Captain partially relieved her predicament since he did consent to pay for her children's board and lodging until such time as they could pay for it themselves. When Patricia received this piece of information from Syria, it dispelled the last vestiges of any hope she had had of regarding him as a substitute father. However, she found she was welcome to his daughters' cast-off clothes. There were 'trying-on' afternoons when she would try on a batch of them which Syria had unpacked from their mothballed cases. She enjoyed doing this, for she never expected anything new for herself, and she liked some of the old dresses. At least they made a change. The hats were a different matter, all being grossly unsuitable for her age group. Syria did not approve of hatlessness, and being forced to wear them made Patricia feel even less hopeful about her appearance than she already did.

Syria managed to squeeze something out of her small income to spend on herself. She was only forty-two when she remarried, and still a good-looking woman. Her Court dressmaker acquaintance provided some elegant, barely-worn clothes and shoes at low cost. She had a weakness for gloves, and bought herself several pairs in fine kid. She took great care of her clothes, and they lasted a long time, though a faint odour of mothballs usually hung about them. She changed at six every evening, and appeared in a variety of gauzy, floating, silk and velvet gowns, worn with delicate narrow pointed-toe shoes and pure silk stockings. Round her neck she liked to wear a long string of beads in ivory or jet or coloured glass. Patricia associated these outfits with her bedtime, which remained for many years extraordinarily early. She thought her mother looked as beautiful as the moonlight lady on the big chocolate box with its deep blue silk walls, where she kept her handkerchiefs.

Syria, in her role of God's delegate, listened to Patricia's prayers, having steered them in the direction in which they should go. She asked for blessings on every person in the household by name, including 'my two Daddies'. She then begged forgiveness 'for anything naughty I've done today, and help me to be better tomorrow.

And I'll try too.' She had added the last bit, to show that she did make some effort, since God didn't seem to be helping much. Syria stooped over her as she lay in bed, her long thick hair pinioned high and bushy with tortoiseshell combs. The modern bob was not to her taste. Sometimes Patricia managed to peer down the front of her dress, and was intrigued by what she glimpsed there. Syria's chest seemed to divide into two slightly raised, yet flattened sections, which Patricia could not recognise on her own chest. Syria would, in fact, have regarded cleavage as indecent, nor was it required by fashion. She was simply, by chance, fashionably flat.

But now, Syria kissed her, any outstanding apologies for sins that day having first been made. Then she hooked up the big black curtains over the ordinary window curtains and left the room, and the long dark night lay ahead. A long night it was, too. Syria aimed to produce a situation like the grave, no chink of light, no storybook, no doll, no teddy, nothing, in short, to offer a diversion from the serious business of getting to sleep. Sleeping children were under control, and she got her two youngest out of the way between seven and eight until Patricia was at least fifteen. Any attempts at departure from the sleep timetable were quelled.

Patricia woke early, sometimes so early that it seemed as though she had been awake all night. She lay in the dark, sheet pulled tightly right over her head in defence against the witch, Grendel's Mother, the skinny hag monster who crept up behind sleeping people and murdered them with her clawlike hands. Then she entertained herself with her own serial stories, or watched the strange procession of hypnagogic images that crossed her vision under her closed eyelids. Sometimes she seemed to hear music. At six thirty the cook and parlourmaid, who shared the downstair bedroom, got up. Patricia welcomed these signs of life. At seven, the gardener arrived from the village to clean shoes and pump water in the scullery beneath. At seven fifteen sharp, the parlourmaid, accompanied by a large neutered tabby cat, took up a tray of early morning tea to Syria. She was fond of the cat, and when, after some years, it was run over by a train, she buried it alongside her little garden plot in the dell, and set up a stone, engraved with a poem of her own composition, on its grave. She broke the news of the cat's death carefully to Patricia, obviously expecting her to cry. But Patricia found that she did not mind, though she regretted that this must disappoint her mother.

She was not expected to put a foot out of bed until Syria came to wake her officially at ten to eight. She unhooked the black curtains, and seated herself on a low wicker chair. Patricia got out of the bed which had been her father's old folding safari bed in Africa. It was spartan, with a wafer-thin mattress, but surprisingly comfortable. Then she knelt before her mother and, as she had done at bedtime, recited a set prayer, composed for her by Syria, in which she begged to 'be preserved from all evil thoughts, deeds and words.'

At ten past eight a warning handbell was rung, and five minutes later a brass gong sounded for breakfast. The Captain stood behind his chair at one end of the table and Syria faced him at the other. The Captain kept Meredith and Jane on either side of him, Patricia and Georgy were next to Syria, at the farthest possible distance from Jane. Glovie sat next to Jane, within too easy distance of the Captain's sarcastic tongue, which caused Patricia much indignation. When all were at home from boarding school, there were ten at table. After the Captain had recited grace, the family started on porridge, which was cooked in a double steamer atop a portable paraffin stove. A wooden spoon was used to stir and serve it, doled out with soft brown sugar and milk. Soon the plateful metamorphosed into a sloppy mush. Patricia tried to keep her porridge pristine for as long as possible, and watched in disgust as her stepfather immediately set about stirring his into a brown sludge that reminded her of the open cesspit in the far reaches of the blackcurrant field. Next came what at a later epoch would certainly have warranted the description of Full English Breakfast. This was one of the few times when the whole family was legitimately together. Georgy was quiet, but Patricia enjoyed joining in the fracas. In the corner the cat finished off the porridge.

Family prayers followed. Chairs were pushed back and the two maids came in from the kitchen and took their places just inside the door. The Captain read a passage from the Bible, and when that was over they all about turned, knelt down, and buried their faces in the chair seats. Together they recited the Lord's Prayer in its rough-hewn seventeenth century language. The ceremony ended with the Collect for the week from the Book of Common Prayer, the only prayer book in general use by the Anglican Church. Its stately language became so familiar to Patricia that, without ever trying to do so, hearing it every Sunday in church as well, she learned whole sections of it by heart. She knew the language was somewhat different from what she used every day, but that did not bother her. It was simply religious language, and religion had its own different ways. Sometimes when she could not sleep at night, she recited whole stretches of the Morning Prayer to herself.

Breakfast over, the family dispersed, the Little Ones returning to their nursery eyrie. Their duty now was to produce Big Jobs in their enamel chamber pots. Not for them the anonymity of a private performance, though the house had three fully operative lavatories. Syria scrutinised their offerings daily before disposing of them. Occasionally she delegated this inspection to Glovie, who was not very interested, and was prone to toss the products in a carefree way straight into the lavatory. Patricia's system was deeply resistant to public takeover. There had already been the enemas in Rhodesia, and many barren half-hours of her life had been spent straining on the pot. Apart from the disappearance of enemas, nothing had changed, and laxatives had become the order of every evening. But she was a match for them. Syria believed in variety. Some tasted foul, others were quite pleasant, but Patricia's innards hardened themselves against the lot. They came in rotation. There were fizzy Sedlitz Powders, which she had trouble in swallowing at all, and which left her with a life-long aversion to effervescent drinks, including, unfortunately, champagne. There was liquorice powder, which caked on the way down. There were Grey Powders, crushed in a spoonful of white sugar, which left her with a lifelong distaste for white sugar. There was the fiery Golden Syrup of Figs, which she enjoyed, but which produced a uniquely agonising stomach ache the next morning. Despite these assaults, Patricia remained constipated for years until boarding school liberated her. Even here, Syria had demanded that the school matron inspect her efforts every morning, but after doing it once, matron declined to continue. Patricia was thankfully relieved of this attention, and her costiveness ceased.

Before this deliverance, Patricia suffered from frequent stomach cramps. She assumed it was the natural order of things, so she continued to sit for many minutes each morning 'trying,' and drawing faces with her finger on the dusty linoleum floor. If successful, she wiped her behind with two statutory pieces of smoothed out orange paper, stacked up in a little basket for this purpose. She often helped Glovie with the preparation of these pieces of paper, which came in white, pink and yellow, and were sold in those days wrapped around each individual orange. Glovie and she sat together at the nursery table working on the paper, and then Glovie cut a pile in half, that size being deemed sufficient for the purpose. Further supplies were left in the lavatories in addition to the toilet roll, which the Little Ones were not supposed to use. Syria did not hold with overmuch expenditure on toilet paper, and what she did buy was of the coarsest kind, off-white and slightly crinkled. Patricia never saw its like anywhere else.

In physical matters, Syria could be surprisingly naive. Although she carried out her inspections with great regularity, she did not perform them efficiently enough to notice, although Patricia did, that for a longish time, Patricia harboured white threadworms. She had identified them from her Pear's Encyclopedia. She mentioned them to no one, and no one mentioned them to her. Eventually they disappeared, fatally discouraged, no doubt, by the battery of laxatives that came their way.

The chamber pot ritual completed, Patricia made her little bed and dusted her room according to Syria's formula. If she forgot, or skimped the dusting, some minor penalty, such as deprivation of the day's sweet ration, was imposed. Ever since the day at Leiston, when Patricia had forgotten that she must not ask for a second helping of pudding on pain of being sent out of the dining room, she had been working hard at not forgetting. But it still happened sometimes. Syria also came down on her hard if she forgot to comb the stray hairs out of her hairbrush.

Georgy did not have to make his bed, or tidy up, or dust.

CHAPTER 23

Syria's hothouse plants, Patricia and Georgy, were segregated from the other children in a large first-floor nursery, close to her bedroom, and between the front and back staircases. It had wall-length windows, facing over the south gardens, and there was a fireplace where a coal fire was lit daily except in summer. Georgy slept in the nursery, out of which a door led to Patricia's much smaller room. This was locked at night to prevent Patricia paying visits to Georgy. They had plenty of toys, which were kept on two long shelves, covered by a black curtain, and put away tidily at night. Georgy had a clockwork Hornby train, and several brightly coloured regiments of soldiers. They shared a large box of wooden bricks made by a local carpenter, out of which they built houses, farms, and some very high towers. Patricia's favourite possession was a large Victorian dolls' house, furnished and peopled in period, which had been made for an aunt. This was kept under lock and key, and she was allowed to play with it only under supervision, on wet days.

The older children's domain was downstairs, a long, one-storey annexe called the Hobbies. Here the boys kept their boxed collections of birds' eggs, butterflies, fishing rods, and air rifles in separate sections. Jane collected books, principally the fairy stories of different nations. It was cold there in winter, heated only by a paraffin stove. They also had the freedom of a big open lounge at the foot of the front staircase. In the evening they spread themselves on inglenook seats, either side of a big anthracite stove, or on oak seats by the windows. Here stood a gateleg table, on which lay the daily newspaper until such time as the Captain appropriated it. On her way through the lounge to breakfast, Patricia sometimes snatched a glance at the front page. There was a great airship falling in flames out of the sky. There was a baby who was kidnapped out of his nursery and disappeared. There was a king who was murdered, and a schoolboy called Farouk, a few years older than herself, who suddenly had to become king in his place. Her mother bought her *The Children's Newspaper*, but it was not exciting. It could not compare with what *The Morning Post* had to offer.

The older children had tray suppers of sandwiches and milk in the lounge. Syria never relaxed her measures to reduce contact, and above all, unsupervised contact, between her two youngest and the dangerous Pearson-Thring mix. They were to be pure Syria culture, her own carefully nurtured creatures. She was already having some difficulty maintaining a hold over Grey, who had adopted the device of putting a distance between himself and his mother, but she could depend upon Peter's devoted need to please her. The two eldest Thrings, Bryn and Meredith, were reasonable to deal with, but Jane remained obstinately out of hand. Their father paid little attention to his brood, provided they minded their manners and turned up punctually for meals. He seemed contented to leave them to entertain themselves in their own ways. There was a degree of mutual trust. No demonstrations of affection were given or expected. It was something the Captain must have had little of himself, having left home at the age of twelve to become a midshipman in the Royal Navy. A small portrait of him at that age, a pale waif of a boy, hung in Meredith's bedroom.

This disinterestedness in the minutiae of his children's lives did not suit his wife. They had been accustomed to relative freedom before their father's remarriage, and were not always of a mind to submit to Syria's regimes. Bryn was the least affected. She had a wealthy, elderly "aunt," a friend of her dead mother, who needed a companion. She paid the boarding fees for Bryn's fashionable boarding school, and took her over for a large part of the school holidays. Sometimes she took Bryn with her for long periods of continental travel. They visited France, Hitler's Germany and Stalin's Russia. But despite all this apparent privilege, Bryn was not happy. She was shy and prim with strangers. The aunt with whom she had to spend so much of her time was an elderly person whom Patricia recalled as big, grey, shapeless and dull. Years later Bryn admitted to Patricia that she had felt guilty about her inability even to like her benefactress. Bryn had known her own mother up to the age of six, and the memories were good ones. She cherished a few odd snaps of a serene and pretty woman with fair hair and blue eyes whom Bryn herself resembled. There was a portrait of her hanging on Meredith's bedroom wall which Patricia thought at first was a painting of Bryn. She was very different from her stormy young sister, and the only Thring youngster trusted by Syria to spend an occasional hour in the upstairs nursery without supervision, when Patricia and Georgy got her to draw pictures for them, especially ones of witches eating babies. She sometimes joined them on the regulation walks with Glovie, leaving the house well after them so as not to arouse Syria's intervention, and catching up with them in the lanes, where she taught them how to vault five-barred farm gates, and balance along the top bar. Patricia relished these occasions, for she hated being cut off from the rest of the family, who seemed to be having a much more exciting time than she was.

Patricia was also keen to get to know Meredith better. He maintained an aloof attitude towards the youngest pair, rather more friendly to Georgy than Patricia, whom he accused of a selfish insistence on getting her own way at Georgy's expense. Doubtless he was right, although not so in the incident which he frequently quoted against her. She had cracked open her boiled egg at breakfast, and cried, 'It's hard! Give it to Georgy!' He took this as a perfect example of her callousness, but she knew, as he did not, that Georgy preferred hard-boiled eggs to soft ones. She sensed that Meredith disliked her, but did not know why. One afternoon when Syria had allowed the Little Ones to play in the garden instead of enforcing a walk, Patricia decided to weed an overgrown flowerbed near the house. The gardener had ignored it, confining his attentions to the more formal beds. Down in the dell, Georgy and Patricia had been given small square plots for their own gardening efforts, and lying protectively alongside them was another plot, which Syria called her garden.

Patricia did not care for her plot. She had sown several rows of candytuft and eschscholtzias but only a few stragglers came up. Her plot remained a stony patch, and she lost faith in the power of seeds to germinate. But the half-wild bed above the dell attracted her and she set to work. This place had plants already growing in it, bypassing the need for seeds. All it needed was someone to care for it, and she had elected herself that someone. At the family lunchtable she drew attention to her labours. Meredith merely remarked, 'What are you expecting to get out of it?'

'Nothing!' retorted Patricia.

'You must be,' he said. 'You would never do anything for nothing!' Patricia was incensed. She had not thought about why she was weeding the flowerbed, but the idea of reward had never entered her head. And she minded because she admired him, but he obviously did not think well of her. From that day on she never touched the flowerbed again.

Despite his freezing indifference, her desire to win his approval lingered on. The best she could get was the ghost of a grin. He was so very unlike her older brothers to look at, neat, of medium height, with a long head, a long spare face, and a quiet composed expression. His mealtime conversation was mostly directed at his father and Jane, and centred on matters which Patricia knew nothing about, such as mathematical formulae and wavelengths. Meredith could even prove that one and one did not necessarily make two. People did not interest him. In this he was unlike Grey, who made Patricia laugh with his ironic sense of humour and his flair for mild ridicule of neighbours and schoolmasters. Meredith excelled at athletics. The Pearsons were not athletic. Meredith could do interesting things, like jumping clean over the tennis net in one remarkable bound. When he went on to Cambridge, he became a rowing blue, and his oar was hung up in the lounge. The Pearsons had loose joints, and Grey and Patricia had flat feet. They were poor runners, and despite all Patricia's efforts, she never succeeded in clearing the tennis net unless it was halfway down. But she was able to twist herself about in several unnatural ways, and her thumb and finger joints bent backwards spectacularly.

When the older children needed to sue Syria for some favour, they elected Bryn to act for all. She approached Syria with the plea that she spare them from having to munch their way through two doorsteps of bread and butter before reaching jam and cake. Bryn obtained a compromise; in future one doorstep would suffice. Meredith remained polite but cool with Syria. Patricia remembered her having penetrated his armour only once. It made her see him as a human being with feelings she could recognise.

It was her habit on summer evenings, after she had been packed away to bed in her heavily shrouded room by a quarter past seven, to creep forth again down the long passage after her mother had gone downstairs to her drawing room at the end of the house. She passed the back stairs, which Syria rarely used, and arrived at the top of the main staircase. Here she could safely settle down to eavesdrop on the older children's conversation until they too each followed his or her individual curfew in order of age. It was a triumph to have defeated Syria's system and to have found a small area of time and space free and unwatched by anybody. The others never suspected her presence because the staircase turned a corner and she was on the far side. She felt less cut off from the mainstream of family life when on the staircase. She noticed that the Pearson and Thring contingents got on together rather well, although the families were in many ways so different.

One summer evening, Meredith decided not to finish his sandwiches. He was not fussy about food, perhaps he was not hungry. Syria, passing unexpectedly through the lounge, noticed the rejected food. This was a challenge to one of her strictest rules. Everything must be finished up. So she ordered him to clear his plate. Meredith declined politely, but it was still a case of defiance. In her sharpest tones, Syria sent him to bed at once, well before his nine o'clock curfew. Patricia retreated hurriedly to her bedroom and stood listening through a crack in the door. She heard Meredith stumble upstairs and into his room, which lay across the passage from hers. He slammed the door, and suddenly Patricia heard strange sounds of a kind she had never heard from him before. He was now a big boy of fifteen, almost grown up. She slid out into the passage again, and realised with a pang of astonishment that Meredith the self-contained, the calmly superior being, was sobbing loudly. She pictured him in his little room, perhaps sitting on the bed (although it was not allowed to sit on beds) beneath the delicate water colour portrait of his dead, fair-haired mother, her dreamy gaze fixed smiling and unseeing on her son. This controlled, sardonic stepbrother was giving vent to feelings that Patricia had never guessed he had. She stood in the passage, her heart wrung for him. She went up to his door and laid her hand on the knob, then hesitated and withdrew it again. It was not only fear of her mother's sudden appearance, it was fear of Meredith that deterred her.

She sympathised with a terrible sympathy and she longed to steal in and put her arms round his neck. But an instinct told her she would not be welcome. He would feel put to shame in front of this small girl he didn't much like. In short, he would be mortified to see her appear on the threshold, and Patricia realised that she did not have the power to console him. Sadly, she returned to her room.

At that moment, she had come near to breaching the barriers of age, sex, family allegiance and temperament, which had always separated them, and probably always would.

Stepsister Jane was a quick, nervous, bright child. She also became a very angry and stubborn person when, at the age of ten, she found herself having to share life with Syria. They detested each other, though Syria made a pretence of virtuous attitudes. Jane did not intend to let herself be knocked into a convenient shape, and Syria had no intention of letting her get her own way. So Jane fought her on all fronts all the time. She insisted in doing what she wanted, which was not really so much what she wanted as what she knew Syria did not want. She was outspoken, or in Syria's language, rude. She was untidy, and refused to put away her belongings. Her bedroom was a marvel of disorder. Secretly, Patricia admired this. She did not much care for Jane herself, for Jane scarcely deigned to speak to her, a younger child, who, as she saw it, was getting preferential treatment. But gradually each was gaining some respect for the other, in their mutual distaste for Syria's unbending rule. But Syria was Patricia's mother, which made a difference. It meant that Patricia's battle was less single-minded than Jane's. After a row with Syria, Patricia suffered remorse. She was anxious about her mother's ailments, for Syria suffered from a fair number of them, including gastric ulcer, varicose veins, hammer toes, toothache, and frequent headaches. Most of all, Patricia was sorry for her for having lost the love of her life and being married to the Captain. She felt her own rebellions merely added to her mother's trials, quite apart from the disagreeable consequences they had for herself. Yet she welcomed Jane's tough defiance. Jane offered cheek and answered back rudely, offences often held against Patricia. Probably Jane never noticed that Georgy was there, but his stepfather certainly did. In terror at his angry roar,

Georgy ducked for shelter behind the power that was Mother. But Patricia was open to contamination, and Syria knew it, and tightened her grip. She regarded Jane as she would an infectious disease which might strike her two most guarded possessions. Patricia resented the special status she and Georgy had been burdened with. Jane was envious of it, and let her know it one day when Syria's precautions lapsed momentarily, and they met alone in the garden out of sight of the house windows.

'Why,' hissed Jane, 'do you two Little Ones have a bath every day while we get them only twice a week? Why do you have better suppers than we do? With hot drinks. And why do you have one of the best rooms in the house all to yourselves? And why don't you go to school like we have to?'

Why indeed? Patricia's feelings echoed her. 'We didn't ask for these things,' she tried to explain. 'We are made to have them. I don't want them. Why do we have to have a wretched bath every day? And why must I go to bed at the same time as Georgy, though I'm two years older than he is? Even you get different bedtimes according to your ages. And why do we have to be shut away from the rest of you, cooped up in a room at the top of the house while you are allowed to go anywhere by yourselves?' More and more unfairnesses kept crowding in as she compared their lives, and she tried to make Jane see that she was not at all pleased herself. A fellow feeling began to grow between them. But Syria clamped down on any pleas for change with her most forbidding pronouncements, such as, 'There is absolutely no question of it!' Or, 'We will hear no more about it! It is for me to know what is best.' Nor would she ever concede to Patricia any seniority over Georgy where bedtime was concerned.

Jane proved too hot to handle at her boarding school and contrived to get herself quietly expelled. The matter was hushed up at home, where she was by now in Syria's opinion, unmanageable. The famous lunchtime incident, never forgotten by anyone who was present, gave some point to this. Jane, now a sturdy thirteen-year-old, sat next her father, gloomily picking the dirt out of her fingernails, and was ordered by him to stop it. She ignored him, and continued to operate on her nails. The Captain, reinforced by Syria, followed up with curt demands. Jane paid no heed. The family watched. What could the parents do about it now? There was a tense silence, broken by a sharp order from the Captain:

'Leave the room!'

Jane made the tactical error of submitting. Slowly and sulkily she arose, and, kicking the table leg noisily, she left, slamming the door behind her. But the parents had regained the initiative, and the manner of her going had incensed them both. The Captain rose and marched outside. Soon everyone heard screams, and the sounds of an energetic scuffle. The listening family realised that the Captain was doing his best to belabour Jane with a stick, and that she, a big strong girl, was resisting successfully. Suddenly the door flew open, and the Captain reappeared, panting and dishevelled. 'Grey!' he barked, 'come out here!' Grey was the biggest and strongest person in the house, but gentle by nature. He walked out doubtfully, as well he might. He was ordered to hold his stepsister down by force while her father beat her. He had never managed direct disobedience to parental orders successfully. In a mental fog he did what he was told. He felt very bad about it, but years later he told Patricia that Jane did not hold it against him for long.

Syria decided that she could no longer be expected to tolerate her stepdaughter under the same roof, and she resorted to her ultimate move, and not for the last time, to eject the offending body altogether.

'I *will* be mistress in my own house!' was a favourite saying of hers, and she said it now. Jane, at this stage, seemed too much of a challenge to ask of any school that the Captain would be likely to choose for her. She was sent to a psychiatrist, who reported that her mental age was well below her actual years. Glovie somehow gleaned this secret piece of information and passed it on to Patricia, who worked out that, according to this, perhaps she herself was older than Jane. A governess was found for her, and this turned out well. Hilary Dalton was a young woman with a kindly temperament. She must also have been sufficiently intelligent for Jane, who harboured a great scorn for stupid people, among whom, she told Patricia, she included Syria. They took up residence together as paying guests on a farm a few miles away, and here at last Jane's nerves had a chance to calm down. Occasionally a much happier Jane came over with Miss Dalton for tea. She seemed to idolise her, and the family was able to take a look at this remarkable person. There was nothing striking about her, though she seemed agreeable. Perhaps, after all, the same might have been said about Glovie by a person looking on from the outside. For some years after her invaluable services ceased, Jane continued to quote her as her mentor. She settled down reliably enough to go on to yet another boarding school, whence she obtained a scholarship to Cambridge. There she achieved top honours twice over, though in those days of the thirties, an actual degree was not conferred on women. She went on to become a distinguished research scientist.

Syria continued to make it her business to know exactly what was going on around her, and to control it absolutely where her two youngest children were concerned. She exercised a special taboo on meetings in bedrooms between Patricia and any of her brothers except Georgy. Patricia was mystified as to why this should be. Once she forgot the rule and visited Grey in his room. Syria materialised behind her within seconds and sent her packing without any explanation. All Patricia had wanted was to make her large brother take more notice of her than he seemed inclined to do. After all, she had been palmed off on him as his ninth birthday present when he had been hoping for a train.

CHAPTER 24

Nine o'clock was school time. Patricia and Georgy sat down in the nursery with Glovie, who now assumed the role of governess as distinct from maid of all work. It is unlikely that enquiries were made about their absence from official school. They were at the tail end of home-based education, especially for girls. Syria herself had been taught by a series of young women, mostly French or German, who came to learn English and were employed for a pittance and their keep by the Rector. Only from the age between fourteen and sixteen did Syria attend a small boarding school in Eastbourne.

In Patricia's time, the local village children had to attend the Elementary School in the village, but the middle classes managed things differently. By now, home education in the "schoolroom" was rare. For large, hard-up families, such as the clerical family Syria had been born into, it had been the cheapest way of providing for girls. Syria's brothers, however, had all been sent to boarding schools and had gone on to take scholarships to University, where they trained in medicine, for the church, or the Colonial Service.

Syria was hard-up, and the Captain had all he could do to afford his own children's education. Syria had contrived, before she had ever met him, to get Grey and Peter covered for their own public schools by various sponsors, but it was not until they had left school that she would feel able to embark upon the wider education of the two youngest. To all appearances she was no longer a single parent, but in many respects she remained one. It had come as a shock to Patricia when she realised her stepfather's reluctance to finance her existence or that of her brothers. She had thought that was what fathers did. But she was aware very early that there was no closeness between her mother and stepfather. There was no shouting, no violence, no swear words. The Captain never used bad language. There was only a controlled chilliness.

Education in the nineteen thirties was dictated almost entirely by class and income. The brighter children of poor families obtained scholarships if they were lucky, and went to Grammar Schools, enabling them to proceed to University. For poor middle class or working class people, it was the only route, but for a family to be accredited in the "proper" circles, the children had to attend "public" boarding school, and boys had to precede this with preparatory school, starting at seven or eight. The Captain had achieved these conditions for his three, and Syria had contrived to get Grey and Peter into the club. So she was outraged when the Captain suggested she could very well send her two youngest to the local Elementary School, indicating a scant regard for their abilities or the social sensitivities of their mother. Syria was not defeated. She had discovered in herself a special talent for twisting the arm of people, such as school heads, from she required special favours. In course of time Georgy was sent to a preparatory school on the Norfolk coast of the Wash, near enough for her to justify the expense of visiting him every term. Patricia was packed off to a girls' boarding school over two hundred miles away on the Malvern Hills, where Syria visited her once a year. She earned a scholarship, which covered most of the fees, at the end of her first year at this establishment. There was, however, a further price to be paid, solely by Patricia, for being a poor pupil. The headmistress, a formidable square-shaped woman with a gruff male voice, took a stronger dislike to her than she did to most of her pupils, all of whom were terrified of her. She liked to remind Patricia how much she owed the school, but Patricia was never able to see the logic of this.

For the time being, it was schooling at home under the benign tutelage of Glovie, who followed the routine of her own mid-nineteenth century schooling. There was a strong emphasis on learning by heart. It was not difficult. Patricia and Georgy learned by heart the multiplication tables and any other tables concerning weights and measures that in those days were printed on the back outside of a penny exercise book. They learned the arts of addition, subtraction, multiplication and long division. They could define the eight parts of speech, beginning with the Noun and ending with the Interjection. They could demonstrate their functions in a sentence by the process of parsing, knowledge which proved invaluable later on when tackling foreign languages.

Geography and History were taught in the same business-like way.

The name of every English county was memorised, together with its county town and principal river. Climate was considered. Those Mediterranean areas, much boosted in modern travel brochures as winter suntraps were disposed of in Glovie's classification as winter rain regions, and in later years, Lettia was to discover that her definition was the right one. In history, Glovie could not let slip such an opportunity for adding the dates of the Kings and Queens of England to the "memory library." She enlivened this with many colourful tales. Even Robin Hood and the Sheriff of Nottingham found a place in her curriculum. History stopped when the young Victoria was summoned from her bed in the middle of the night to learn that she was now Queen. Anything later than that was too modern for Glovie.

The favourite lesson was English. Glovie concentrated on poetry, and Patricia soon learned by heart Gray's Elegy in a Country Churchyard. She recognised the churchyard. It was just down the lane and across the fields by the ruined flint church with the round tower, where white collar doves circled. Glovie loved churchyards, and had passed on her fondness for them. She had a penchant for melancholy poems, and had composed quite a few herself, which Patricia got off by heart, not distinguishing between them and the work of Thomas Gray. All Glovie's works, like Gray's, rhymed and scanned with a beautiful regularity. Many were stories about children who sickened and died early in life. Patricia fully expected to meet with an early death herself.

To a mournful air, Glovie sang:

'A mother sat nursing her dying child, Her face was wan and her heart was wild...'

It ended, as they often did, on a note of consolation. Mother believes that one day they will be together 'for evermore.'

Even more poignant was King David's lament for his infant son.

'I shall go to him,
I shall go to him,
But he will not return to me.'

'Like my father,' thought Patricia.

Glovie retrieved many sentimental ditties from her girlhood in the mid-nineteenth century, and sang them often to Patricia. The voice was quavery but the words were clear:

'O meet me when daylight is fading,
And is darkening into the night,
When songbirds are singing their vespers,
And the day has far vanished from sight;
O then I will sing to you, darling,
Of the love I have cherished so long,
If you will but meet me this evening,
When you hear the first Whiporwill song.'

The simple tunes haunted Patricia, and she would sing them through under her breath as she crouched in her nightie on the lamp-lit staircase at night. She realised that the songs Glovie sang were very precious because no one but Glovie and she now knew them. They would be lost and forgotten. No one after her would ever know of the old street lamp which watched over lovers:

One evening late in winter
I was shining down the street,
When a lover came beneath me
And read a letter sweet;
I watched him come this way,
I heard the words he said,
'My love, my love, the golden day
When we at last are wed.'

'O all the young, the happy, and the far and quiet dead, The old street lamp remembered all, And this is what he said' (Refrain)

It was heavily charged stuff, and Patricia soaked it up. No wonder that her mother clung so tenaciously to her father's memory. It would not have seemed right to have deserted him, and given those feelings to the Captain instead.

Glovie's songs made it clear to Patricia that a man's first duty to a woman was to adore her. That was what must have been wrong between her mother and the Captain. She could not imagine the Captain adoring anybody. One of her favourite songs evoked this golden romanticism, although Patricia could not be quite sure whether it was about a mother or a lover. Was it, she wondered, about

Glovie remembering her own mother?

'And I dream I see her walking,
With her stately grace of old,
And the perfume and the powder
In her hair of sunny gold;
I remember, I remember,
'Tis a lifetime since we met,
But her sweet face, pure and lovely,
Lingers in my memory yet.'

Patricia understood that love's last duty is to remember. That was what her mother was doing. And the songs touched Patricia's own childhood with a Victorian afterglow.

'When I'm dead and gone, you'll remember my songs,' Glovie used to say.

CHAPTER 25

The Captain insisted upon verbal accuracy. The Grace which he recited before the family sat down to a meal was carefully phrased: 'For what we are about to receive may the Lord make us truly thankful.' He liked to point out that he said 'about to' rather than 'going to' receive, since they were not going anywhere. He reprimanded anyone who said, 'Can I do this?' 'It is not a question of can. Of course, you can do it. But may you do it?' If in the flow of some family discussion, Patricia interrupted her elders to say, 'I think that....' the reproof, accompanied by a sardonic smile, was swift. 'Think? Few people are capable of thinking. What makes you think that you can think?'

Patricia thought thoughts that were critical of her stepfather. She imagined life without him, and the more she lingered on the vision, the more she liked it. She wondered if it might be possible to dispose of him in a manner that would appear to be an accident. She discussed this idea with Georgy. During that week the Captain was spending time up a ladder doing a repair job on some upper windows. Perhaps while he was perched up there, they could suddenly shriek at him from down below, startling him so that he would lose his balance and fall and, as happens to people who fall from heights, break his neck and die. They considered this for a day or two. Georgy did not discourage it, for the Captain could hardly bear the sight of his youngest stepchild, and roared terrifyingly at him from time to time, when Syria was not at hand. Unfortunately for the execution of their plot, Patricia discovered that the penalty for murder was hanging. The police might discover that the affair was not an accident and track her down. She decided sadly she dare not risk it. and the Captain was saved from her murderous impulses.

There were sometimes parts of her lunch for which Patricia felt far from truly thankful. On Fridays she and Georgy were served an insipid dish of steamed fish sent for them by special order on the train from Norwich. Jane cast envious eyes on this preferential treatment, but Patricia would gladly have given hers to Jane. Maud the cook had a good line in pies and steamed puddings, but on bad days they got cold stewed prunes and figs, which Patricia loathed. No allowance was made for personal tastes, except for Georgy, who was excused marrow. The older children devoured everything put in front of them, but Patricia could not overcome her abhorrence of red meat and fat. She usually managed to get rid of it by slipping the reject to the edge of her plate and waiting till Syria's attention was elsewhere, when she slid it off onto the open handkerchief ready for it on her lap. She quickly wrapped up the lot and disposed of it in her elasticised knicker leg. She was never caught though there was one narrow escape when she forgot to throw it away afterwards and Syria found the bundle and shook it so that dried pieces of fatty meat fell out on the floor. Patricia gazed in horror, but fortunately Syria did not recognise those desiccated scraps for what they were. Years later she made use of the same technique during a school lunchtime crisis when soft herring roes were served up. None of the girls could bear them except Patricia, but those at her table were able to dispose of theirs by passing them to her clandestinely. Her elastic knicker legs and open handkerchief accommodated them, ready for her later consumption. Alcohol was never drunk save by the Captain who had an occasional glass of Burgundy. He gave no sign of enjoying it, so Patricia assumed that it tasted nasty. Some years later, Grey, who had just turned eighteen, dropped into a pub for a pint of beer. Syria smelt it on his breath and saw it as confirming the fears she had always had about his moral weakness. There came the day when Grey's godfather, an ex-wartime cabinet minister who paid his school fees, was entertained to lunch. He would have received the customary teetotal menu. Syria's father had not seen fit to entertain his Bishop, of whose line in theology he disapproved, to anything more special than sandwiches in the vestry, and his daughter saw no reason to accommodate her distinguished guest with wine. She disapproved of it so it would not have been honest.

On this occasion Patricia and Georgy were relegated to lunch in the nursery with Glovie, but afterwards they were brought down and formally introduced to this tall grey man who, their mother had told them, would scarcely have been able to see them. He stood on the rug in front of the fire and gravely shook hands with each of them. Syria did not lack a sense of history.

At lunchtime, each of the offspring, on finishing, had to ask permission to leave the table. Had anything been left on a plate, permission would not have been granted until it had been eaten up. Peter had his own ritual. He went round behind Syria, and kissed the back of her neck. He called it a butterfly kiss. Patricia felt irritated by this. She would not have wanted to do it.

After lunch there was compulsory bed rest for Georgy and Patricia while Glovie and the maids washed up. They not only had to go to bed, but for the first half hour they had to draw their curtains and lie down in the dark. Patricia used this period to shut her eyes tight, bring her knees up under her chin, and disappear into her secret serialised life. It was becoming so enthralling that she was almost reluctant to draw back the curtains and start reading. Syria prescribed set books for this period. Patricia dutifully read with her eyes every book she was given, but her attention did not always follow her eyes. The option of rejecting a book was not available. What she preferred was *The Boys' Own Paper*, *Alice in Wonderland* and *The Wind in the Willows*. What she most often got was books about the sea. Everyone, including the Captain, who interested himself minimally in her doings, seemed determined to thrust nautical books at her. She was bored by the sea and ships, and mystified by the language of navigation. She could never remember the difference between starboard and larboard, or between port and stern. What was a lanyard or a yardarm? How far was a knot? How long was a watch? She did not know and she did not want to know. But she had somehow to toil her way through the pages of *Mr. Midshipman Easy*, *Westward Ho*, and the odd Conrad. Nor did she appreciate love stories. She could not imagine why they cropped up all the time. What did people see in them? The only kind of romances she enjoyed were Spenser's *Faery Queen* and the Arthurian legends. Bunyan's *Pilgrim's Progress* had a religious effect on her. For a week or two it transformed her world. She strove to preserve the feeling, but it slipped away and could not be recovered.

An important part of Syria's routine for Glovie and the Little Ones was two daily walks. One was usually dedicated to shopping in the village and took place after lessons. Until he was six, Georgy was cocooned in woollen garments. He was permanently cossetted as delicate, in the image of those vulnerable little Victorian children. Syria had lost three brothers and sisters in infancy. Patricia, too, was thoroughly fastened up, complete with one of the hated hats. In winter they both wore knee-length leggings. These had buttons all the way up which had to be fastened one by one with a buttonhook.

They walked to the village along lanes that had never yet known tar, and were as they had been in past centuries, rutted and sandy in dry weather; muddy and puddled in wet, often with a ridge of grass straggling down the middle. There were the deep marks of cartwheels and the big hoofmarks of farm horses. Glovie was still active at sixty or so, despite the fact that she had been up early, lending a hand everywhere. She seldom complained, though she frequently uttered a dirge about her painful feet and weak arches. In the early days, when she was still pushing Georgy in his wheeled chair, a cumbersome black object with a hood and pramcover, she often took off at a trot. Georgy squealed delightedly, and Patricia ran and hopped alongside. If Glovie was in walking mode, Patricia ran ahead and clambered up on a five barred wooden gate and sat waiting for her to catch up, while she gazed across the fields to tall woods beyond, which harboured a great many untidy rooks' nests. In the opposite direction the view was of the grey-green marshes, criss crossed with reed-fringed dykes, and beyond them the half-ruined flint Saxon church with its round tower. Over all hung the huge sky which takes up much of the world in Norfolk. Sometimes the fields were being ploughed or farrowed by a pair of great horses, steered from behind by the ploughman, a slow but steady job, with special care taken in the turning at the end of each row, sometimes they were clothed in growing corn in all its variations, from tender early green to the burnished copper of August, no longer seen in later years. Some fields were left to grass for a season, when they pastured the heavy horses. Patricia knew several by name. They were curious rather than aggressive, but they inspired a certain caution, for they were so big and she felt so small. Glovie was scared of them all. She regarded any animal as a potential biter, and horses had very large teeth. But the ploughman taught Patricia how to offer these amiable giants a lump of sugar or piece of apple on the flattened palm of her hand, so that all she felt was a velvety snuffling muzzle brush delicately across and skilfully whip away the titbit. Sometimes, meeting them as they drew a wagon loaded with beet or deliciously smelly farmyard manure, so different from the chemical product of later years, the farmhand stopped and let her stroke them, or if the harness had been discarded after the days' work, he lifted her onto a broad back and gave her a ride.

The main purpose of the walk to the village was to deliver Syria's household orders. In the grocery section of The World's Largest Village Stores, Patricia watched fascinated as the assistant painstakingly wrote down in pencil on a duplicated order pad the long list of goods required, which would later be sent up to the house in a horse-drawn van. Most of them had handwriting that was beautifully shaped, even when viewed upside down. They were all very kind to Georgy and Patricia, and decades later Patricia found she could recall each of their faces as clearly as if she had seen them the day before. They slapped and pounded butter taken from a large mound into the shape of small bricks, each weighing one pound, and they deftly turned and twisted them with two grooved wooden spatulas until the butter had been persuaded into perfect form, and patterned with narrow lines. A big red bacon-slicing machine stood at the end of one counter, and a diagram showing the various thicknesses of bacon rasher available, was displayed on its front. All the groceries for Seven Acres were ordered this way. Telephones were rare and they did not have one. So long orders, at least twice each week, with plenty of top-ups, were a necessity. When Glovie had finished reading out her list, the assistant invariably said, 'Might you not be wanting?' and then ran through a litany of further supplies. It would have been unthinkable for Glovie to add to Syria's instructions, so nothing more was ever ordered, but this did not discourage the assistants from following the same routine each time.

The butcher's shop and the ironmonger's often had to be visited too. For a treat Glovie sometimes took the children into the forge. This was a busy, noisy place, right in the centre of Coltishall, and the muscular, red-faced farrier moved around, wielding red-hot iron rods and horseshoes in its flaming depths, while horses of every size and colour stood waiting to be shod. The farm horses stood patiently, stamping their heavy feet and shifting their weight from one haunch to the other. The farrier was also the village saddler and the place was hung about with metal-studded leather harness, heavy collars, bits and bridles and riding saddles, as well as a big collection of the decorative brass circlets that any fully equipped working horse had to wear on its forehead. Patricia saved up and bought one to hang on her bedroom wall and she tried to memorize how the harness sat upon a horse so that she could improve her sketches. Once, in an open field, she saw a huge chestnut animal, shining like the sun, galloping round and round, unbelievably long mane and tail flying. She stopped in awe. 'What work does he do, then?' she asked. It was not made at all clear what he did. 'That sort of horse savages people,' said her mother. His function remained a mystery to her. It would not have been one to the village children, from whom, by the class mores of her family, she was completely cut off.

This exclusion from local child company gave rise to awkward situations, and it was tiresome because it meant that Patricia had no real friends of her own age until she went to boarding school. She was scared of these forbidden and forbidding children and yet wanted to make contact with them. She was being trained as a little snob, but curiosity diluted the effects of that training. It landed her in uncomfortable situations. If she and the village children met in the lanes, she was not supposed to acknowledge their existence. But where was she to look? The boys, there were never any girls, knew where to look. They stared straight at Georgy and Patricia and they made embarrassing noises. And if she chanced to turn her head after they had passed each other, their heads were twisted back to front too. They thrust out their tongues and made faces. Their aim, in which they succeeded, was to intimidate the stuck-up Seven Acres children, but the rule of the village policeman and the ingrained habit of generations, restrained them from anything worse. The entrance to the village was the trickiest hazard. It was guarded by a posse of boys who seemed to challenge their right to enter the village at all. They uttered hoots and jeers, and occasionally threw small stones which always fell short. Patricia wanted to throw stones back but was restrained by Glovie, who advised her to walk on as if nothing had happened. In Glovie's eyes, throwing stones was a grave offence. She told stories of children who had been blinded after being struck in the eye by a stone. Patricia must ignore absolutely all signs of hostility by the village boys and maintain a ladylike demeanour.

The boys were stationed at points throughout the village too, and one such place was outside the cobbler's workshop where Glovie often took the family shoes for repair. The children usually accompanied her inside his small, stuffy den, with its strong smell of stale feet and its grey pewter last, polished by use, on which the shoe was placed upside down for repair. The grimy, weary-faced cobbler did not go out of his way to make friends with the children, but held aloof, distantly polite. He had muscular hairy forearms which fascinated Patricia. But one day, lacking foresight, she stayed alone outside his shop. Three or four of her well-known tormentors appeared and stood around her, dangerously close, grinning and grimacing. She stared straight back, petrified with fright. The one she feared most, a boy with ginger hair and a freckled face, began to kick up the dust in front of her with his boot, like a small bull preparing to charge. Something needed to be done. So Patricia kicked back, and the dust flew between them. He stopped, and the first and last words ever to pass directly between Patricia and the posse were uttered.

'You're *silly*!' he said, loudly and clearly. It was not as bad as she had feared.

'So are you!' she retorted.

The dialogue ended there, for Glovie and Georgy emerged from the cobbler's shop, and this promising start to an understanding was interrupted, never to be resumed.

On their way back from the village, Glovie and the children often met cattle being herded along the narrow lanes. Glovie was even more terrified of cows than dogs, and had some alarming anecdotes about bulls who broke loose and gored people to death. To be on the safe side, they treated any solitary horned beast advancing towards them as a bull, and once it was in fact one. Patricia remembered how, quaking with fright, she and the other two had scrambled over a low churchyard wall they happened to be passing. The bull was meandering along, quite alone, having escaped from some yard.

Often they stopped, to pick a bunch of hedgerow flowers for Syria, who loved receiving these tributes from her children. Patricia could not then know that, behind Syria's disciplinarian self, so pre-occupied with keeping the house and everyone in it under her control, there was another self, avid for evidence that she was loved. She accepted the flowers fondly and lost no time in putting them in water and arranging them in some favoured position. The tangled hedges had something to offer in most seasons. Patricia particularly liked the deep crimson ragged robins and campions. They lasted well. The silken petals of poppies wilted as soon as picked, and flamboyant dandelions sulked and closed up for ever. Speedwell, too, with its summer-sky blue flowers, did not live up to promise, for the heads fell off almost at once, disdaining to survive their rape from the hedge. But buttercups and daisies lasted well, honey suckle was a generous flower, and in late spring, a foray into the marshlands rewarded with the supreme prize of golden mallows, which grew freely along the narrow dykes.

CHAPTER 26

The Captain spent much of his first year at Seven Acres constructing a grass tennis court. He was mechanically ingenious and prepared for this operation by making a strange contrivance for ploughing up the ground. It was powered by a motorbike engine and moved at a smart walking pace, steered by the Captain. Once the ground had been churned up, stones, big and small, littered its surface, and one afternoon the Little Ones were pressganged into collecting up these stones and removing them in baskets. Syria was away at the time, or she would not have allowed the Captain to draw Georgy into this exhausting work. The sun beat down that hot afternoon, and he soon felt sick and had to stop. After the ground had been de-stoned and rolled flat, it was sown with grass, and within a few months it had been transformed into a fine tennis court with plenty of spare lawn at the sides for deck chairs and croquet.

The homemade plough was developed into a grass mower with a seat atop, from which the Captain steered his capricious creation up and down the lawn.

To one side there stood a rustic type wooden summerhouse, a friendly place in which to spend an hour reading. In high summer delicious flower scents floated through it. It was embraced by a tangle of old-fasioned red roses which shared it with a giant buddleia bush, whose deep purple, honey-scented blossoms attracted hundreds of peacock and red admiral butterflies, giving the illusion that the buddleia itself was literally alive with colour. It was a temple of butterflies. On the far side of the lawn there was a boundary of tall, lombardy poplars, whose light, silvery leaves let a muted sunlight through, and whispered softly in even the stillest weather. Beyond the tennis court was a paddock where Silver, a bad-tempered Iceland pony spent much of her time, and alongside the court and the paddock rose a steep bank leading to an upper paddock. In the spring this bank was white with flowering blackthorn, and its verges were thickly carpeted with primroses.

The upper garden round and beyond the house was more formal. It was reached from the dell by a steep path, and separated from it by a rose and honeysuckle hedge. About the house were rosebeds. The nursery windows at the back looked out beyond the rose garden and its sheltering lilac and laburnum hedge, to the fruit and vegetable gardens. There were two orchards of different ages, home to apples, pears, damsons and Victoria plums. Then the territory grew wilder. There was a screening avenue of tall woodland trees, the residue of some ancient copse, which crossed the width of Seven Acres land and cut off the view beyond. Syria christened this wood Shady Lane. The area beyond it was invisible from the house except in winter when the trees were bare. This could be useful. Finally, there were two or three acres of open ground, bordered by thick field hedges and, on the western side, by the London North Eastern Railway Line from Norwich to the coast. This was used two or three times a day by leisurely passenger trains and a couple of very slow, interminably long goods trains. It was one of these which had run over Syria's tabby tom, whose age and deafness had impaired its hearing.

Most of this area was covered by blackcurrant bushes. There were also several large henhouses which the Captain had built on a frame set up in the yard outside his carpentry workshop. Nearly all his time was spent either in carpentry or in the care of his five hundred hens, whom he fed with two good meals a day, one of corn and one of kitchen scraps, such as potato peelings and the remnants of porridge which were mixed up together in a galvanised iron bucket and warmed on top of the kitchen range. By comparison with the hens of later generations, his hens were living in the Ritz. In the spring he bought a couple of hundred day-old chicks. He kept them in a circular house, raised well off the floor and warmed by a special curtained lamp in the centre which was left on day and night. After three or four weeks, coloured feathers began to appear. His chicks grew up at their own pace. Several months later, when they had become slim, adolescent birds, they were known as pullets and were pecking freely in the runs. Soon they began to lay small, delicate eggs. They did not graduate to adult status for about a year. Most of the cocks were destined for the Sunday lunch table.

The Captain's mood was at its best when he was carpentering. He made his own henhouses singlehanded. They were large structures, palaces for hens, with plenty of room inside for the birds to perch at will, and with a row of cosy nesting boxes which opened from the outside for the convenient removal of eggs. The children could walk about inside the houses without bending their heads.

Enclosing this little kingdom stretched the flat and fertile Norfolk fields, a chequerboard of hedges and trees. Myriads of birds and small animals shared this territory; some, such as badgers and foxes, not so small. Where the fields surrendered to the wetlands, half a mile or so away, otters were occasionally seen.

In summer, the cuckoo sounded from dawn to dusk.

Patricia gazed out of her bedroom window and watched the late sun slanting over the trees in Shady Lane. In autumn they were all colours. Yet behind this loved country world, a kind of sadness lurked. Here she was, aware that her life still lay in front of her, and yet she felt that she had already lived for a very long time, and life seemed precarious. Sometimes she lay in bed and listened to her heart beating and wondered how many years there would be before that steady clock ran down. They sang in church about Death but she was not tempted by the prospect of the heavenly kingdom. She sang, 'O for the pearly gates of Heaven, O for the golden floor,' and was not persuaded. She wanted Life, and more of it. She wanted it without black curtains and so much bed, especially when the sun was still high and the voices of the labourers and children were ringing in the next-door fields. She wanted it for herself, all of it, but bits of it were always being snatched away by this or that rule, and she didn't like having things taken away from her even if it was for her own good. It didn't feel as if it was. It seemed that more and more got taken away until, at death, everything had to go, in exchange for a life that no one really wanted to reach. 'I feel sad, but I don't know why,' she said to her mother as she was being tucked into bed. Syria simply said, 'We just have to accept it. Your Daddy always said that everything good has to be paid for.' It was a favourite saying of hers, so Patricia sighed and decided that you were only allowed to enjoy anything for a short time, after which you had to start paying for it by not enjoying it any more.

There were the lighthearted times too, and she could not help noticing that they were most likely to come when her mother was away on her visits. Syria's departure once over, Patricia dried her tears and very definitely made the best of it. Syria was usually absent for about three weeks, and as she always went when the other five children were at boarding school, the only people left at home were Glovie, the Captain, Patricia, Georgy and the maids.

The Captain never accompanied Syria on her travels, maintaining that he could not afford such luxuries. The fact was that he much preferred his introverted life in his workshop, the chicken runs, and his study, where he read books from Norwich Public Library, and busied himself writing nautical novels that were never published. He went to bed at exactly ten o'clock. During Syria's absences all he required was to be left alone by his stepchildren, and they were only too pleased to co-operate, especially the timid, pale Georgy. Syria said she thought he was jealous of Georgy, and perhaps he was. Patricia felt a bit jealous herself. But the idea of a grown-up being jealous of a little boy was strange to her.

The children were deeply bonded with the garden and its creatures. For Patricia, night and early morning were the best times of all. She made of these hours a world of her own, in which she led an entranced private existence to which only Georgy was admitted. Glovie was welcome on its periphery, but she never sought to probe. She seemed to know by instinct not to intrude, and was not in the least interested in regulating things.

She never made the children recite prayers to her. 'Do you believe in God'? Patricia asked her. She noticed that Glovie did not give a direct answer. 'I believe in the Golden Rule,' she replied. 'What's that?' 'Do unto others as you would be done by.'

So when Syria was away, visiting friends from a past life in various parts of the country, there seemed no reason for Glovie or her charges to live by any rulebook at all. Routine walks, afternoon rests in the dark, and early bedtimes were forgotten about. Nothing was said. They understood each other perfectly.

So Patricia and Georgy played in the garden to their heart's content and at all hours. If it was wintertime, Patricia spent long cosy evenings reading in front of the nursery fire after supper. Sometimes she read to Georgy. They went to bed when they felt tired. These respites gave Patricia ideas. She began to see that things didn't necessarily have to be so tiresome. The sort of changes she wanted could actually take place, and no one was the worse for them. Indeed everyone felt a great deal better. Next, she got the idea that perhaps she could help on such changes if certain precautions were observed. Perhaps, secretly, she could do anything she wanted. And what she most wanted was to be able to move around privately, without anyone having to know, every second of the time, where she was and exactly what she was doing. She wanted a world that was entirely her own, to be shared only if she chose and with whom she chose.

She discovered that this world could best be attained when everyone in the house except her shadow, Georgy, was asleep. So she began night wanderings, which in spring and summer, developed into even more magical dawn wanderings. This always had to happen when her mother was away, for Syria slept lightly and had incredibly acute hearing, as well as the ability to move about as silently as a snake, so that no warning of her approach was given. But Patricia quickly honed her skill at creeping about and opening and closing doors noiselessly. The earliest wanderings were confined to the house, Patricia bearing a lighted candlestick, with Georgy in tow. They crept past the bedroom door where the Captain coughed his asthmatic cough, and descended the front staircase into the lounge, where the anthracite stove, glowing orange-crimson through its mica window, grunted its comfortable way through the night.

Sometimes they went to Syria's bedroom, at a safe distance from the Captain's, and pried and poked their way through her drawers. Everything had to be left exactly as found, for she had a detective's eye for the slightest alteration in the position of anything. Many of her drawers she kept locked. They never found anything interesting anyway, but the mere fact that they were trespassing in such forbidden territory made these investigations irresistible. Patricia was tempted to try out one of Syria's Rhodesian cigarettes, but had to decide against, for Syria would probably have counted them. It was disappointing that the only sweets they found were candied ginger. They shared a piece between them and found it disgusting. On Syria's return, she detected its absence and accused Patricia of stealing. Unable to tell a barefaced lie, Patricia had to undergo a penalty. She had to learn a couple of Collects from the Book of Common Prayer and recite them to her mother. Any of Syria's possessions which promised to be interesting were locked away in little boxes or drawers which defied penetration. She became even more mysterious to the children.

They searched the kitchen at night. The larder, or pantry, was a 'walk-in' one with leftovers laid out on a marble slab, and covered with domes of white muslin stretched across a frame. The kitchen range at night was out and cold. Syria did not allow Patricia to linger in the kitchen, let alone the pantry. So the sight of generous supplies of butter, sugar and bacon from the World's Largest Village Stores, side by side with half-finished roasts, puddings, and bowlsful of eggs from their own henhouses, excited her. She decided to try her hand at the forbidden art of cooking. At that time, Syria laid out twopence a week for the regular purchase of *Bubbles*, a child's paper which, as well as serials about King Alfred, Robin Hood, and the Bunty Boys, included a recipe page for girl readers. Patricia consulted this and decided to make chocolates. Flour, milk, cocoa, sugar and an egg were required, also vanilla, which she would have to dispense with. She collected small quantities of the first four ingredients from the kitchen at night, and early in the morning she raided a henhouse for the egg. The cook would not miss anything that way; she had not yet reached that stage of intimacy with Maud and Mabel which she was later to enjoy.

When everyone had gone to bed, the children crept down to the kitchen. They had hoped that the fire in the range would still be alive, but it had gone out and Patricia was not able to use a saucepan on it for the mingling and heating of her hard-won ingredients. She settled for a compromise. Among her toys was a scarlet tin moneybox, shaped like a postbox. Into this she stirred her ingredients, heated the box on the grate of the nursery fire next day when no one was about, then hid the whole unpromising concoction at the back of her toy shelf, in hope that it would set, as forecast by her recipe. As nothing had been heated to the required temperature, nothing happened. After a few days of anxious waiting and probing, she was obliged to recognise that the mixture had gone bad.

At night the house was a different and mysterious place. All possibilities seemed open, and where Patricia led, Georgy was happy to follow.

In the daytime they were never allowed to linger by the anthracite stove downstairs, or to settle down on the comfortable seats built in on either side of the big brick fireplace. At night it became a favourite roosting place. Holding the lighted candlestick, or sometimes a paraffin-filled fairy light, Patricia led the way there and they ensconced themselves in this shadowy, red-glowing night world, in the company of the creaking stove, which sounded so much as though it was alive. Books could now be filched at will from the big bookcase and transferred secretly upstairs. Patricia's favourite was a complete *History of the Great War of 1914 to 1918*, in several big brown volumes, illustrated with photographs and black and white drawings. The War Memorial in the centre of the village, with names engraved all round it, took on meaning.

They were the brothers, fathers, sons, of the people who served in the shops, who worked in the fields, who did mending for her mother, who came in the summer to pick the blackcurrant crop. They were people like the gardener Rob, who had not been killed but had come back suffering with his nerves. She was to encounter surplus women throughout her growing-up years. At boarding school there would be mistresses, pretty, fading women whose fiancés had been killed and whose moods on November 11th, Armistice Day, were treated with fascinated tolerance by their pupils. Patricia had often wished she was a boy, especially when her mother badgered her to keep her skirt down, hissing such admonitions as, 'You're showing dreadful sights.' But there was another side to it. Being a man was dangerous. Their lives were more at risk than women's, and she was relieved to think that she would probably not be required to sacrifice hers. She could not foresee the age of the bombing of cities.

From the War History she learned also of the wretched fate of horses in that conflict. A picture which moved her very much was a painting entitled: 'Goodbye, Old Man,' it showed a Tommy on a devastated battlefield bidding farewell to his fallen horse. She acquired a copy of it which she pasted into her prayerbook and when she went to school, her friends wept with her over it.

She learned of the formidable fighting qualities of the "Hun," and read frightening accounts of their murdering of civilians. It was therefore a relief to read of at least one noble German officer whose men had fought an obstinate platoon of British soldiers until all but one of the British was dead. A picture showed an exhausted Tommy stumbling from his dugout and coming face to face with the steel-helmeted "Boche," who extended his right hand to him in acknowledgement of a brave enemy. So after all, not all Germans were bad, but in those years not long after the war, that was what most people seemed to think they were.

On those same bookshelves were volumes of late nineteenth century *Punch* Magazines. She was not pleased with the short straight fashions of her time. How much more beautiful women must have looked in her mother's childhood. Even Syria wore these plain, straight things, though in Patricia's eyes she managed to look beautiful whatever she wore. What mattered most was that Syria had retained her mass of long hair, of which she was quietly proud. She washed it in rainwater from the soft water barrel outside.

There were two other books which Patricia decided she must read for reasons of self-improvement. She longed to make herself better informed so as to catch up with the older children and participate more knowledgeably in their conversations at mealtimes. The books she chose for this purpose did not prove to be the help she had hoped. One was *The Search For Bread*, by Prince Kropotkin, a socially enlightened pre-Revolutionary Russian aristocrat, and the other was Olive Schreiner's *Women and Labour*. In her nine-year old ignorance of the issues involved, neither book meant much to her, though they said something for her perseverance, and they did at least teach her that many people had to exist in a poverty greater than any of the blackcurrant-pickers. After this experiment she gave up setting herself improvement courses.

One night as they sat in the lounge at about two in the morning, poring over a book by candlelight, her hair caught fire. The smell of singeing alerted her first. She had never been on fire before, but had the presence of mind to snatch up a cushion and smother the smouldering before it took proper hold. Georgy gazed at her with his mild blue eyes, not quite understanding. The smell of burning hung over the lounge for a day or two, and no one could account for it.

Sometimes at night the dining room attracted them, though it was a cold place. Here there was a long mantelpiece covered with shooting trophies won by their father, and a number of silver christening mugs and beakers. The most elegant piece was a heavy pint silver tankard with a lid, presented to Grey by his beneficent godfather. He had done well. So had all three of her brothers. Patricia was the only one not represented. On the sideboard was a large oval silver tray, inscribed to her father by medical colleagues in Africa and on display in a room with a French window which was locked only at night. There was nothing unusual about this. Burglaries were rare in the country. It was only after the Second World War, when cars introduced strangers into every neighbourhood, making quick get-aways easy, that break-ins became a plague. Before then, the expending of spare time in constant movement from place to place was not a common ambition. Everyone knew who lived in their own world, who was peculiar and who dishonest. There were four outer doors at Seven Acres, and not one was locked in the daytime.

The chief attraction of the diningroom was the sideboard's supplies of white lump sugar. It was easy to tuck into these without leaving traces.

Only once were they nearly caught. They must have made some sound which disturbed the Captain, while they were sitting by the stove in the lounge, for they suddenly heard the handle of his bedroom door turn. Patricia promptly extinguished the candle, whose dim glow, reflected up the stairs would have reached him almost at once, and seizing hold of Georgy, she propelled him through the open diningroom door, and thence through to the servants' quarters. They hurried on till they came to the back stairs. They could already hear the Captain thumping down the front stairs, and the chance of being caught was real. They scrambled up the stairs and sped along the landing to Patricia's bedroom, managing to close the door noiselessly.

They squeezed themselves together in her narrow camp bed and lay, listening anxiously. After a time, having presumably inspected the ground floor thoroughly, the Captain returned to his bedroom. It had been a scaring episode, and led to even greater care.

CHAPTER 27

Syria decreed more fresh air when the afternoon rest was over, and she preferred this to take the form of a walk. None of the nursery trio much cared for this. Glovie had only just finished helping with the washing up. Shopping had usually been done in the morning, so now it was a matter of tramping the lanes. That at least was what Syria assumed they were doing. Glovie found ways round it.

They often slipped down the hill to the bungalow, set in a large garden among the fields, where lived the two Irish spinsters, Margaret and Mary, and their noisy cairn Cuddy. He had become the only dog Glovie was not afraid of. They were always given a great Irish welcome. Margaret and Mary were really two elderly children themselves, and they enjoyed including Patricia and Georgy, with their friend Glovie, in a life that seemed practically all play. In weather when the clouds raced and the wind blew cold, they were made at home in the cosy sittingroom, and treated to Mary's delicious sticky toffees. Sometimes they clamped earphones on their heads and listened intrigued to the crackling voices. There was no wireless at home. When the weather was fine, Margaret, the younger sister, led the children on a scamper across the fields and marshes. She showed them what she claimed was the ruin of an old castle, but there was little to suggest a castle on that slight grassy mound, though she did point out something that might have been a bit of ancient stone wall breaking through the undergrowth. She showed them the best places for finding buttery gold marshmallows, and a clear pebbly tributary of the River Bure where there were shoals of tadpoles. This led to innumerable happy afternoons for Georgy and Patricia, spent playing in the transparent shallow water with whole fleets of tadpoles, while Glovie sat on her folding stool nearby, knitting, or reading her favourite magazine, *Modern Woman*.

Patricia came to feel an intense attachment to the country round her. She felt close to a past which seemed still to touch the present. The 'far and quiet dead' of Glovie's song might have been dead, but they were not far. She knew where they were. She was very close to them in ruined Great Hautbois church, with its round tower, standing isolated on the very edge of the marshes. When they did not visit Mary and Margaret they often went there. Local tradition held that it was Saxon, and it was obviously very ancient. Its nave was only partly roofed, and the main entrance was barred by a locked wrought iron gate. The east end, which remained roofed, was completely closed to the outer world by another locked door. It was unlocked only on the rare occasion of a funeral service for one of the few people on Great Hautbois' parish register.

The church stood, flinty and stalwart, alone among the woods and fields bordering the wetlands, and the hot summer sun and the fierce gales and snows of an East Anglian winter beat upon it and left it slowly crumbling away, but still able to serve those who wanted to make their last rest in its shadow. Patricia seldom returned to Norfolk in adult years, but whenever she did, she made straight for the old church. Forty years after the afternoon walks with Georgy and Glovie, she found the roofless entry to the nave unlocked, and she went in for the first time. Under the open sky inside the walls, she found three gravestones. They belonged to the elderly friends of her childhood who had spent their lives within sight of the church.

There was a benign aura to the overgrown graveyard when the sun shone. While Glovie sat reading or knitting on her camp stool, Patricia and Georgy wandered about among the grey-green stones. Many of them had late eighteenth century rococo shapes. Butterflies flitted about them. Some leant at strange angles. Lettering had often been worn away by a century or so of winters, so that the histories of those they recorded had faded out of sight. Patricia brooded on the names and dates of others, and wondered at the many who had died as children. She herself was rather afraid of dying as a child. In the midst of this necropolis stood a grander monument, a tall broken pillar with a stone border and a rusty iron railing surrounding it. Glovie explained that the broken pillar symbolised a life suddenly broken off. Like my father's, thought Patricia.

She walked among the gravestones, in this place of graves so decorously gay, with its wild flowers and its butterflies, and felt the shortness of life. She imagined, though she wished she did not have to, the dead, lying skeletal in their coffins six feet down; people who had been as alive as Maud the cook, as Mabel the parlourmaid, as grumpy Rob the gardener, as Glovie, as Georgy, as herself. From here it was a short step to pondering on the grave under its granite slab thousands of miles away, on a hill in Africa, in a place even lonelier than this. Would he still be recognisable or was he by now a skeleton, no more a person than the bare branches of a tree in winter? She asked Glovie how long people in coffins lasted, and Glovie said she thought about five years.

In dreams he stood there, a dim shape, and she knew it was he, but he never turned his face towards her. She longed for him to look at and recognise her. In her night-time saga, she altered this. They were rich with re-unions, after long separations. He was the hero-King, he was Arthur, and she the lost daughter, searching for him, and beset by dangers. Through these tales flitted a sinister old witch, but her father turned up at the last moment and rescued her. She always arranged to be in a very tight spot when, god-like, he broke upon the scene. This was not allowed to happen too often, lest it lose its drama. In keeping with Arthurian legend, she was clad in a flowing medieval gown, and had long golden hair, taken back under a becoming wimple.

The time came when these adventures were on the verge of being more interesting than ordinary life. She was turning her back on the humdrum world from which her hero, stolen from her earliest childhood, was missing. There was no man to take his place. Her stepfather had no interest in her nor she in him. There was no warmth between them. Nor did she care for his appearance. He was small in stature, shorter than her mother. Her own father had been big and handsome. Peter had told her something she valued above all. 'You could do no wrong in his eyes. You were his favourite, make no mistake about that!' Years later she realised how generous Peter had been to have told her this. He had seemed happy for her, and not at all envious, and yet no one could really like being in second place. She hadn't liked playing second fiddle to Georgy. So she dreamed of being alone with the father whose favourite she had been, and trying to fight off the truth that never again would she set eyes on him. But reality pressed, and she could not keep up the pretence indefinitely. She awoke from it suddenly. One morning she was practising on the piano the music for an old song Glovie had taught her. It was *Robin Adair*.

'What's this dull town to me?

Robin's not near;

Who was it I longed to see?

Whom wished to hear?

Where's all the joy and mirth Made this town heaven on earth? O they're all gone with thee, Robin Adair.'

The sad little ditty was telling her something that halted her in mid phrase. She had just grasped unmistakeably, in one instant, once and for all, that her father was in fact quite dead. Her re-creation of him was a waste of time, and she could not believe in it any more. He was not real in the way she wanted, and never would be. He had gone and she had to accept the meaning of the words, 'for ever.' It was useless to go on pretending. And there was a sadness in not feeling able to go on doing it.

Despite rows, and knowing that she took second place to Georgy, Patricia was still as afraid as she had ever been that her mother would die too. Every time Syria left for one of her progresses up and down the country, Patricia pleaded with her to be careful. And yet she caught herself beginning to imagine a different life, with Glovie in her little Cambridge cottage, and not at all disliking the idea. Perhaps if her mother died, that was where her stepfather would send her. But this was still hardly thinkable about. One dull spring evening after tea, Syria suddenly stopped the hymn tune she was playing on the piano.

'When Jesus calls Mummie,' she began, and hesitated. Patricia was surprised. She had time to speculate how Jesus the remote, the truly unreal, could possibly call her mother anything. They must be on much better terms than Jesus and herself.

'When Jesus calls Mummie to Himself,' resumed Syria, 'You won't mind too much, will you.'

Patricia was shocked. Her mother must be going to die, and she must be expecting to die soon. She could not find any voice to reply to her. She buried her face in the armchair cushions, trying to suppress the sobs that welled up. After a moment's silence, Syria turned round on the revolving piano stool and realised the effect of what she had just said. She tried to unsay it. 'Don't worry, darling. He won't call me for years and years.' But Patricia did not know what to think.

So unhappy must Syria have been in her marriage to a man with whom, apart from a an orphaned family and a sense of duty, she had nothing in common. Patricia could not remember a time, and she could remember very early times, when she had not been aware that behind everything, including so much that she took delight in, there lurked a vague sadness that she could not explain. She thought it might disappear if she could return to her lost home in Africa. She cherished the memory of it and took care to keep it alive by thinking about it often. She remembered the sunshine, the red earth, and the brilliant flowers. She kept on hoping that they would return. In the early 1930's her mother told her she might have to go back. What Patricia did not know was that it was proving impossible to sell the place, and Syria thought a personal visit from her might stir things up. The great Depression had brought about a disastrous fall in her share values, and she could no longer sustain the mortgage. Many years of drought had followed their departure in 1924. Arthur had paid an inflated price for the Farm, and now the agents were saying they could not get rid of it at any price. No one was willing even to rent it. The Captain showed no inclination to help Syria out with the mortgage payments until times should improve, so there was nothing for it but to let it go. Enough money had already been thrown away. So the Farm, together with Arthur's grave, went out of their lives for good. At the same time, Syria sold, for next to nothing, the few small houses along the Cape Town shore which Arthur had bought as an investment. Some twenty years later, they rose astronomically in value.

So Patricia had to give up hope of seeing her paradise again. Georgy would go back to Africa after the war as a medical missionary, and in I955 Syria paid a last visit to friends there, now grown old, but Patricia postponed her return for many years.

CHAPTER 28

An outing to Norwich was a serious expedition, seven long miles of fields and woods away. Syria always took them there. They went by bus, or by train from the local branch line station. Syria had given up trying to drive since a disastrous lesson with the Captain, when she had landed the Austin in a ditch. The children preferred the bus anyway. It drove past the historic wooden Domesday Book Mill across the Bure. The Mill's long life came to an end in the fifties, when it was gutted by fire. The drive to Norwich was pleasant in its green ordinariness and its stomach-churning little bridge at Crostwick Common. In Norwich they disembarked at Tomblands, a big open area just outside the Cathedral. One of the Norwich treats was a visit to Bowhill and Elliot's, a long-established shoe shop. Syria suffered from hammertoes due to wearing hand-me-down shoes in her hard-up childhood at the Rectory, and she was as conscientious about the children's feet as about their excretory habits. Patricia's feet were dead flat. A buildup of a quarter of an inch was carried out on her shoes by this shop. She and Georgy enjoyed standing on their x-ray machine, long since banned, which enabled them to study their own foot skeletons. Later on, they were taken up a narrow staircase to the Corner Tearooms opposite Jarrolds, where firm-looking middle-aged ladies served cupfuls of creamy, foaming hot chocolate, and exquisite home-made meringues. Those meringues were to mark the lifelong peak of meringue experience for Patricia. After this there was usually a visit to the dentist. He wielded his horrid instruments with some humanity, promising the children that if the pain became too severe, they only had to raise a hand, and he would stop for a moment. Patricia was very susceptible to him.

A spell in the galleries of Norwich Castle Museum came next. Extra money had to be paid out for visiting the dungeons, so they did not visit the dungeons. Patricia would have liked to inspect them, but Syria was not open to persuasion. She left them to wander round the galleries while she hurried off, unencumbered, for a quick visit to her favourite doctor. The children were specially intrigued by a female Egyptian mummy, several thousand years old. She lay there in a glass case, her face and her little hands uncovered. A thin black leathery skin was stretched across her facial bones, splitting in places, and the fine fingernails on each hand looked less old than her face. Strands of coarse reddish hair escaped from her head wrappings, and the rest of her was swathed in yellowing bandages. Patricia took an interest in the condition of the dead, but this woman was more than simply dead. A menace seemed to hang about her. Patricia turned away from her to the manuscripts of Rider Haggard, a Norfolk man, for she had been greatly stirred by *King Solomon's Mines* and *She*, and wanted desperately to believe in the wild Africa that Rider Haggard had conjured up.

Sometimes, instead of in the Castle, Syria deposited the pair on Jarrold's toyshop floor. This contained toys that Patricia keenly desired to possess. What she wanted most was a pedal car. These came in all sizes and colours, and Patricia would have settled for quite a small one. Unhopefully she persevered with strong hints to her mother, but it would have been an outrageous indulgence, and Syria remained true to her principle that to give in to a person's whims was bad for the character, and she must have found Patricia's character imperfect enough without any further help.

Small pleasures did give much enjoyment, and had the advantage of being cheap. The children never returned home without each bearing a copy of a child's comic, such as *Bubbles* or *Tiger Tim*. They carried serial stories about Red Indians, Robin Hood, and King Alfred the Great, as well as cartoon tales of a series of goons known as the Bunty Boys, and a family of humanised animals.

One day Syria went off to Norwich by herself and returned with the two children's papers. She gave Georgy his *Tiger Tim*, and then summoned Patricia for a serious dressing down. There had been trouble between them that morning before Syria left. She had not succeeded in getting Patricia to own up to a piece of naughtiness. Not only had she not owned up, but she had denied having done the deed at all. 'You will not get your *Bubbles*,' she now told Patricia, 'until you have owned up to taking out those safety pins which I fixed to your sheet last night, and hiding them in the wicker chair.'

For once Patricia knew herself to be entirely innocent. 'I didn't take out the pins and I didn't hide them,' she insisted. Looking disgusted, Syria turned away. The previous night, desperate to find some way of stopping Patricia pulling the sheet tightly over her head and face, completely covering it before going to sleep, she had taken two large safety pins and pinned the sheet firmly down to the blanket beneath. She had tried everything, emphasising how bad it was for Patricia's health to shut off the air in this way, and even offering a bribe in the form of a green bead necklace. Patricia simply would not stop doing it. The fact was, she could not stop doing it, for she was too frightened of the dark. She knew that if the sheet was not firmly tucked down under her head, she would be open to attack by the fiend, Grendel's mother. The clawed hands would grab her. Therefore she had to stick to her habit, much as she would have liked to gratify her mother. After Syria had pinned down the sheet and left the room, Patricia was left with no choice but to pull the blanket, together with the sheet, right over her head, which made the atmosphere even stuffier than usual. But she dared not unpin the sheet. Syria always came in at ten o'clock for a last inspection, and would be very angry with her. Uncomfortably hot, she managed at last to get to sleep.

Early next morning she woke up, and to her surprise the sheet was free, the pins were no longer there. She assumed Syria must have relented and removed them when she came in at ten. But Syria had not done so. The pins must have been still in place then. When she came in the next morning and found the pins gone, she was very annoyed and demanded to know what Patricia had done with them.

'I haven't done anything,' Patricia told her. 'I didn't unfasten them.' Syria did not believe her. 'I don't like children who tell lies,' she said. She hunted about the room and soon found them, tucked behind a cushion in the wicker armchair.

Syria knew that Patricia longed to have her *Bubbles*, but as afternoon turned towards evening, she still refused to own up. Nor would she confess at bedtime. This was an unheard-of situation. Syria must have begun to wonder. What conclusion she came to, Patricia never knew, but her conviction that Patricia had deliberately removed and hidden the pins was obviously shaken, and next morning she handed over *Bubbles*. Patricia's private opinion was that Glovie had crept in and taken them and hidden them in the chair. She knew that Glovie, who must have had some idea of the situation, would have sympathised with her. She did not enquire, and Glovie said nothing.

Patricia did not know that such things can happen somnambulistically, and that after all, she might have done it herself in her sleep. At any rate, Syria never pinned the sheet down again.

Syria was subject to the kind of ill health in which a person keeps going but never really feels well. She had a number of complaints, and she talked to Patricia and Georgy about them because they showed more concern than anyone else. The Captain enjoyed straightforward health himself, apart from bouts of asthma, but he believed rather heartlessly in the commonsense remedy of ignoring the passing symptom, in Syria as well as himself, until it went away. What she yearned for was something like the attention her late husband had given her during her convalescence from typhoid fever. She wanted a fuss made of her, a medical programme arranged, and possibly a tasty soup made from game shot specially for her that very morning. The Captain was no Arthur, in this as in many other respects. She was visited by a rotation of discomforts and maladies, ranging through toothache, headache, incapacitating corns, sciatica, and, to cap them all, duodenal ulcer. This cleared up almost overnight years later, after the Captain's death. Patricia and Georgy were very aware of the sufferings through which she so bravely carried on, and worried constantly about their mother's survival.

There was something catching about this. Mysterious bouts of nausea began to afflict Patricia. She often woke at night, vomiting. Next day she could not eat, and was made sick all over again by tablespoonsful of castor oil, washed down with segments of orange. She could never keep this down, so the dose was repeated. She wondered why her mother persisted with this surefire recipe for sickness, and she made such scenes over it that at last Syria desisted. The days in bed dragged on, however. Sometimes she felt like getting up, but she was not allowed to. Her temperature was taken frequently and she was fed tasteless beaten-up eggwhite or Sanatogen, a pulpy white tasteless gruel. She forgot what real food was like. Christmas came and went, and she was still on starvation diet and still in bed. It had been decreed that she was ill, so there she stayed, and stayed, and stayed. By now she felt quite weak from lack of food and exercise, the boredom of living in a shaded room with nothing to do and very little company. At last, after what had seemed like years, Syria decided to risk getting her up again.

Shortly after her recovery, it was Georgy's turn. He had been reporting aches and pains in his legs, and the village doctor diagnosed rheumatic fever which was serious, if correct. After a sufficient period in bed, agreed between Syria and the doctor, he graduated to convalescence, and was gradually restored to a normal way of life. From now on he was regarded as even more delicate than before. He was indeed a pale little fellow. Syria remained anxious about his heart, though he had been cleared of heart murmur at the age of four months. Now she had another anxiety to endure, since rheumatic fever frequently damages the heart. Fortunately for Georgy, these fears were not borne out. He developed into the only Pearson child to have any athletic pretensions, turning out to be a very fast runner, and to enjoy such robust health that these early apprehensions were quite forgotten.

Around the time that Georgy was making a welcome recovery from rheumatic fever, Patricia was entering into a supremely hypochondriachal phase. As the Bible was the only book allowed in her bedroom, it was inevitable that she became acquainted with leprosy, that punitive disease which gradually ate a person up and cut them off forever from family and friends. One day she noticed that a scab on her leg was not clearing up. The unwelcome truth struck her. She was suffering from leprosy and would soon be snatched away from home, mother, Glovie and Georgy, to live in isolation until she died an early death. She passed a despairing few weeks until Glovie told her, in reply to her anxious, probing questions, that leprosy was not a disease which occurred in England. The reprieve from banishment was tremendous. The scab cleared up at once.

Respite did not last. Patricia began to notice that she was getting pains on both sides of her chest. She must be suffering from consumption, a serious condition which at that time carried with it the sentence of banishment from home to a sanatorium. At last she confessed these fears to Syria who, prone to take alarm at any kind of symptom, was not hard to involve. She sent for the village doctor, who examined Patricia and pronounced her to be suffering from nothing worse than muscular stiffness.

After a brief relapse into health, Patricia noticed that curious, semi-transparent shapes were forming in front of her eyes. Everything she looked at bore faint traces of them. They were like ghostly pieces of meccano. Recently she had heard about cataract. This must be it. She was starting to go blind. She endured for a while and then reported it to Syria. She was expecting the worst when Syria arranged for her to see an eye specialist in Norwich. She dreaded that consultation, but her fears were laid to rest as quickly as the others had been. All she was seeing was faint traces of blood vessels in the eyes which had come into existence before she was born and faded not long after birth. This was normal.

Patricia was not through yet. There was the alarm over uneven heartbeats, which convinced her that heart failure was on the way. The village doctor was sent for yet again, and she learned that she was experiencing extra systoles, a common, and in her case, harmless condition. Needless to say, this symptom, too, disappeared. She still had to deal with tetanus, or lock-jaw, as Glovie called it, a fatal condition which was liable to strike you if you cut yourself between the thumb and first finger. It did not take Patricia long to bring about this accident, but Glovie assured her that the scratch was so slight it had not gone deep enough for infection. With this, the series ended. Leprosy, tuberculosis, blindness, heart failure and tetanus had been a formidable catalogue of disasters. By now, Patricia realised that she was prone to fears about her health, particularly anything which carried threats of banishment. Before admitting any of them to Syria, she had always extracted a promise that, whatever happened, she would not be sent away. Syria took every one of these crises seriously, and consulted that essential exorcist, the doctor. She needed his reassurance as much as Patricia did. In former days, she had not had to look further afield for it than her husband. Even now, he was helping her posthumously. She had perfected a method of getting medical attention without having to pay for it, in days long before the

National Health Service. She invariably begged doctors off their fees on the ground that the children's father had been a doctor, and that she was a doctor's widow. Although they could see for themselves she was no longer a widow, nor the children technically fatherless, professional gallantry, allied to Syria's unashamed persuasions, still worked for her. She was never embarrassed by that sort of thing. It was her right, and other people's privilege, that they should come to her aid.

Patricia finished by nearly inflicting real damage on herself. She decided to create a salad of greenery from the garden hedge, and her recipe included leaves from the plant Lords and Ladies, which unknown to her were mildly poisonous. The effect was startling. Soon the inside of her mouth, including the underneath of her tongue, became inflamed and stung painfully. She said nothing to anybody, but drank a great deal of water to cool things down, and in a couple of hours the symptoms had subsided. She had given herself a bad fright. She had been afraid she had fatally poisoned herself, and she did not want to die. She had only recently learned from Glovie that some people killed themselves on purpose. It astonished her that anyone could possibly want to die. She could not imagine such a state of mind.

During Syria's regular absences from home, Glovie's position as the calm centre of the children's lives was reinforced. So imperceptibly did this happen that Syria was unaware of it, for she was supremely possessive and could not knowingly have put up with any kind of rival. She aspired to the status of perfect Mother. Not for nothing had she left a sheet of paper among her effects on which she had written a quotation from the Book of Proverbs:

'And her children shall rise up and call her blessed.' The truth was that Glovie was the most adaptable, hardworking, cheap and uncomplaining mother's help that she had ever had. It allowed her to space out regular contacts with her two youngest children with the precision that was so important to her, laying down "rules" which were never questioned by Glovie as earlier Nannies had questioned them, and she remained unaware of Glovie's quiet evasions of them in a happy conspiracy with the children. She made sure that hers was the first face that Patricia and Georgy saw every morning when, as she assumed, they awoke. Except in coldest wintertime, Patricia had been sitting on the windowsill since dawn, watching nature come to life, but as the moment of Syria's entry approached, she leapt back into the darkness of bed. At mealtimes, Syria kept Patricia and Georgy under close watch, next to her. Sometimes she took them for specially favoured walks. She rode her large bicycle, while the two children proceeded on scooters, which registered a satisfying speed when freewheeling downhill. Syria, crowned with an impressive hat, usually of Edwardian vintage, preceded them in dignified fashion, dismounting regularly to allow them to catch up.

She gave them an hour of her time after tea. They sat with her in her drawing room, or rather cosily in her big bedroom, where in winter there was always a fire burning in the grate. She was usually in mellow mood, and ready to play for them on the piano, or to play card or board games. Syria liked cards, and having an excellent memory was very good at them, though she would not allow them on Sunday. Patricia loved hearing her mother play the piano, and she remembered these times for Syria's happiest moods. She threw off her preoccupations and laughed occasionally. She talked to them about her own Victorian childhood and showed them fading photographs of impressively severe and ugly forbears, overdressed in voluminous dark robes, or with heavy beards and side whiskers. The women all wore white lace caps. She recounted treasured memories of the years spent with their father in Africa and read them Arthur's own articles about big-game hunting in the bush, written in the early years of the century and published in *The Empire Review*. They attended closely to these articles as they sat on the floor at their mother's feet, on the worn skin of one of Arthur's lions. She left them in no doubt that her heart was still with him. She kept framed photographs of him in all the Pearson bedrooms, some as far back as his schooldays. Patricia studied them, wishing as ever that she did not have to manage without him. Syria monopolised their bedtime too, a ritual that was brisk but thorough. She gave them their daily bath together in the big bath. She had no qualms about washing them intimately, not troubling to use a flannel, and there was a certain unwelcome feeling associated with her soaped hands, which left no part of their anatomy unexplored. The situation became further embarrassing to Patricia when she was reaching puberty, while Georgy's physical development trailed a long way behind. Syria seemed not to have noticed that Patricia was growing up, and in the end she had to take matters in hand herself and gain a reluctant permision to wash her person herself and without the company of Georgy. He must have benefited too, for of late she had taken to kicking him quite vigorously in the crutch when they were seated opposite each other in the bath.

Their mother had rarity value, and the children enjoyed these times alone with her unless one of them, usually Patricia, was in disgrace and being sent to Coventry, that is, being pointedly ignored and not spoken to until she apologised.

Syria always tucked them into bed herself, and disposed herself to hear their evening prayers. The praying completed, there came the moment when any apologies outstanding got their last chance. However resistant Patricia might have been during the day, she could never hold out at night, but had to swallow her pride and force the untrue words out of herself, for she knew she would not get to sleep with Syria's unforgiveness hanging over her. Yet how was it that she seemed to be so very naughty? Georgy wasn't. She hit at last on the expedient of finding some small propitiatary gift from among her possessions to give her mother every night. It could be difficult sometimes to know what to give, but if she ran out of inspiration, she did a drawing for Syria. The daily offerings were an insurance against the bad times. Syria accepted them graciously. The child could be very trying, but at least she was affectionate.

When Syria was away, Glovie took over their bedtime. Nightly gifts were not necessary for her. There was no need to placate her, for she never got angry with them. It was not that she had no grounds. Patricia could be a tempestuous pupil, and when her hand would not obey her intention or she was unable to spell out the sense of a word or get the long division out, she often flew into a temper and shed tears of rage at herself and Glovie, who remained unperturbed, or at worst expostulated, 'You'd try the patience of Job!' Georgy never lost his temper either. He just sat there, watching Patricia do it.

Glovie's good nature had to stand up to tests from another quarter too. Syria never accepted that anything was beyond repair and some demanding tasks were laid on Glovie. She expected fast work, and Glovie produced a fairly constant trickle of meek protest at the endless stream of jobs that came her way. The children noticed a pattern in her complaints which they chanted back at her, 'Now you know, Mrs. Thring, I can't do that, so it's no use going on!' But in fact she could 'do that,' and grumbling gently, accomplished marvellous fcats. They saw sleeves replaced, skirts lengthened by false hems, large holes in pullovers picked up on knitting needles and mended in situ, invisible repairs to lace, jumpers with new lengths knitted straight onto the base, not to mention such tedious jobs as turning worn sheets side to middle and joined together down their whole length by a double hand-seam. She had the special skill of picking up ladders in stockings with a fine crochet hook. It was never finished. As soon as the pile was diminished, it was refurbished. Glovie's ineffectual protests must really have been about the frustration of never seeing her work completed.

As demands on her increased, she made less of her own clothes and bought more. This meant exciting visits to the World's Largest Village Stores. When Glovie set out on a buying spree, having presumably saved up several months' pay, Patricia was as interested as if she had been buying for herself. Upstairs into the Hat and Dress Department they went. Glovie favoured long, loose-fitting woollen cardigans of a style then in vogue, and she preferred soft blues and greys. They both studied the array of choice intently, assessing each garment as it draped itself about her small, round-shouldered little figure. Together they considered it critically in front of the long cheval mirror that was the pride of Dresses and Hats. Patricia liked best the garments had had some bit of satin or silk trimming.

Glovie adored trying on hats. They were twitched this way and that, with much mirror glancing from various angles. She could not resist feather trimmings, and if a hat did not start with one of these, it very soon acquired one. Pheasant or pigeon feathers, picked up on walks, were destined to find a place in her millinery.

New shoes were the most constant necessity. The feet that caused her so much trouble were flat, and as she often reminded them, had weak arches. Most of her small income had to be expended on them. Patricia and Georgy enjoyed dawdling in the Shoe Department downstairs, as box after box spilled its contents on the floor, with the shop assistant and Glovie deep in conversation about the defects of her feet. Patricia liked hearing Glovie chatting with the assistants in a way that she had never heard Syria do. Some of the shoeboxes contained small coloured story booklets, and these were passed over to the children as negotiations went on. Most of the shoes failed to live up to Glovie's hopes. They were scarcely worn after purchase, and were kept crammed into a bedside chamberpot cupboard.

Glovie was not beautiful and never had been. She had a head that was slightly large for her small spare body, her skin looked even older than its years, her feet had a tendency to turn outwards. She had a hair problem too. At first she wore it long, fastened in a bun, and then she decided to catch up with the times. A "shingle'"was what she desired. She greatly admired Syria's abilities. 'Your mother's a very clever woman,' she often said, and so she assumed that hair styling would fall within the range of her accomplishments. Syria sat her down on a kitchen chair and swiftly scissored off all her hair to within an inch or so of the head. An Eton crop, she called it, maintaining that it suited Glovie perfectly, heedless of the cries of distress uttered when her too-trusting client was able to reach a mirror. In time, the shorn hair grew to a more becoming length about halfway down each side of Glovie's face, and she kept it that way, brushed dead straight, indeed, there was not a natural wave or curl in it. Patricia and Georgy delighted in Glovie's quaint appearance.

She seemed them like a sort of elderly elf or brownie, with kind hazel eyes. A visit to the village shops often ended with a present. They would return home, each with a brightly coloured rubber ball, or a celluloid windmill which turned in the breeze. Their mother continued to disapprove of these impulsive gifts. But Glovie was a giver, a habit she never tried to lose.

CHAPTER 29

The web of lanes reaching out from Coltishall into the country around had few visits from strangers. Even people who possessed motor cars used them only for major excursions, such as a twelve-mile jaunt to the seaside or the seven-mile drive to Norwich. People walked or cycled shorter distances. Some stabled their own horses and rode everywhere or got about in pony carts and elegant little traps. Patricia and her mother spent an unforgettable summer evening being driven by an elderly bachelor admirer of Syria's in his neat equipage around the Broads. The smart little pony trotted them briskly along the evening lanes, quiet save for birdsong and voices in the fields. They passed through villages thatched with Broadland reeds. The few tourists negotiated small houseboats along the waterways, and intrigued the locals by doing their shopping in what appeared to be thin pyjamas, forerunners of slacks. A rare form of transport was a coach, drawn by a high-stepping grey, a top-hatted coachman upright on the box. Sometimes Glovie and the children met it on their walks. In the coach sat an old lady in her nineties. A coachman had driven her round the lanes in the afternoons since early in the reign of Queen Victoria and a coachman was doing it now. She lived near the River Bure in a graceful house which had a spectacular copper beech tree in the front garden. Living with her was her gentle, middle-aged niece and a friend, maiden ladies all. Patricia went to her ninety third birthday party. She had ninety-three candles ablaze on top of a huge cake.

All the farms had three or four shire horses who drew the plough, the harrow, the heavy wains. The bright chestnut Suffolk Punch was a common sight. One of Patricia's chief joys was watching the harvesting of the twelve-acre field opposite her bedroom window. They began reaping at six in the morning, not stopping until dusk. Round and round went the horse-drawn binder, felling the corn with its sharp blades and throwing out the sheaves, which were picked up and heaped into tent-shaped "stooks" to dry out for the next four or five days, longer if the weather turned wet. As the binder went round, the standing corn became an ever-smaller island in the middle of the field. Boys and men stood around with dogs, waiting for rabbits and other small animals to make a dash for safety as their refuge was stolen from them. Most were quickly caught. The stooks made perfect, sweet-smelling places for a quiet afternoon read.

After the corn had dried out, the thresher was towed into the corner of the twelve-acre field, near the five-barred gate off the lane, where it began its day-long work, generating a low, musical hum across the Seven Acres garden and the surrounding fields. The stooks were dismantled, and workers with two-pronged forks lifted the bound sheaves onto wagons. They were brought to the thresher and threshed, to separate out the grains of wheat, barley or oats. The straw left over was forked into piles the size and shape of a cottage, and thatched against the weather. Sometimes the field had a rest from corn crops, the grass was left to grow long, then cut and dried out as hay. The harmonious forms of sheaves, stooks, and stacks no longer grace the countryside; by the 1960's they were gone, replaced by mechanical farming.

Glovie and the children could walk for miles along winding lanes without seeing a vehicle, and the few people they did meet were nearly all farm labourers, whose faces they knew well. 'Top o' the marnin' to ye,' the men greeted them, dragging out the words in the consonant-swallowing sing-song that was then Norfolk speech. Patricia and Georgy tried hard to copy it, but though they mastered several phrases tolerably well, they never acquired facility. Georgy was best at it, and took special pride in one phrase which he maintained he had heard in use. Patricia was not sure. She tried to decode it.

'Do I do, do you don't do,' intoned Georgy, in exactly the right sing-song mode, and they translated it, 'If I do it, then you can't.'

Every farm, like an isolated sentry post in this lonely field-world, had its own guardian dog which, on their approach, rushed out at them, barking frenetically. The children learned not to be intimidated, but for Glovie, each encounter was torture. She never got used to them. As her unwilling feet dragged themselves nearer to the dreaded animal, she began to chatter her rune: 'Yes, yes, yes! I can see he's a nice dog. Don't worry!' Usually they were not worrying, but she was, and the tempo of her rune increased until the danger was passed. It was the same with geese, sometimes encountered near ponds. The birds advanced towards them in single file, hissing aggressively, but Patricia discovered that if, instead of retreating at their threat, she walked straight at them, they always veered off.

Every season had its flavour. In winter, the hard lanes crackled with ice and the hedges sparkled in the frost. Norfolk is a cold country in winter, but it is also a sunny one. Winter light there is very bright. On the short afternoon of Christmas Eve, they always made the plunge into a special field, where the hedge was full of pine-scented fir and berried holly, and came home with aromatic armfuls of greenery to decorate the house.

There were certain mid-field copses, long since swept away by modern agriculture and a large airfield, there were tangled dells and remote places where only wild animals and birds came. A favourite hideout was off a narrow lane close to the Bure. Scrambling over a bramble-entwined fence or squeezing through a seldom-opened gate, they descended a wooded slope through a dense wilderness of undergrowth lit suddenly by sun-splashed glades. Under tree roots, badgers had excavated their setts, and in spring, primroses filled the woods with gleams of pale ivory. Here they constructed a little home out of fallen branches. It had two rooms. No one knew it was there, and they returned to it again and again. They never saw another human soul, yet it often seemed that some benign watcher was present. After she had read *The Wind in the Willows*, Patricia knew that the presence in this wood and the Piper at the Gates of Dawn were one and the same. Glovie brought a trowel and basket and they uprooted a few primroses and replanted them along the slopes of the Seven Acres dell, where they multiplied, so that some of the enchantment of their hidden origins was conveyed to the garden at home.

Sometimes they wandered through the water meadows of the Bure which went on for miles. There were drained grassy ways, and fields where cattle browsed down to the water's edge, though Glovie would never enter a field if she saw cows in it. Coots and moorhens glided along the water, and in deep lanes close by, pheasants strutted and partridges paraded their chicks. Some birds ended up on the Sunday lunch table when the Captain and his retired doctor friend went on their shooting expeditions together. But the children liked the river most of all. Undoubtedly Ratty and Mole lived their secret lives under those willows. They have departed long ago, for since those days, the airfield has devoured great stretches of land nearby, the sky is torn with the shriek of low-flying monsters, and peace has forsaken that place.

Glovie and the children particularly enjoyed picnics. They usually went to one of the partly-demolished haystacks to be found just inside field gates Glovie set up her folding stool in the shade of the stack and brought out her knitting, or the doll's dress she was sewing for Patricia's favourite Jane Sprogg, or she would immerse herself in *Modern Woman*. Jane Sprogg herself, with her stiff wooden body, jointed peg legs and painted face and hair, was a special *Modern Woman* bargain which Glovie had bought for her, together with a set of Jane's clothes, cut out and ready to sew. Glovie did the sewing. Georgy amused himself burrowing in the hay. Or they both just listened to Glovie, recounting stories of her life during what she called "the olden days". The picnic tea they had brought with them, the plain jam sandwiches, the Swiss roll slice of cake, brown tea straight from the Thermos, all tasted deliciously different out of doors. Thermos tea was always to remind Patricia of their picnics. The afternoon sun travelled slowly through its arc, and the mellowing light subtly changed the mood of the countryside, moving patches of shadow towards their evening stations. Birdsong sounded out more clearly. In autumn they usually did some blackberrying after tea. Glovie had a long hooked stick, cut for her specially by the gardener, which enabled her to bring triumphantly within reach heavily fruit-laden briars from the tops of hedges, and high and thick those hedges were. Pruning them was a skilled, time-consuming task, carried out every two or three years in winter, and done by hand, beautifully, with a small scythe, with respect for the life and shape of the hedge, very different from the cruel mechanical trashing and ripping which too often replaced it in later years. Pies and jam were the harvest of those hedges, with sometimes the bonus of mushrooms, which Glovie and the children became experts at finding, hidden away in secret places in the grassy lower levels of the bank. The delicate characteristic smell, the soft white caul, covering close pink pleats, assured them that these were mushrooms and not poisonous toadstools.

They were good times. 'Tell us about when you were young' the children often said, and she did, sharing with them the events of her distant Victorian life. She had been born in 1867, and the nineteen twenties and thirties were too modern for her. So far as she was concerned, the coaches and carriages, the governess carts and dogcarts, and the people who went about their daily business on horseback, had scarcely left the highways and byways. There were in fact a few such people still to be seen in Norfolk, there were still horse-drawn cabs lined up outside Norwich station. Glovie herself told how she rode sidesaddle, a seat she recommended as being safer. She told of times when the Lincolnshire fens were frosted so hard that you could skate on them for miles. There had been prosperous times before her father, a rich farmer, lost his money in crop failures. That year they had skated over ruined potato fields. There had once been a carriage and pair in his stables, and she had danced the gavotte, the waltz and the polka at country parties. She demonstrated the steps of these old dances to Patricia, humming suitable tunes as she did so in her slightly quavering voice. She had shown talent as a pianist and been promised studies at Leipzig, but the financial disaster put an end to this plan. There had followed her engagement to a young chaplain who was destined for duty in a British embassy, but he had fallen ill suddenly and died. The wedding dress was ready, said Glovie, but she gave it away, knowing that she would not want to marry anyone else. Then she had been obliged to earn her own living, a difficult situation for a middle-class girl of those days, to whom few doors were open. Teaching was one way through, and she had taught in girls' boarding schools. At one of them she met Edie, Syria's eldest sister, who was a sixth form pupil there. They had stayed in touch, and it was through Edie that the introduction to Syria had come. Before that, Glovie had worked some years as a "companion"; in other words as a respectable dogsbody to an elderly woman, Mrs. Peters of Bromley. A real friendship had developed between them, and when she died, Mrs. Peters had left Glovie most of what small capital she possessed.

Glovie had a grand instinct for a riveting story, and her own history probably missed nothing in the telling. It seemed to have been strewn with disasters; big and small. One of the biggest concerned the collapse of the bridge over the River Tay in Scotland as a train full of people bound for England crossed over it. 'Hundreds of people drowned!' said Glovie impressively, and the children were awed by the terror of such a sudden end, and in the dark, too. There were several smaller tragedies. She told of a little child who had choked to death on a peach stone, of another who had died after being stung by a queen wasp. There was the distressing tale of the lady whom she had had to accompany to the "lunatic asylum" and whom she had had to deceive a little in order to get her to enter quietly. There were people who had been bitten by dogs, so that the threat of rabies and the mad horror of water hung over them, an illness which Glovie emphasised was incurable. Patricia began to realise how dangerous the world was. Death could also come through a cut between thumb and forefinger. The victim was destined to die a slow death from 'lockjaw' through inability to open the mouth wide enough to eat anything. There was the toddler who had drowned in his parents' ornamental garden pool, and sick babies who had died in their sorrowing mothers' arms. So much of her life seemed to have been permeated by these sad events, or at least, by reports of them, that it was as if she was a kind of one-woman Greek chorus, celebrating the chancy cruelties of fate. She sang mournful Victorian ditties to the children, and her own long poems scanned and rhymed with restful regularity as they gently pointed to some moral to be learned from life's troubles. In spite of all, Glovie was a placid and even cheerful person who was able to be content with very little.

Patricia could, and did, imagine life continuing without her mother, painful to her that such a possibility was. but she could not grasp the idea of it without Glovie. She hoped that if her mother died, her stepfather would send her and Georgy off to live with Glovie in her tiny two-up-two-down cottage of yellowish brick in Grantchester Road, Cambridge. Syria, needing to dispose of both children during a period of family quarantine, had sent them away for a blissful three weeks to stay with Glovie in this modest haven, whose purchase had been made possible by Mrs. Peters' legacy.

Here they settled down, in a state of perfect, harmonious disorder, day and night smoothly merging, most of their time spent listening to Glovie's wireless or reading from the mountain of women's magazines which she kept in her bedroom. Back home in Norfolk, their only experience of a wireless had been in the bungalow of the Irish ladies down the lane. It was magical, with its gasps and snatches of music at the twist of a knob. *No, No, Nanette* was the popular London musical of the moment, and the children spent many hours listening to its catchy songs. There were no regular walks, in fact, scarcely a walk of any kind; no fixed bedtime, not even any getting up time. They all simply did what they felt like doing, when they felt like it, day and night. Buttered toast was available whenever Patricia wanted it. There was no fatty meat to be surreptitiously disposed of, no hateful stewed figs or prunes. The house was gloriously untidy, and probably a little grimy too, but they did not mind about things like that. There was no dusting to do, and consequently no penalties for forgetting to do it. Everywhere, things lay about in piles and heaps; clothes, books, shoes, magazines, skeins of knitting wool, china and crockery. There were framed photographs of Georgy and Patricia too. as well as of the three other children in her life to whom Glovie was devoted. She was the godmother of the one and the adopted auntie of the other two. Her godchild was a "blue baby," with a defective heart valve, who lived to the age of eighteen, and died not long before Glovie herself. She was forced to live the careful life of an invalid. Little Jenny was pale, with a blueish tinge, and she could only get about out of doors in an invalid chair. Patricia and Georgy were regularly brought up to date on the progress of this child, as well as hearing about the doings of the other two. They were the daughters of a local lawyer who lived in the Barton Road nearby, in a roomy modern house with a big garden. Glovie had met them through her surviving relative, a brother who farmed in the village of Barton, a few miles down the road. Patricia and Georgy were taken to meet the girls and spend the afternoon playing and having rides on their pony, a sedate animal which Patricia somehow managed to fall off. The warm friendship of this family meant a great deal to Glovie, but her dearest love was Jenny with the weak heart, and when, years later, she died at the age of nineteen, Glovie lost heart too.

Her house was tiny, with a narrow staircase, and a small bathroom with a noisy, smelly gas water heater. In the miniature back garden there was a shed which was an Aladdin's cave of treasures for which there was no space left in the house. It sheltered a medley of china teasets, jugs and vases, which reminded Patricia of King's the ironmonger's. Glovie presided peacefully over this crammed menage. Life during those three weeks was triumphantly disorganised and satisfying. Patricia would have been more than happy, had she been orphaned, to have stayed there forever.

The children received no pocket money until Patricia was nine. Syria's reasoning was that Georgy was too young until he was seven, and if he was not having it, Patricia could not have it either. So neither child had any money to spend except what they received for Christmas and birthday presents, when aunts and uncles, and even the Captain, gave them small handouts. Syria impounded most of this and put it into Post Office Savings accounts for them. They were each left with about a quarter of the total received, to spend on approved purchases. Patricia wanted books, crayons, and a doll from the village toyshop.

The dolls cost too much for her resources, though one Christmas she received a fine one from Glovie, which she had been longingly gazing at in the shop window. Georgy wanted additions to his Hornby Railway and his Meccano set. A good deal more could be bought in those days with what, after decimalization, were to become insignificant sums of money.

Georgy was good at saving. His temperament was not averse to it. But Patricia found it frustrating. The books she wanted were often beyond her means. A book costing ten shillings usually came to more than half of her gift money, more than she was allowed to spend in any one season. So it would have to be saved up for a long time. If she began saving for the book at Christmas, there would be eight months to wait until her birthday in August. But Syria was adamant. About three-quarters of gift money had to go into the Post Office. Patricia envied the three Thring children who kept receiving legacies from ancient unmarried relatives. Theirs was not a very fertile family, and the three reaped the benefit. No one left anything to the Pearsons. Almost all of them for generations had married and produced plenty of children of their own, ready to inherit anything that was going. It did not help that Syria was unable to get on well with any of her in-law relatives.

One morning, when wandering with Glovie round Roy's the ironmonger's, Patricia's eye fell on a small tin of gramophone needles. Her hand fell on it too, and surreptitiously transferred it to her pocket. No one noticed. She did not need gramophone needles for they did not have a gramophone. She did not even know what they were when she took them, but she liked the idea of possessing something that no one else knew anything about. She hid them in a doll's cot, and subsequently purloined several more boxes. She was becoming quite a collector. She began to wish her gains were not quite so useless. From there it was a short step to finding a solution to her need for more sweets. Most particularly, she wanted chocolates, which she had been forbidden to eat by doctor's orders, since Syria had called him in for an embarrassing examination to investigate the cause of Patricia's wandering stomach pains. She had had to lie down completely naked on the drawing room sofa and submit to his proddings, an exquisitely tiresome episode. The good doctor reassured Syria that she was not suffering from appendicitis, but to be on the safe side, he prescribed an embargo on chocolate, and the substitution of hateful rocky lumps of a sweet brown glassy substance, with pieces of string running through it, misleadingly called barley sugar. She was also allowed to have something called fudge, but which tasted of aniseed. Patricia loathed it more than anything she had ever tasted before. Now there was an obvious use for her well-honed light-finguredness. For months, it obtained for her all the chocolates she could possibly desire from Roy's the bakery. Laying an innocent-looking little hand at rest on an open box of chocolate bars on the counter, she waited until the assistant was immersed in conversation with Glovie, and then slid a bar or two deftly out of its box and up her sleeve. Soon she found she was stealing more than she could eat, so she let Georgy into her secret. He was happy to have more chocolate too, so she trained him as her working partner and they shared the loot.

Fresh possibilities opened out at home. Patricia possessed a round-ended pair of scissors, given to her purposely because they could cut nothing worth cutting. With them came two boring reels of black and white cotton. Bryn, in her workbox downstairs, had some beautiful blue cotton and a lovely little shining pair of sharply pointed scissors, shaped like a stork. Patricia stole the lot and hid them at the back of her toyshelf. She reckoned that if she put her toys away tidily every night, no one would find them there. She became even more ambitious. She had always admired Glovie's silver wristwatch. It had a silver link bracelet and an appealing round face. It was easy to take that, and she hid it away carefully. Now and again she took it out secretly and looked at it, and wound it up. One day it stopped ticking, and not all her winding efforts would start it up again. This was a crisis. Everyone at home knew Glovie's silver wristwatch.

Patricia was on friendly terms with the two young women serving in the Post Office shop, so next morning she ran far ahead of Glovie on the routine walk, hurried into the Post Office, showed the girls the watch and asked them to make it go. They tried but were unsuccessful, and lingered over it, puzzling. To Patricia's shame, the crime was uncovered by Glovie herself when she entered the shop a few minutes later and found the assistants still poring over her watch. It swiftly became clear that Patricia was in unlawful possession. The girls stared at her, tut-tutting. From being her friends, they turned hostile. She did not know where to look. Above all, what would Glovie think of her?

Glovie took back her watch, remarking casually, 'Dear dear! I'd been wondering where that was!' She did not refer to the matter again. It was as though it had never happened.

But Syria discovered a cache of chocolate bars, and when she realised that Patricia had embarked on shoplifting, she took fright. She searched every inch of the toy shelves, the dolls' cots, and the dolls' pram. All the hiding places came to light, and in them a collection of gramophone needles, pencils, rubbers, and penknives, lifted from the village shops, together with Bryn's stork scissors and blue cotton reel. All the shop goods were returned and Syria gave

Patricia a solemn lecture, saying that if she had come from the farm labourer's family nearby, she would have been banished to a sort of prison for child thieves, called Borstal. A village boy had recently been caught stealing just like Patricia, and had been sent there. Patricia's greatest dread was to be sent away from home. She felt ashamed too. Everyone in the family must have heard what she had been up to, though none of them said anything. But it seemed to her that they looked at her with scorn in their eyes, all, that is, except Glovie, to whom she felt she had done the greatest injury of all. She could not understand it herself. For three weeks she was not taken to any of the village shops. Walks were confined to country lanes. Syria explained that she was too ashamed of Patricia to let her be seen by the villagers at all.

The cure was not yet complete. Patricia stopped stealing at home, but as soon as she was allowed back inside Roy's the bakery, she and Georgy, her undiscovered accomplice, continued to help themselves. However Patricia's impulse had been weakened. She ruminated uneasily on her misdeeds. An inconvenient inner voice would not leave her in peace to enjoy her booty. One morning in Roy's the bakery, that inner voice took command. She had just filched a bar of chocolate, and was watching Georgy steal another. The assistant had gone to the back of the shop, and Glovie was studying her list. There was no risk, but the voice of what she supposed must be conscience had become insistent.

'Put it back!' she hissed at Georgy. Surprised, but obedient, he did so. Patricia retained her bar, and they shared it together on the way home. It was the last bar, and from that day, she never stole again.

CHAPTER 30

Patricia longed to go for a walk by herself. She felt irked at never being allowed to go anywhere on her own outside the garden boundaries. The five older children, of whom Jane was only four years her senior, had been liberated. They had bicycles and combed the countryside. They cycled to the sea twelve miles away. They rowed on the River Bure in a dark green canoe made of elephant hide brought back from Africa. They fished, too, and were constantly pleading to be allowed to eat their catch. At last Syria decided to put an end to this idea, so disruptive to kitchen routine. She agreed to have Grey's catch cooked specially for him. At lunchtime it was placed before him, a tiny perch, all alone in the centre of a large plate. Grey's appetite was a byword. Meredith called him a human incinerator. That day the famous appetite went unsatisfied. He got his fish, and that was precisely all he did get. The others laughed and he took it good-humoredly, but Patricia did not see the joke. It seemed like a punishment for something, but for what?

He did at least get freedom to roam at will, but no matter how much older Patricia got, she never seemed to qualify for hers. She treasured one happy escapade when Syria was away. It was a sunny autumn morning when Peter fixed a cushion to the crossbar of his big bike, arranged Patricia astride it, and swept her away on an unforgettable jaunt along miles of country lanes. Apart from Bryn he was the only older one who ever put himself out for her, and never teased her. Sometimes he came into the drawing room when she was practising the piano, and sitting quietly beside her for a few minutes, offered encouraging comments.

Patricia went on imploring her mother to let her go for a walk by herself. Syria prevaricated. She asked strange questions, such as, 'If you were playing just inside the drive gates and a gipsy came up and asked you to go with him, what would you do?' Patricia knew that the required answer was, 'Say no,' and so she gave it, although she was pretty sure she would say, 'Yes.' It was just another of those irritating ways in which her mother treated girls differently from boys. But Syria had suffered one great unforeseeable catastrophe in life, and she clung tenaciously to these two child possessions of hers.

At length she agreed to let Patricia take a walk on her own. and she prepared for it. She sent a message to Irish Mary and Margaret in their house at the end of the lane, which was in sight of the upper windows of Seven Acres. She told them that at a certain hour precisely, Patricia would leave her home and walk down the lane unaccompanied. She requested them to turn her straight round and send her back to her mother. Patricia felt cheated by these terms. It was not a real walk at all, and not in the least like what Jane was doing. But she hoped that if she passed this trial satisfactorily, she would be given her freedom. But it turned out to be the only solo walk she would be allowed to make until she was fifteen.

She found secret ways of evading house arrest. Escape from the ever watchful eye had to be snatched by stealth. It had a special flavour. Midnight prowls became more ambitious. The children stole right out into the garden as early as four o'clock in the summer, and shared the dawn with its creatures. The sky, with its growing light, was the pathway of many foraging birds. Early bees from the orchard hives buzzed by.

In the fields, cows lowed, a horse neighed. A cockerel crowed in the farm down the lane. The footfalls of bad-tempered Silver sounded in the front paddock. She had been up for sometime cropping grass, or noisily crunching the small turnips laid out for her. It was too early yet for the farm labourers. The children liked to get out before the stars had quite faded. In those early morning hours, there was no man-made sound, no wheels, no engines. This was the everyday stillness, centuries old, so ordinary then, soon to be so rare, the country as people had known it from earliest times. Patricia and Georgy were participators, without having the least idea of it, in the last days of natural peace.

So Patricia worked her way through with Georgy to some degree of freedom. What further might not be attempted? They roamed together the length and breadth of their little kingdom, garden and orchard, dell and field. In Patricia's imagination it became the land of King Arthur, his knights and ladies. Those long-ago woodlands, those green swards, might even now be conjured back into life, and the Red

Cross Knight and Una be glimpsed riding down the dell, under its white may trees, or across the lawn, striped, as the sun rose, with dappled poplar shadows. The world of imagination became so strong that it seemed at any moment to merge with the world of reality. Inner and outer worlds did fuse, to some extent, and dawn pathways took on a dreamlike quality.

Though Syria went on her progresses to friends fairly often, and for several weeks at a time, she was still at home most of the year. Then Patricia, having tasted a rare quality of freedom, had to make the best of getting up early and sitting on her bedroom windowsill. House prowls when her mother was at home were too risky a challenge, for Georgy would have been a great hazard. She experimented with getting out of one of her windows which opened onto a sloping roof. It was good to be out of doors, but the shape of the roof prevented movement in any interesting direction, and there was a distinct risk of falling ten feet into the flowerbed below, without any way of re-entering the house. So it had to be the window seat, which offered its own satisfactions and was safe from discovery.

The Dawn Watch began with the first pale intimations of light round the edges of the black curtains. It was still heavy darkness in her room. Patricia got out of bed, and dashing across to the window, tucked herself onto the broad seat on the far side of the black folds. Here was a safe world, for the black curtain, cutting off the dangerous darkness of her bedroom, was her friend instead of her enemy. It was hours before a soul in the sleeping house would move. Outside, before her eyes, the world was opening itself to light.

It seemed to her that the waking birds accepted her presence among them. Sometimes their wings, as they darted by, brushed, with a soft ringing sound, the iron bars that Syria had fixed across the window. The eastern sky beyond the twelve acre field over the hedge was dark, broken by ivory streaks. Gradually, colour infused them, and Patricia, watching, realised that in a matter of moments, night had withdrawn, though she could never pinpoint exactly when it happened. The shadow masses in the sky gathered themselves together and became oceans of crimson and gold. The birds were now really on the move and filling the air with their calls; there were more wings beating, more close swoops and curves. There was a growing volume of small sounds, the voice of the hedgerows. There were sudden disturbances; the cacophony of a cock pheasant out in the paddock, the cry of a peewit in the field opposite, the clear call of a cuckoo. Last, in a massed crowd, came the sky armies of rooks, making their way from tall, elm-cradled nests in the wood near the village. Patricia loved the drama of the rooks' arrival. Their feeding ground was the twelve-acre field. They came in all seasons and weathers, predictable as dawn itself as they swooped earthwards in one great untidy settling movement. They came at the time the sun was edging over the horizon in a blaze of gold. Its imminence had been heralded by a curious liquefaction of the skyline. As Patricia watched, the sun climbed above distant woods and fields, and filled the world with clear-cut light and shadow. She treasured and never tired of the Dawn Watch.

Then things quite quickly resumed their ordinary appearance, and after lingering a little so as not to miss anything of the departing wonder, unwilling to accept that it was over for the next twenty-four hours, she re-entered the darkened hole of her bedroom and found her Bible, the only book allowed there. Then she settled herself back on the window seat and immersed herself in the history of the Israelites, and the savage events that accompanied their conquest of Canaan, that land of milk and honey. She worked her way from Egypt, through the wilderness of Sinai, the establishment of stern, demanding laws, and the building of that lavish structure, the Ark of the Covenant. She read of wholesale slaughters condoned, indeed, commanded by God, not sparing man, woman or child. She aimed to read every word of the Bible, beginning with the Book of Genesis, but she was in no hurry to finish it, for she had a presentiment that on the day she reached the last word, she would die. On fine mornings she stayed on the window sill until she saw the gardener arrive, heard the dead ashes in the kitchen range being raked out by Mabel, and the regular beat of the pump handle in the scullery below, where Rob would be ensuring the day's water supply. When she heard Mabel's footsteps on the backstairs, as she carried up Syria's early morning tea, she replaced the Bible on its shelf and went to bed.

For sometime after their arrival at Seven Acres, Syria made a half-hearted attempt to get Patricia on horseback. On the Farm in Rhodesia her older brothers had done all they could to avoid riding. They had been threatened and even beaten into it. Peter had received ten strokes from a rhino-hide whip for evading this duty, and been promised twice that number if he were caught cheating again. But in Patricia Syria met with willing co-operation, for there was little she liked more than the idea of having, at her own command, a pony, or palfrey, as she preferred to think of it. There was not much command about it. In the first stages, the gardener took hold of the reins and led her at a tedious amble round the far reaches of the blackcurrant plantation. Soon he left her to get on with it by herself. The palfrey, Silver, had come with the house, together with a sturdy pony cart, and she proved an unsatisfactory steed. She was quite handsome, with a white coat, a very thick mane, and a tail that touched the ground. But her temperament was deplorable. The village boys amused themselves by throwing stones at her from the lane above her paddock, and gradually she became unmanageable. Patricia was frustrated by Silver. She did not wish to be ridden, her preferred pace was a casual walk punctuated by stops to pull at clumps of grass. Nor did Patricia consider herself properly equipped. She did not have jodhpurs, which was what other girls wore for riding, but instead, Syria dug out an unbecoming pair of black, knee-length trousers in stiff, unyielding serge. She knew she did not look right, not that there was anyone to see her, for she was not allowed to go anywhere except round and round the blackcurrant field, and certainly not beyond the drive gates, which was where she longed to be. The only time she had an audience was in the blackcurrant-picking season when the bushes were heavy with clusters of ripe fruit, filling the air with their sharp, sweet aroma. From nine in the morning a procession of women from the village came up the drive, past the house and orchards and hen runs, to pick the fruit. The Captain handed out lightweight chip baskets and the women were paid a small sum for each basketful. Patricia rode her mount round the field as they picked. No one spoke to her, nor did she speak to them. She would have liked them to talk to her, but she felt they might not be friendly if she tried to open up a conversation. She wondered what they were thinking of her.

She was extremely envious of three ginger-haired sisters around her own age, who lived on the far side of the village. She sometimes met them at children's tea parties; they were the daughters of a successful local businessman. The girls' parents encouraged their riding, providing each of them with a delectable pony, and allowing them to compete in gymkhanas, where they won rosettes, while Patricia watched, narrow-eyed with jealousy and hopelessly fantasizing about how she might persuade her mother to replace that bad-tempered Silver and support her own ambitions. She knew it could never happen. Syria's principle number one barred the way; it does a child good to learn to go without, thereby achieving the twin goals of strength of character and economy. In any case, elegant ponies and gymkhanas were beyond the sights of a child living in what was a mere veneer of affluence. She had already picked up that if you were not a riding child, you did not count for much. She did not belong with the blackcurrant pickers and their children, but nor did she belong with the ginger-haired girls.

She longed at least to acquire their expertise. She wanted to harness, or rather, caparison her palfrey herself. As things were, it was left to the surly gardener to do. He disliked Patricia for a spoiled child, and was always telling her so. She realised by now that Silver was vicious. She had been trying to rub Patricia off against a tree trunk when they were going down Shady Lane and she would move persistently sideways as Patricia tried to mount. Having at first refused to go beyond a walking pace, she would suddenly bolt through the plantation and round it again at full gallop, completely out of control. Patricia clutched the pommel with both hands, leaving it to Silver to decide when to slacken speed. The ginger-haired girls would not have clutched their pommels. Their palfreys would not have shot out of control. Somehow Patricia stayed on board, and strangely, no one noticed these goings-on. She took good care not to mention them, for that would mean the end of any sort of riding for her.

She could still not relinquish her longing to wander at will through the world on horseback. Syria had always vetoed an expedition down the lane as far too risky. Patricia realised that if she was to realise this goal she would have to find some way of being in control of Silver. She made one last effort at mastery. She waited until a fine May morning when her mother was away from home. Her intention was to mount Silver bareback and take her out of the paddock and down the lane. Syria was due to return that afternoon, so it would be the last chance for sometime. Under the spell of her Arthurian dream, she proceeded with her plan. Ignoring Silver's nasty expression and laid-back ears, she approached her in midfield, seized her mane, and propelled her towards the gate. Georgy skilfully induced her with stolen sugar lumps to stay there, while Patricia scrambled onto her back from the top of the gate. She was persuaded to move off at a faint-hearted dawdle, and Patricia, bridleless, gripped her mane. No one would see them, it was about five in the morning, and in the house, the Captain, Glovie and the maids were still asleep. Silver meandered along the edge of the paddock in the general direction of the drive exit. Suddenly, Georgy, correctly guessing that Patricia wanted her to put on speed, darted out, gesticulating, from behind a bush. She swerved sharply, throwing Patricia straight over her head, and then stopped dead, to survey her fallen rider. Patricia lay there long enough to feel grateful to Silver for not having trampled on her. A fierce agony shot through her left arm. She could scarcely move it and was convinced she had broken it. Apart from that, she was all right, and cured, finally, of palfrey-riding. It was difficult, that evening, when her mother returned, to conceal her disability. Syria's sharp eyes, ever on the alert for something out of order, missed little. But they missed this. Perhaps it was a greenstick fracture, perhaps just a bad strain, but it had to look after itself until it cleared up.

CHAPTER 31

Occasionally, on a fine summer afternoon, the obligatory post-lunch rest was cancelled and everyone went down the River Bure together in the family boat. It was moored in a culvert off the main river and was a strong, versatile wooden craft built by the Captain himself, plank by plank, on a frame he set up just outside his carpentry workshop. There were seats along the sides and seats across it, with enough room for Syria to sit in comfort, facing the stern, legs outstretched. There were duckboards to keep feet dry and steady. There was a mast and a big canvas sail, and the boat also had rowlocks and shipped sturdy oars. There was a large peg on the edge of the stern for a Yulo pole. The Captain preferred movement by sail and on breezy days he manipulated his craft skilfully between the river banks, gliding along with a gentle rippling sound. If there was no wind, he could set the boat in motion by another favoured method, 'yulo-ing.' He was the only person who could do it competently. He did not like sharing the handling of his boat with anyone else. To yulo, he stood in the stern, grasping the long pole set loosely over its peg, and with a steady side-to-side movement, he brought the vessel forward. Down the Bure he took them, ten in all, when with full complement. They seldom met another boat. After about an hour they moored and had a picnic tea on board. There were jam sandwiches and rock buns and sensible current cake, made by Maud. The Captain did not like icing. Patricia always longed for them to go further down the river, but they were forced to turn back at the same spot every time, blocked by a great old wooden corn mill which stretched from bank to bank, its wheel driven by the current. So they returned home in the late afternoon, happy with river sounds and smells and sights, arguments and altercations mellowed. Even the Captain, though still an infinitely distant being, seemed a bit more likeable, for the boat and the voyages were all due to him.

The process of boat-building had been a slow and fascinating one, and it was repeated once more for the neighbour with whom he went shooting game. The Captain was always working away at something in wood. The floor of his workshop was covered with aromatic golden shavings, sculpted and curled, so that Patricia wanted to pick them up and keep them, but she could never find a use for them. They lay there, simply to be admired. The Captain made breadboards and bookcases, penholders and bedside tables, of his own unique design, and he fashioned small domestic objects from left-over chunks of wood, with some familiar feature carved upon it, such as the tom cat. He used his skill for some ingenious repairs. Syria had a china coffee pot shaped like a green woodpecker, the crown of the head forming the lid. The lid got broken, and the Captain fashioned a new one, of great wit and charm, in the shape of a tricorne hat.

He was a man in whom all kinds of talent lay dormant, none of them brought to full fruition. He was sent to sea in the eighteen eighties as a very young midshipman. Judging from a photograph taken at that time, he was a mouse-size slip of a boy with a slightly receding chin and an introverted expression. He told of how he disliked his midshipman years. Yet he did well in the Royal Navy, becoming an expert in Naval gunnery, and this expertise took him all over the world. Syria hinted that he would have risen higher in the Service if he had not had such a prickly personality. He was a man of simple integrity, but in his sardonic, intellectual way, he intimidated people. He barely drank and never swore. This trait at least must have satisfied Syria's highest standards. During a train journey to Norwich, Patricia heard a man utter a word she did not know, and told her mother.

'What did he say?' asked Syria.

'Bugger!' said Patricia. Syria leapt as if she had been stung. Sternly she said, 'Let me never, ever hear you say that word again!' The Captain was of a compact and athletic build. His children called him a pocket Hercules, which appealed to his dry sense of humour. He was an artist of talent and sketched his way round the world, in his depiction of people and animals showing a sensitivity not apparent in his indifference to Patricia and Georgy. He reached the rank of Captain and served on several renowned battleships, before retiring, officially for health reasons, just before World War One. For the rest of his days, and he lived till 1949, he remained a not too well-off gentleman of leisure which he did not know how to use. He was perpetually worried about money though he must have had his share of the bequests which constantly trickled down from aged relatives to his children, and of which Patricia and Georgy were enviously aware. Everyone knew when he was filling in his Inland Revenue forms, and he never bought any new clothes or travelled further afield than Norwich or Cromer. He managed to spend virtually not a penny on his stepchildren save that entailed in providing them with board and lodging, and Syria made it clear to each of them that as soon as they were earning any money themselves, he would expect them to pay their way whenever they came home. Both parents seemed harassed out of their minds by money, and Syria strove to imbue her children with her own passion for economising in all directions. Georgy was willing to co-operate, but not so Patricia, who desired things with greater urgency than he did.

The Captain, having settled at Seven Acres, buried himself there among his hens, his blackcurrants, his carpentry, shooting in the season, and the odd bit of watercolour painting. He also wrote a few children's stories, which revealed a hidden side of him. They were exciting and adventurous, just the kind of stories Patricia liked, and he read them to her and Georgy one winter by the fireside after tea, when Syria was away on her travels. The stories were never heard of again. He spent some months writing a nautical novel about war at sea, which was tried out unsuccessfully on several publishers. When in communicative mood, he could be relied upon for a few entertaining yarns about his time in the Navy. Patricia's favourite was the one about being on a cricket field in Japan during an earthquake. The ground, he said, rolled in waves like the sea.

Early in his career he had grown a neat pointed beard, and despite his small stature he managed, when in uniform on formal occasions such as Armistice Day, to look quite distinguished, with a resemblance to George V, the monarch of the day. The beard made an excellent camouflage for the receding chin. He seldom smiled, but Patricia felt surprisingly gratified if she managed to coax a tardy rictus out of him. Every night the children gave him a goodnight peck, as instructed by Syria, and received a token gesture in return. There was no warmth on either side, but it was a ritual in a family where rituals were a landmark of existence. In those years, Patricia assumed that she hated him. Syria's attitude of longstanding forbearance towards him weighed with her. But as she grew older, she realised that she felt sorry for him. He seemed so solitary in his tenuous and irritable contacts with people. His own children respected him, as he did them, though he went through a turbulent period with Jane. The ground they met on was intellectual. He would have made an excellent University professor, but it fell to his son, who in so many ways, resembled him, to take up that role.

Bryn confided in Patricia that he seemed to have enjoyed an idyllic first marriage to her mother, a pretty, fair-haired woman, who in her portrait, resembled Bryn. She had been an early Cambridge blue stocking, and in course of time, would be followed there by all three of her children. Her early death from tuberculosis was a disaster for the Captain. Bryn herself never married, but her father once shed his reserve enough to try to encourage her, telling her that a good marriage was the surest path to a contented life.

CHAPTER 32

The parents seldom invited anyone to lunch, and no one at all to dinner. They did rise to tea parties and the best ones were held in the garden in summer. The Captain kept the grass tennis court in good condition, marking it out regularly with whitewash and mowing it with his remarkable grasscutter, on which he perched, steering it noisily up and down. It often looked as if it was going to run away with him. He then went round the court with a long stabbing instrument, and impaled every incipient dandelion and daisy plant that he could see. He completed the effect of a well-valeted lawn by pushing a heavy iron garden roller up and down every inch of it.

Visitors to tea were the few young people considered to be of a suitable class living in the area, and their parents. The afternoon was spent playing doubles, while the others rested on garden seats or in the buddleia-bowered summerhouse with its retinue of red admirals and peacock butterflies. Sometimes a game of mini-cricket was played out by the younger children in the wide grassy space alongside the court. At four o'clock Mabel and Maud brought tea down into the dell, and everyone settled in deckchairs around the three-tier trolley and cake stand, under the light mottled shade of the poplar avenue.

Tea parties in winter could be tricky. There was the time when Syria had invited the two children of that rare species, a divorcee, to tea with Patricia and Georgy upstairs in the nursery. Mrs Bowes-Harding could not stay to tea, but it was arranged that she should bring the pair, Archie and Annabel, at four o'clock and return to collect them at six. Not being an expert timekeeper she arrived early and deposited her children with Syria at a quarter past three. Glovie reported their arrival at the house to Patricia and Georgy, but the children did not appear. Not until the grandfather clock in the hall had struck four were they admitted to their friends in the nursery. Syria had shut them into an unheated empty bedroom until the time at which they had been officially invited. Mrs Bowes-Harding, who had left them at the front door and departed immediately, would not get to know of this until she fetched them later on. Her reactions were not reported, but there were no more tea parties with Archie and Annabel.

Patricia regretted this, for they were the liveliest children she knew. Archie was a particularly jolly and rumbustious boy. He made up for his confinement in a chilly bedroom by running completely wild in the nursery. He jumped up and down on the furniture, and finally pulled down the heavy curtains that hung on their wooden rail the length of the big window.

The whole lot descended on the floor in a confused mass, to Patricia's appalled delight.

Syria could not tolerate early arrival by guests. Her youngest brother, recently returned to England from Central Africa with his newly married wife, arrived half an hour before the appointed time for lunch, probably anticipating a warm welcome from his long-parted sister. Years later, his widow told Patricia that they were given the freezing treatment for being early. He was, so Syria always maintained, her favourite brother, and when he died a couple of years later after eating a bad sausage, she went around pink-eyed for days. But rules were rules, and no exceptions could be made.

As she grew older, Patricia became ever more curious about those children who were never invited to tea, but who shared the countryside with her. She and Georgy had always been uncomfortably aware of the little posse of boys who manned the village entrance, and of rows of grinning faces who stared at them when they arrived late to church. But so far the only spoken communication between them had been that brief challenge outside the cobbler's shop, launched by the red-haired boy. She wondered what it would be like to know them better. There was the son of a nearby farm worker who looked about her age, but a little taller. What was he like? How would they get on if they could only speak to each other? There seemed no way of knowing. Family mores did not allow of conversation between them, though the reason for this embargo was not clear. Patricia could see that the boy down the lane had many more friends than she had, for she didn't really have any. Archie and Annabel had disgraced themselves, and none of the other teaparty children, who were as shy as she was, counted for anything at all. She had a hazy idea about class. It both threatened and intrigued her. She felt willing to try and bridge the gap somewhere, but she was under such constant surveillance that any overture, even if she had been brave enough, seemed impossible.

It happened that one unique incident brought about a fleeting contact with the labourer's interesting son. There was a black iron bridge about fifty yards from the drive gate, where the lane crossed the branch line between Norwich and the coast. Occasionally a face would appear on this dark surface, a primitive face, grotesquely sketched on it with white chalk, with some mis-spelled caption, such as "A stoopid boy," "an ugly gurl". Though the artist had never gone so far as to name these portraits, Patricia and Georgy were convinced they represented themselves, and had been drawn there by some ill-disposed village boy. Soon after they appeared, such pictures were removed, rubbed out by a person unknown, though they guessed the gardener had been sent to do it.

One morning the bridge offered an exceptionally provocative spectacle. From end to end, on both sides, it was covered by a picture gallery of idiot faces, and this time they were named. 'Silly Georgy,' "Ugly Patricia," "Fat Georgy," "Stupid Patricia," proclaimed these disagreeable captions. Georgy was by no means fat, and Patricia did not think she was especially stupid, but she had long suspected she was ugly. The bridge made her feel bad. Georgy, as yet barely able to read, could hardly take it in. Family speculation as to who had done it was the main topic of lunchtime conversation that day.

In the afternoon Glovie took the children on an unfamiliar route to the village. Through field gates, along back garden ways they went, bypassing the usual point of entry and its lurking posse of boys, by now chief suspects of the crime. She led them to a house they had never called at before. It was the village police station. Here she delivered a letter by hand, remarking to the policeman who took it from her that she had been charged to do this, although she, personally, felt it was unnecessary. After a friendly chat they returned home.

On their morning walk with Glovie a couple of days later, Patricia noticed that as they made their way up the last lane before home, the farm labourer's son was walking alongside them on the far side of the hedge. They were approaching a field gate, and Patricia hung behind. The boy slowed down too. At the gate he beckoned to her, and she walked right up to him. He had quite a nice open face, she thought, and she did not recognise him as one of the worst persecutors. She had instant ideas about making him her secret friend.

'Those faces on the bridge,' he began diffidently, 'you think we did them, don't you?'

'Well, yes,' she admitted, but not crossly.

'We didn't do it,' he said earnestly, in the broad Norfolk accent that Patricia and Georgy had been at such pains to acquire. 'It was your big brothers that did it. I saw them at it. We've been blamed.'

'My brothers?' exclaimed Patricia, astonished. 'Are you sure?' 'Yes,' he said. 'I saw them doing it. That be the truth.' Patricia could not help believing him. She hesitated. She wanted to hear more, and above all she wanted to go on talking with him, but Glovie was some way ahead and was calling to her and she felt she had to catch up. They were very near home. As she turned into the drive Patricia looked round. The boy was no longer to be seen on his side of the hedge. He had disappeared, and he never emerged again from his other world.

She told Glovie what she had heard, and suddenly the matter of insulting pictures on the bridge, which had enlivened the last two family meals, died. Patricia could scarcely believe what proved to be true. Grey and Peter had confessed. They had carried off the deception for two whole days and made Syria look foolish in the process. The story must have delighted the village. Glovie confided that she had always felt that the letter to the law was a mistake, and advised Patricia not to refer to the matter again. They never heard what happened to Grey and Peter, but Patricia was sure the penalty for such perfidy must have been severe.

CHAPTER 33

On Sunday mornings the bells of St. John's church rang out in prolonged peals for the eleven o'clock service of Mattins. Their clear sound summoned the congregation from far and wide, Coltishall was a scattered parish. It had some competition, for among those fields, woods and marshes, there were many grey flint churches with squat, square towers, all singing out at the same time. No one could escape the sound of bells. They were as much a part of nature on Sunday mornings as the birds. Patricia welcomed them on Tuesday evenings too, when the bellringers of St. John's had their practice, and their voice, reaching her ears from a mile or so away, comforted her, immured in the stuffy depths of her blacked-out bedroom. On some days, usually in winter, they reached her as a slowly-paced single bell, and this toll, at stately intervals, told of someone being tucked into their earthy bed in the churchyard. But the Sunday peals, from thatched-roofed Coltishall, from Horstead across the near fenlands, from Lammas, from Belaugh down river, competed in cheerful cacophony. At five minutes to eleven St. John's changed down from the octave to the Five-Minute Bell, warning laggards to hurry up.

Grey had taught Patricia an irreverent jingle:
'On Sunday he goes to church
To hear the Parson shout;
He puts a penny in the bag
And takes a sovereign out.'

The penny for the collection was given to Patricia at the last moment by Syria, in a small red leather drawstring bag which had belonged to her grandmother.

People put on their best clothes for church, and Patricia was becoming clothes-conscious, which proved tiresome, both to her and her mother. Her worst trial was Sunday morning hats. Most were adult cast-offs from the early 1920's. Her keenest distaste was reserved for a couple of summer straws with tiny brims, worn well pulled down over the forehead. One of them was tight as well. With these monstrosities clamped down over her hair, eyes barely able to peer out from under the narrow, low-slung brim, she felt herself to be a laughable spectacle. She did not aspire to beauty, but she resented being forced to look a frump. How was it that her elegantly dressed mother could not see what a fool she was making of her daughter? She concluded that Syria thought it was good for her, in the same way that it was good for you to go on doing things and wearing clothes and eating food you didn't like, and it was very good indeed for you to practise going without things you did like. The hats made her look worse than she already did. She despaired of her face, particularly her nose, which her mother said looked like a piece of putty flung on from a distance. She hated it when people gazed at her with a faraway expression, and said, 'She's just like her father.' It would have been different if they had said she was like her mother, but they never did. All she could do was to remind herself that an age ago, there had been a fatherly man on a train who had told her she was pretty.

One Sunday morning she took the red straw out of the tissue paper where it was carefully preserved, and decided she would not wear it. In the backyard the Captain was cranking up his gaunt old Austin, which resembled an outsize pram because it had a hood which could be folded back to give an open car. It was capacious, and could swallow five or six people in the back, two of them on folding seats. The Austin's problem was that its starting powers were erratic, and the Captain was still having trouble with a resistant starting handle.

Patricia remained hatless, and her mother arrived upstairs to chivvy her on.

'It is the turn of the red straw this week,' she said testily. 'Hurry up and put it on. You're keeping everyone waiting.' Patricia begged to be allowed to wear a pink linen hat that she disliked less.

'Not this week,' said Syria. 'It is the turn of the red straw. You are to put it on at once, and stop being silly.'

Patricia burst into tears. 'I won't put it on!' she shouted.

'You will do as I say!'

'I shan't!'

'Glovie,' snapped Syria, in her most ordering-about voice. 'See to it that Patricia puts on that hat, and then comes down at once. I will take Georgy. The car is waiting. I do not intend to be late for church.' In fact, the Captain had not yet succeeded in turning the engine over.

But all the children had already arranged themselves inside, and Patricia knew their ears were cocked. She felt ashamed of these rages which made such havoc of her face. She stamped her feet and roared.

Glovie made her quiet voice heard somehow through Patricia's sobs and hiccoughs. 'I know how you feel, darling,' she said. 'But it's best to put it on.' She always did know how Patricia felt on these occasions. That she understood made all the difference. She would wear the hat to save Glovie from getting into trouble too. She jammed it on, and went angrily down to join the church party.

It was one of those days when the Austin refused to move at all. Georgy, Patricia and Glovie would have to walk, setting out far too late to arrive at the beginning of the service. The others had cycles to fall back on. Hot and embarrassed, the little party finally made it to the church door. At such moments, Patricia needed to disappear altogether. The large congregation was seated with a view to class distinctions. Those unregarded persons who could not stomach this attended some place called Chapel. The most prestigious families occupied the front pews right across three aisles. The top rankers from the Hall occupied the centre front, the retired Admiral and his wife the front aisle on the left. They all had their own distinctive hassocks, and seat runners to take the hardness off the wooden pews. At one end of the pew a printed visiting card was inserted in a brass holder, recording the name and address of the family in possession, and effectively warning off newcomers. The Pearson-Thrings qualified for two front seats in the sunny south aisle. Syria had furnished them with visiting cards, scarlet seat runners, and hassocks. This degree of seating priority had been awarded on account of the Captain's Senior Service status.

The humiliation of being late to church was not compensated for by this mild degree of social elevation, for on entering, Glovie and the two children had to walk past a three-row phalanx of village school children at the very back of the church, a position so lowly that there was a gap between it and the main body of pews. Now they had the advantage over those uppity children from Seven Acres. Patricia hurried past them, head down, aware of broad, jeering grins, sniggers and suppressed giggles, and knew that she and her hat were under judgment from a merciless audience.

The Service of Mattins followed strictly the order it had followed in that church since 1662. It began with the lengthy peroration 'Dearly Beloved Brethren....' and was followed by a Confession of such utter personal unworthiness that Patricia never ceased to be amazed to hear her proud mother reciting it by her side in unrecognisably subdued tones, she who would never allow that she was wrong about anything. Yet now here she was, confessing to sins; here she was, humbly admitting that she had done things she shouldn't have done, and not done things she should have done, and that she was a miserable offender with no health in her. Clearly, what she said to God and what she said to Patricia were entirely different things.

There were other interesting matters to attend to. Patricia was quite carried away by organ music, the more earth-shaking the better. There was the choir to look at, a big white-robed assembly of men and boys. She knew each of their faces, and noticed if anyone was missing. There were little boys no bigger than Georgy, and others of her own size. Some of them she would have liked to meet. It perplexed her that there were no girls in the choir. When she asked why, her mother said that though girls' voices could be quite nice, boys' voices were better. Patricia was offended by this. She herself could sing as robustly as anyone, and she loved doing so. She knew all the hymn tunes and chants by heart. She and Georgy had their favourites. She got annoyed and sulked if a familiar hymn tune was changed, and refused to sing it. She preferred the majestic ones, such as the hymn for sailors 'Eternal Father, Strong to Save,' and 'Jerusalem the Golden,' blest as it was with milk and honey. She was particularly drawn to 'Ten Thousand Times Ten Thousand,' because it promised a time when children would no longer be fatherless, nor widows desolate. Though her mother was no longer strictly a widow, she was still missing Arthur, so in a way she was one. Patricia herself felt distinctly fatherless; the Captain and she were mutually distant from each other. There was just one advantage to be gained from the connection with him, and that was that his uncle had contributed several hymns to Hymns Ancient and Modern. They were laden with gloom, concentrating on the perils of the Deep, the shortness of the day and the transience of earthly joys. She could understand that. She was young now, but how much longer would it last? Already the golden light was shadowed by the Approaching Last Judgment. So she shared with her great step-uncle a sense of the brevity of life's joys. It was true. Nothing she enjoyed lasted long enough. It was always snatched away. One Sunday she was invited to choose a hymn for Mattins, and she picked her current favourite, 'Jesu, Lover of my soul.' It told of tempests and gathering stormwaters, and the music was solemn, to match. It was a thrill to hear the elderly vicar announce her hymn in church, but three weeks later, he was dead.

Patricia enjoyed Mattins. She accepted the archaic English of the Book of Common Prayer and the Authorised Version of the Bible as a matter of course. They were old-fashioned, she knew, but she was familiar with the language through hours spent reading the Bible on her early morning window seat. But there was much that did not make sense. Why, if Heaven was so desirable, was everyone, including herself, unwilling to die? To her, death meant just one thing, being incarcerated, in lonely silence, inside a narrow box six feet below the green grass and sunlight, and in the unpleasant company of worms. That was the only certainty. Heaven was an unreal dream. But when it came to Hell, she changed into a trembling believer. She knew she qualified for eternal damnation, for she had committed the Unforgiveable Sin against the Holy Ghost, and she had done it on purpose. One day, while practising the piano, and unable to get the notes right, she had banged the piano keys and shouted, 'Damn the Holy Ghost!' Somehow it was Its fault. At once, she had wanted to unsay it, but that could not be done. This episode was to cause her much anguish in the future, when the time came for her Confirmation. She then realised the full horror of being Unforgiveable, cut off from everyone. It had haunted her for two whole terms. At last, in her despair, she was driven to confess her Sin to the school chaplain, whose was fortunately a man of common sense as well as a Religious Authority, and her fears were relieved.

For the present, serious trouble from the divine quarter was kept at bay by the practice of a few rituals, such as doing everything possible with the right hand and outlawing the left. It could be a nuisance at times. To her relief no one noticed these odd ways.

There was one shaming church occasion when she laughed out loud as the vicar arrived in the pulpit and was intoning, 'In the name of the Father and of the Son and of the Holy Ghost.' She had just seen the well-behaved Georgy poke Grey, who was in the pew in front of him, in the rear as he was about to sit down. Grey leapt and turned round with an enraged glare. Patricia's laugh was not discreet, but a loud, clear belly laugh, and everyone turned their heads to see who had committed this sacrilege. Amazingly, Syria never realised who it was.

After church people met in colourful groups in the churchyard, politely greeting one another in a gentle social pavane. There was the large and stately mistress of Coltishall Hall, overweight but so handsome that Georgy managed to make Syria quite jealous for insisting how pretty she was.

Patricia did not find her pretty, and was more apt to remember the day they had called on her at the Hall and been shown round the big heated greenhouses with their spreading vines, from which bunches of ripe purple grapes hung down. The Lady of the Manor, having basked in their admiration at this sight, led them out again without offering a single grape. In church this woman was accompanied by her thin, white-haired husband, and sometimes by a small shy boy, probably a grandson, who seemed overwhelmed by his awesome grandmother.

There was immensely tall Colonel Sands and his tiny wife, who, even in late middle age, really was pretty. Their garden by the river was given up for a day every summer to the annual village fete. There was the big family who lived further along the riverbank. Their sons were in their teens, and the mother gave fine tea parties, to which the whole Seven Acres clan was invited, with games of murder in the dark all over the house, and plenty of iced cakes for tea. The parties always ended up with presents. These people and many others met together to exchange courtesies in the churchyard, and then drifted away. Many walked, but a few from outlying areas, like the Pearson-Thrings, drove home in rarely used motor cars.

It was on a ripe afternoon of late summer that Patricia attended her second* wedding. For once, Syria left Georgy at home. The young auburn-haired cousin of the people at Great Hautbois House was being married at Coltishall church to a good-looking young clergyman. They were both tall and stately. Patricia was full of wonder at the glamour of the event. The Church was full, and the usher gave them good seats near the front. The groom was enviably handsome, and the bride, her expression calm and glowing, looked unbelievably beautiful in her long ivory satin gown, her red-gold hair shining through the folds of the wedding veil. The reception was held out of doors on the wide terrace overlooking the watermeadows of the Bure. Did life hold such an event in store for Patricia, she wondered. She fervently hoped so. The bride and bridegroom seemed destined, so far as she could see, to a life of perfect bliss.

She never forgot them. A great many years later, news reached her that the bride of that summer afternoon had become a widow, and, not long afterwards, that she too had died. Patricia would never think of them as other than they were on their wedding day, young and glorious.

* The first was her mother's wedding to the Captain. (Part II)

CHAPTER 34

Patricia loved her little brother Georgy. It went without saying that she did. She never dreamed of questioning the fact, though very early she realised that Syria had shifted her main interest to him. She even accused Syria of loving him more than herself, just as, some years back, Grey had accused her of loving Patricia more than him. Syria always denied it, but she made her signs of preference obvious. He was "Our little boy." One day Aunt Annie, sister to the Captain and an accomplished watercolour painter, came to stay. The next morning Georgy did not accompany Patricia and Glovie on the routine walk. He had been summoned downstairs to sit to Aunt Annie for his portrait. There were two more sittings. She made an excellent job of it. His guileless blue eyes gazed out of the picture, his face was framed in soft brown hair, and he wore a smock which matched his eyes, and Syria framed it and hung it on her bedroom wall.

The summons for Patricia to go downstairs and have her portrait painted never came. She felt disbelief and then annoyance that her mother could quite so clearly want a picture of Georgy but not of herself. Obviously she loved Georgy more. Similar episodes were to occur. A few years later, when Patricia had returned to her boarding school a few days before Georgy went back to his, Syria visited the studio of the best portrait photographer in Norwich with him, and had themselves immortalised together, side by side.

Although always maintaining that she could not afford special treats, she paid up to send Georgy abroad on a European tour with a school friend and his parents. But it proved impossible for her to afford Patricia's train fare to Edinburgh to stay with her Aunt May, although she would consider doing so if Aunt May were to include herself and Georgy in the invitation. Aunt May declined to do this, so Patricia did not go anywhere at all. There were inconsistencies here which no one could fail to spot.

Syria composed a love song for Georgy O'Reilly Pearson, which went:

'My little O'Reilly,
He's a dear little boy,

He's Mummie's little darling,
Her pride and her joy;
And when he's a big boy,
How happy we'll be,
For Mummie loves little O'Reilly,
And little O'Reilly loves me.'

There wasn't a song for Little Patricia. She didn't exactly begrudge Georgy his song, but it was unfair. When she pointed this out to Syria, she said, 'But of course I love you both equally.' Patricia knew it wasn't true.

Georgy did not get away with his favoured status. After all, Syria had recorded whipping him when he was two years old, and it still happened now and again. One day he boasted to Patricia that when he was positioned face down across Syria's knees and being rhythmically struck on his bare behind, he had laughed instead of crying. This was a subtler defiance than anything Patricia had thought of, and at first she did not believe him. But she suspected Georgy of being a truthful child, and came to the conclusion that Syria must beat her harder than she beat Georgy, for she really hurt, and Patricia always bawled loudly, though not only out of pain. There was fear, too, on account of Syria's grim beating face.

Patricia never solved the riddle of Syria's assertion that she loved them both equally, when her behaviour showed quite clearly that she did not. This was from a person who punished lies with whippings, but who told lies herself. She began to abandon the illusion of her mother's perfection, for this was an instance where she could not, as she usually did, accuse herself of being in the wrong.

Jane's summing up of Syria was that she was simply stupid, but this Patricia could not accept either.

She remained faithful to Georgy, though she exacted a price for his crown prince status. She made him play the required parts in her games, her make-believe dramas and her illegal enterprises. She was still bigger and stronger than he, and on the rare occasions when they fought she could rely on knocking him down. She already suspected that by virtue of possessing a small, ludicrous appendage which she had not got, he was on the way to being accorded special privileges, not only by her mother but by the world in general. She did not consider he had earned them. It mattered not that she was braver and more adventurous than he, that his reading and writing were behind what hers had been at his age, and that he could not draw to save his life. He was a boy, so advantages would come his way, and were already coming. She could not forget that the God of the prayerbook and the Bible was masculine, and there were no girls in the church choir.

As for his little pipe, she regarded it as a joke, and as a target for her attacking toes when they sat opposite each other in the bath. She was fascinated by the way he peed, and tried it for herself several times. It did not come easily, but doing it that way did seem to lend her a slight sense of power which was lacking when she crouched. She was ashamed of the way she could treat him. She often blamed him for her misdoings though happily for him, she was seldom believed. But he had not yet discovered how to stick up for himself. One chilly night, when Syria was away from home, Patricia, feeling lonely, insisted that he come and join her in bed. where he repeatedly awoke her with his restlessness, until she threw him out and made him lie under the bed instead. She never quite forgave herself for this piece of cruelty.

CHAPTER 35

Patricia got Georgy fun in ways he would never have found for himself. There was the matter of the Grand Midnight Feast. Girls' school stories had made Patricia long to have one, but it seemed an impossible hope. She had no access to the kind of food eaten at Midnight Feasts now that she no longer plundered the World's Largest Village Bakery. Then it occurred to her to go to the source of food, Maud the cook, with a proposition. The maids were by now trusted friends, and often, when she was supposed to be asleep on sunny summer evenings, exiled in the gloomy depths of her bedroom, she would sit tucked up on the daylight side of the black curtains, and from the window seat watch Maud and Mabel playing together in the back yard with racquet and ball, after their day's work was done. They knew she was there and never sneaked on her. So she confided in Maud her longing to have a midnight feast the next time her mother was away.

'But I can't get hold of an iced cake,' she told her. 'No iced cake, no sweets. How can I ever have a proper feast?'

'I'll bake you a cake,' said Maud promptly. 'And with icing and cherries on it.' It seemed that a midnight feast was one of her dreams too. Mabel joined cheerfully in the conspiracy. The prospect of an iced cake of her own, and with cherries on it, surpassed all Patricia's hopes. It was too perfect for words. Iced cakes, which she adored, never appeared save on Christmas Day, or at other children's birthday parties. And here was Maud, willing to create one specially for her.

At last Syria departed on another round of visits. A night was fixed, and a rendezvous arranged for Patricia and Georgy in the maids' bedroom at two o'clock in the morning. Maud undertook to bake the cake the day before, and to provide other goodies, and they would all share it together. 'Mind you children wake up for it,' she giggled. 'We'll be expecting you.'

That night Patricia felt unusually tired. Both children fell fast asleep. Patricia woke up suddenly and looked at the luminous dial on the clock her godmother had given her. It said one o'clock, an hour to go. She no longer trusted herself to stay awake, and she dared not risk falling asleep again and missing that cake. Maud had shown it her in the scullery that evening. It was a beautiful little cake, completely coated in white icing, with a border of fat red crystalled cherries all round the top.

When Syria was away, the door between the children's rooms was not locked. She dragged the sleepy Georgy out of bed. 'Put on your dressing gown and slippers,' she ordered. We're going for a walk.'

She led the way through the sleeping house. Her stepfather was making too much noise with his asthmatic cough to hear anything, and Glovie always slept soundly. The children were adept at the noiseless opening and closing of doors. They went out through the French windows into the freshness of the rose garden. It was a warm night, and the sky loomed enormous, its immense blackness spangled with tiny stars.

She led Georgy down through the vegetable garden, across the orchard, and into the chicken runs, with all the hens bedded down in their wooden mansions. On a previous nocturnal visit they had penetrated right into one of the big henhouses, high enough inside for them to stand upright, startling the plump occupants into a few squawks and shuffles on their sleeping perches. But this time, they pushed on past the henhouses and the treeline of Shady Lane, and reached the loneliest ranges of the blackcurrant plantation. They were now out of sight of the house. They had never been so far as this at night. They came to the wilds at the end of their land, where it bordered on the railway common, an uninviting place. It was excitingly alarming being out there at dead of night. Patricia decided they had gone far enough, and suddenly she realised that they were not alone. Someone was moving about on their land, and by starlight she could just make out the form of a slightly built man, accompanied by roving dog shapes. This was a man she had seen before, a solitary poacher whom she had sometimes glimpsed crossing a field at dusk with his seven dogs, three of them lanky greyhounds, gambolling round him. He was ageless in appearance, lean and leathery. He always had a pouch slung across his back, and he wore a battered hat. They met up together on the grassy pathway by the hedge. He showed no surprise at meeting two children in their nightclothes out of doors and at such an hour.

Patricia walked right up to him 'What are you doing?' she asked with interest.

In his sing-song Norfolk accent, he explained to them that he was setting traps for moles. By the light of his big torch, he showed them a tin of writhing brown worms, and another tin filled with what looked like small pieces of fine string. 'They're poisoned,' he told them. Then he seized a glossy worm in his thick rough fingers, and with a sharply pointed little instrument, he threaded a length of string into the unfortunate creature. Next, he stooped, scooped out a hole in a molehill nearby, and buried the worm inside.

'That there'll catch him,' he said. 'The poisoned worm kills quickly. I'll be back to pick him up.' I'm off for now. I've work to do with this fine fellow.' He opened the lid of a basket he was carrying in a small sack, and the children glimpsed the vicious, glittering eyes of a ferret. Then he was off through a gap in the hedge and away across the next field, all his dogs around him, sniffing and searching, and the torchlight bobbing. Patricia never saw him again close up, but several times after that, looking out of her bedroom in the first dim light of dawn, she caught sight of his bobbing light crossing the field, and knew that the poacher and his dogs were busy about their affairs.

The children turned and set off back to the house. Suddenly the night was rent by an outbreak of terrifying wails and screeches. They rose and fell, up and down, like some diabolical scale.

'It's babies falling out of prams!' blubbered Georgy. Patricia feared it might be something worse, like a tiger. They had certainly earned punishment. Courage deserted them both and they took to their heels and never stopped running until they reached the French windows, rushed in, and locked the door behind them. Still gibbering with fright they at once made their way to the bedroom next to the scullery, and the safety and comfort of Maud and Mabel, who lit a small oil lamp and pulled them into their beds. Patricia described how they had just escaped from a fierce wild animal which had got loose in the garden and was following them, howling terribly. The maids only laughed.

'It'll be foxes having a bit of fun. Or maybe tomcats,' they said. It should have been cosy, in bed with Maud and Mabel, but somehow, when the iced cake with its glacé cherries was produced, together with sweets and lemonade which the maids had bought for the occasion, Patricia found she had hardly any appetite. Still, she felt very grateful to them for all the trouble they had taken and for the warmth of their welcome after the fright she and Georgy had had.

Patricia had long envied Mabel her early morning job of cleaning out and polishing with bootblack the big iron kitchen range before it was lit. All the dead ashes of the previous day had to be riddled out through the bottom grating and carried away for disposal in a heavy iron bucket. The whole range then had to be rubbed down with blacking and polished hard to give the surface a satisfying dull gleam. After this, the fire was made up of sticks and newspaper, and lit. When well alight, anthracite was poured in through the top from a hod, filling a large space, so that the inside soon became a creaking inferno, and remained that way until after supper when the fire faded and gradually went out. The time came, when Syria was once more away on her travels, that Patricia made Mabel promise to let her do all the cleaning out and polishing of the range herself. She would creep down early in the morning to do it. Mabel agreed good-naturedly with this plan, and, which was just as important, she promised that she would not do it all over again herself. So Patricia energetically cleaned and polished for the next few days, and was proud of her work. Her next goal was to arrange with Maud for cooking lessons, but this was never to happen, for her luck ran out. Every morning at seven the gardener arrived to begin his day's tasks, and one day he arrived unexpectedly early, before Patricia had finished her kitchen range chore, and found her at it. She made him promise not to tell on her, but as she knew, he had never liked her, and he did not keep his promise.

The consequences, when Syria returned home, were far-reaching. She had not intended to send Patricia and Georgy away to boarding school for another couple of years, but now she decided, not without some reason, that neither the Captain nor Glovie could be relied upon to know, at all times, where the children were, and what they were doing. The threat loomed again of the gypsies at the drive gate, as well as of the utter disruption of her system. So it came about that in

Septcmber of that year they were packed off much earlier than they would have been had Rob not ratted on them. It was probably just as well. It was hard enough, at the ages of ten and eight, to adjust to the foreign country and alien inhabitants of boarding school. As it was, Georgy's miseries were so acute that even Syria, accustomed as she was to this form of child reaction, was distressed, and Patricia had to grapple for at least a year with being regarded as hopelessly eccentric. The earlier stages were not helped by Syria's refusal to buy the regulation uniform. She provided what, in her opinion, but not that of the other girls or the Headmistress, was a good enough approximation from her store of reach-me-downs. Everyone else wore black stockings; Patricia was given brown ones. The oddest item of all was a straw panama hat, a shallow-crowned creation of Edwardian origin, which was much too large for her and shaped like a shallow basin. Syria padded it with a billowy lining of khaki-coloured silk, stuffed with thick layers of cotton wool. People beheld this hat with disbelief and it became the joke of the whole Junior House. At last the Headmistress herself insisted that it be replaced without fail the following summer.

The first night at this school, two hundred miles away from home, among complete strangers, and sharing a small chilly room with another girl, hostile in her own loneliness, was an experience that always froze Patricia's heart to remember.

Syria was greatly smitten at having to part with Georgy. She said she had never seen a child cry so much as he did the night before he left home. Both children had cried, but Georgy's tears were the ones she could not forget.

Such were the long-term consequences of those happy misdeeds with which, for so long, Patricia, with Georgy in her train, had outwitted Syria's regimen. The immediate penalty was surprisingly mild. Georgy himself was relieved of sanctions, for Patricia was regarded, quite rightly, as the ringleader. She had envisaged the severest forms of retribution, but she did not even get a whipping. All that was visited upon her was a long, reproachful lecture, impressing upon her how much she had let down her dead Father, who, watching from above, must be deeply disappointed in the daughter who, he had promised Syria, had been born to be a comfort to her Mother. The withdrawal of sweets for a month was only to be expected. Patricia was relieved to find that the rest of her punishment consisted in having to learn by heart the Ten Commandments, and to repeat these, word perfect, to Syria. She had a good memory, so it did not take long. Hoping to recover some lost favour, she threw in the 4th century Nicene Creed for good measure.

Maud and Mabel stayed on together until Syria left Seven Acres with her half of the family four years later. After her mother's death in 1968, Patricia was surprised and delighted to find Maud's address among her papers. They had, she realised, exchanged Christmas cards all that time. Maud now lived in a small village outside Norwich, and they remained in touch for some years until, two Christmasses running, there was silence, and Patricia understood that her old friend, who had played ball in the yard on summer evenings, had allowed her to help in the kitchen and had baked her an iced cherry cake, had retired from all her labours.

CHAPTER 36

After Patricia and Georgy started boarding school, Glovie returned every year from her Cambridge cottage to help during the holidays. Jane was now at University, but she returned for the vacations until matters between her and Syria deteriorated completely. The Captain suddenly abandoned his habitual aloof stance and accused Syria of despotism. He said she should have made efforts to understand Jane. She had failed to do this, and it had made life impossible. His children seldom came home now, and it was because of her. She had brought it all on herself, and there was no longer any point in keeping a large house going. He intended to sell Seven Acres, and to look for a house in Somerset near his sister.

He assumed that this would suit Syria too, since she had been planning to rent a house for herself and her children near Gresham's, so that Georgy could attend as a day boy.

It was true that Syria saw living in Holt as a solution to the boarding fee problem. Gresham's for Georgy outranked any other priority. She had assumed that the Captain would obligingly stay on at Seven Acres until, at the end of Georgy's school days, she would be ready to rejoin him. But he, to her amazed surprise, saw things differently. She had not anticipated that he would seize on this as a pretext for a marital separation, and she vigorously defended herself against the accusation of despotism.

'You have said to me recently,' she wrote, 'that I know Jane is difficult and different, and that her mental development has been retarded by five or six years. What am I to understand? One minute she is grown-up, and must be treated as such, another minute she is a child, and one must humour her. You say the cause of all this is my despotic methods. I don't think so.' She continues, in characteristic Syria idiom, to defend her stance in a recent showdown with Jane.

'I corrected Jane. I spoke without temper, and fairly, to her. She became very angry and insulted me many times that evening, hurting me in all the ways she knew would hurt most. I was quite ready to forgive this, however, and to try to start with fresh hopes, as on a score of previous occasions. I maintain that I handled the position on the correct lines, and had followed a plain principle. But what she wanted was to crush me. I was therefore forced to report the matter to you.'

The Captain had not responded with the required co-operation, and Syria chided him: 'It was your plain duty to have corrected Jane. I can but say again that I have not used despotic methods with your children, unless it is despotic to say a thing and mean it, to give a direction and see it is carried out.'

Syria felt herself to be most unfairly treated as the Captain failed to acknowledge her judgment of events. She was shocked and angered by his outburst but she needed to believe that she wished him well despite his wrong-headedness, and she continued her letter: 'I pray for you every time I wake in the night, and I hope it may help you to sleep, and miss the asthma attacks. I hope we shall one day be feeling something approaching peace and happiness again. A big effort is what we shall both have to make.'

Mustering all her financial resources, she bought a small villa close to Gresham's. With the greatest difficulty, and reproachful reminders as to his moral duty towards his wife, she talked the Captain into paying her a small supportive income.

She no longer needed to accommodate Peter, who was now a certified schizophrenic, with the prospect of lifelong detention in a large mental hospital in Norwich. Grey, to whom she held out no hope of financing in Cambridge where all his step-siblings had gone, was hustled into a job as a preparatory school master, with instructions to work for a degree by correspondence course. She needed every penny she could lay hands on for Georgy, and the medical training she planned for the future Doctor Pearson. Grey seldom came to Holt during his school holidays, much to Patricia's regret. He preferred to stay in Edinburgh instead, with his Aunt May and her three sons.

The transfer to Holt marked the final parting from Glovie. She had been with them for twelve years. Patricia missed her greatly. At Holt, Georgy dropped his allegiance to Patricia and he and his mother formed a closed pair together. By now Syria had despaired of that idealised mother-daughter relationship she had hoped for. 'You're a Pearson really,' she said to Patricia, and the unspoken bit was clearly 'That's why we can't get on.' She had never taken to her in-laws.

Patricia made the best she could of the isolated position in which she found herself, and she escaped from it as soon as she was able to finance herself. Life opened out, offering much to explore, and soon, despite the restrictions of war, she would take advantage of new freedoms. She remembered her old friend sometimes and wrote to Glovie occasionally, receiving affectionate little replies in increasingly wobbly handwriting. In the spring of 1945, feeling uneasy, she travelled across country from Bletchley, where she was engaged in war work at the Government Code and Cypher Station, to see Glovie once more.

She was very old by now. The hardworking years had worn her out, and the frailties of age had obviously overtaken her. She had the pleasure of living close to her friends in the Barton Road, but that year the blue baby god-daughter had died, and it was a blow to her. She liked the local vicar at St. John's church, who sometimes visited Patricia was always to be thankful that she had listened to her intuition. She arrived at the cottage without notice, bringing with her a cake she had made. The old lady who opened the door was tinier than she remembered, more bent and more slow. Her face lit up with welcome.

They sat together for an hour in the parlour, scene of "No, No, Nanette," on the radio, many years ago. Glovie showed her a plain exercise book in which she was writing her thoughts on St. John's Gospel, the subject of a study group at the church which she was still attending when she felt strong enough, and when someone could give her a lift. She must have found St. John in harmony with her Golden Rule.

The time passed quickly. Patricia had to catch a train back to Bletchley to work on the evening shift. Glovie stood at her garden gate, waving goodbye. Patricia waved back and walked on, then turned to wave once more. But already a heavily blossomed tree hid her from view. They could see each other no longer, and Patricia felt a premonitory pang.

August 15th was a day of celebration. It was V.J. day, Japan had just surrendered. The Second World War was at last over. A good day, but a clouded one for Patricia. It was the day a letter came, telling her that

Glovie had died.

A quarter of a century later, Patricia visited her grave, way out of Cambridge, on the road to Barton. She was not in an ordinary cemetery, but in a garden-like little field, bounded by a high lilac hedge. There was no chapel, only a green potting shed and an old-fashioned water butt. It was quite high for the county, and she looked across acres of green barley towards the towers of the University. She sat on the gravestone kerb and remembered Glovie; her songs, her poems and stories, the history lessons, the country walks, the picnics, the long afternoons in haystacks. She remembered the shopping they had done together in The World's Largest Village Stores, the time, magpie-like, she had stolen Glovie's silver wrist watch and not even been scolded for that crime; the unspoken sympathy when life went all wrong, the little surprise presents.

She put the deep blue cornflowers and three white carnations she had brought with her in a jam jar, together with some white sheep's parsley, some ears of green barley and some buttercups. A few wild flowers seemed right for her, after all their walks in the country.

Then she said goodbye.

During Patricia's fourth year at boarding school, Peter disappeared. Unknown to her, he had been burdened with deep anxiety for much of his life, perhaps even before that afternoon when, at nine years old, he had stumbled upon his father lying dead under the kitchen table. Soon afterwards he was sent to a preparatory school near Bulawayo, where the matron had shamed him before the whole dormitory for wetting his bed. Almost as soon as he got back to England, he was packed off as a boarder to Christ's Hospital. There had already been too many changes of scene and people in his short life, and he had his mother's grief to contend with as well as his own.

He was at Christ's Hospital for eight years. He wrote affectionate letters to his mother which gave clues to an alarming degree of misery. He was obsessed with her state of mind, with what he perceived as her unhappiness since his father's death, and he laboured to make it up to her. He tried to please her by schoolboy achievements, and felt compelled to confess to her all his imagined shortcomings. Where Syria's children were concerned, confessions abounded, and Peter could not lose the habit. He loses an exercise book but does not admit this to the master. Instead, he confesses it to Syria. He tells the master he has finished his homework when he hasn't. This, too, has to be shamefacedly confessed. He tells his mother that he has had to write out ten lines for going upstairs without permission, and has fallen back a place in class. He writes that he knows he has spent too much on chocolate, and promises to cut down forthwith. 'Please,' he begs. 'Will you forgive me all these things'? Syria's absolution is essential to him.

He did quite well in class, and was outstandingly good at woodwork. But he failed to shine at rugger. 'However hard I try, I cannot enjoy rugger. It is an awful shame. If you are good at rugger it wins you respect and makes you popular.' After three years, he can still write home, 'I am afraid I am simply miserable.' Then he worries about the effect of this confession on his mother, and tries to reassure her.

At sixteen he went on a school journey to Germany, and sent her pages of marvellously detailed descriptions of cathedrals, villages and rivers. But tucked into the body of these letters, there are hints of a profound desolation.

The first effort at adolescent rebellion came when he startled Syria by taking a firm line about Confirmation, which she was pressing upon him.

'About Confirmation. I could have joined the class, but I don't want to be confirmed unless I have a distinct call to be, which I have not had. I have never understood the teaching about drinking Christ's blood and eating His body, as it comes in St. John's Gospel. I think the disciples must have made a slip or something when they wrote that down as Jesus' wish. I can never associate that teaching with Him. It is an awful shame we know so little of His life, for there is unlimited room for errors even by the earliest manuscripts. The earliest were written in the fourth century. They are the Codex Sinaiticus and the Codex Vaticanus. It is just the same as if no books had been written about Henry VIII until the beginning of this century. I hope you won't think badly about my ideas on Confirmation.'

Whatever Syria thought, he was confirmed within the next two years. His depression, spoken about only to Syria, and unrecognised by her for what it is, clouds his life. 'Sometimes I'm afraid, in spite of all the comforts and pleasures which I should enjoy, I feel so desolate and hopeless that my only pleasures, though very beautiful ones, are thoughts of Jesus and of the life to come. I think them every Sunday in Chapel, and whenever I see a beautiful sunset, or hear some divine music. I may be awfully miserable and sentimental but I have tried to tell you some of my thoughts, which I could never do by word of mouth. Please don't be unhappy about me, or think I lead a life of misery, because I shall always be happy, though not in the worldly way, while He takes care of me, which I feel He will always. You will always be my darling Mummie, and I am sure you will understand.'

Syria could not have understood. She would have been impressed by his devotion to her, and not seen how dangerously sick it was.

Many years later, after half a long lifetime in an institution, Peter came close to the matter when he wrote to Patricia, 'I suppose it is a definite handicap at the age of nine years losing one's Dad, and having to carry on from then, without the male parent influence. Not in the sense of trying to make excuses, but the loss in itself was at least half the explanation. Dependence on one's mother alone, and feeling responsible for her, can possibly detract from one's self confidence. Disadvantages from losing one's father when young are formidable, the more so when he was such a thoroughly good sort. I am to blame for having caused Mum so much trouble, though I feel that if I had been able to leave here, I might have been better able to turn over a new leaf.' While still a schoolboy, Peter had borne an oppressive sense of responsibility for Syria's mental state, and his own was sacrificed to it. Grey had managed to shake this off quite early. She had never liked him much, and it made life easier for him. As for Patricia, it was in fact fortunate that Syria preferred boys to girls. She must have been the only person at Seven Acres, bar Jane, to have kicked Syria in a fit of rage.

Patricia was fond of Peter. He never teased or mocked her. But she saw little of him during her school holidays. Syria had found him a post as a junior clerk in her Norwich bank, a job that must have shrivelled his soul. He had an aptitude for art and languages, but now he spent his day closeted with figures. Syria set him to study for Bank examinations in the evenings, and obediently he did so, failed them, and had to work for them again. Patricia remembered glimpses of him studying, a shade over his blue eyes which were suffering from close work. He had taken to pressing spiritual advice upon the family at Sunday mealtimes. His opinions were tenacious, and he was beginning to make a point of disagreeing with Syria. She had always been conventionally devout, but Peter was managing to outdo her, and even to tell her where she was in error. Religious attitudes in the family were confused and confusing. The Captain attended church and presided over morning prayers after breakfast only because that was in his background tradition. He enjoyed taking digs at religion in such a way as to proclaim that he was a rational being, whereas Syria was merely a wishful thinker. He was particularly prone to air these views at Sunday lunch immediately after church. Patricia could not make out why he went there at all. She herself longed to 'believe,' but it was becoming ever harder, for she could not help being impressed by his arguments.

Peter still attended Coltishall church, but had now taken to lecturing the family on the superior virtues of Chapel. He threatened to secede there. This seriously perturbed Syria, who regarded Chapel as a place attended only by the lower orders.

How long she would have continued to tolerate his diatribes is uncertain, but when he took to standing up in the bus that carried him to Norwich every morning, and preaching to his fellow passengers, she became alarmed. Public exhibitions could not be allowed. He was not open to persuasion and declined to stop it. This was not the Peter Syria had always known, and she could draw only one conclusion. He must be off his head. Psychiatric advice was sought, and one morning he was removed, protesting, from his home, and placed in a "lunatic asylum" in Norwich.

When Patricia returned home for the holidays, Peter had gone. 'Why?' she asked. 'When I said goodbye to him at the end of last holidays, he wasn't mad, as far as I could see.'

Peter had not been in the asylum long before he obliged everyone by acting unmistakeably "mad". A great change took place in him. His weight fell from ten and a half to seven stones in a few weeks. He became aggressive towards the male attendants, and was restrained in a straitjacket and kept in solitary confinement until he became amenable. The diagnosis was schizophrenia, or dementia praecox, often known as "madness of the young". Syria went to visit him and he was brought before her, firmly restrained by attendants. He swore obscenely at her, and the Medical Superintendent, who was umpiring the encounter, scolded him and sent him away again. He apologised to Syria for the shock she had just suffered. Peter's language was not fit for the ears of a lady, let alone his Mother.

Peter was misdiagnosed. He was a very angry, unhappy young man who had been traumatised by the sudden death of his father and dominated by a mother who needed him as a consolation for her own loneliness. He had no social or sexual outlets. But he never showed the prolonged breaks with outside reality of the true schizophrenic. The reality of his own life had been full of abnormalities. His remote, provincial asylum treated him to the best of its ability and soon gave up on him. Schizophrenia in the early thirties carried a sentence of life incarceration. The Superintendent wrote to Syria from time to time, and his prognoses were not hopeful. Peter, young, angry and confused, remained unruly. He even threw a book at a picture because, as he explained to Syria, 'I felt I might do something desperate.' So they put him to bed, for fear he might do something worse. The Superintendent reported to Syria that he used nauseating and disgusting language relating to sex. That alone was enough to confirm Syria's resolve not to have him at home again. The Superintendent impressed upon her that Peter would be very troubling to her two younger children. His letters give a distinct impression that he disliked Peter and had no patience with his kind of breakdown. He arranged with her that all letters sent to Peter at the hospital should be intercepted and forwarded to her so that she could censor or withhold them.

Patricia did not understand was happening to Peter. Although she had never seen him behave in a way that was seriously crazier than what was normal in her family, her mother very early on conveyed the message that he had an incurable mental illness, and would never return home. What was a mental illness anyway? Her own worst fears of abandonment were being lived out by Peter. Her mother told her never to speak of him or his condition at school. His existence must be kept a secret, and if she was asked how many brothers she had, she must admit to only two.

She concluded that this must mean that her family, and perhaps even she herself, was tainted by the awful flaw of insanity. Syria could not account for it, but offered the theory that it might have been caused by Arthur and herself loving each other too much. Patricia could make no sense of this.

Above all, she could not associate the kindly brother she remembered with madness.

'I don't know why they took him away,' said Glovie, who had been in the house at the time. 'He was no more mad than you or I.'

So the mystery of Peter's madness remained. One thing did emerge clearly. It was exceedingly dangerous to defy Syria beyond a certain point. It meant you were mad, and she would get rid of you as surely as if you had been one of those lepers in the Bible.

Peter made one unsuccessful bid for freedom. Outwitting locks and warders, he set off on the long walk home. He had left Norwich and its suburbs far behind, and was several miles into the country before a member of staff, passing by chance in his car, recognised and retrieved him. It would not have made much difference. Syria would have sent him back anyway. The punishment for naughtiness such as this was sedation and being put to bed. They kept a careful watch on him after that.

Peter was a handy guinea pig in various trials which were carried out, sometimes fatally, in the search for a cure for the schizophrenia from which he was supposed to suffer. This was an umbrella term for various types of flamboyant psychotic breakdown, especially in young adults. He was tried out with electric shock and insulin coma treatments, and, most drastic, the prefrontal lobotomy operation, where a fine rod was driven through the temples from one side of the head to the other, disrupting the brain tissue of the frontal lobes. The commonest consequence was a change of personality which, with luck, lessened the intensity of the symptoms. At the very least, the patient would become less troublesome to the hospital. On Peter it had little effect save to produce a cramped style of handwriting. It also had, in a subtle way, cramped his perceptions, so that his letters to Patricia became bizarrely stilted. Over some years, these distortions gradually righted themselves. He continued to be resistant to authority, and what Syria described as tiresome. But his splendid memory and general intelligence were not impaired. He immersed himself in English literature and history, and taught himself Polish, having struck up a friendship with a doctor on the staff.

For some years Syria insisted that letters sent to Peter by Patricia be sent to her first for censorship, until one day Patricia simply decided not to comply any more with this demand, or indeed with any other attempts to control her life. Syria could do nothing about it but disapprove and warn Patricia not to unsettle Peter by saying anything which might make him feel that life outside hospital was preferable to life inside. This was in direct response to a letter she had received from the Medical Superintendent. The months of Peter's imprisonment had become years, and the Superintendent wrote:

'I should not take any notice of his appeals. He is quite unfit to leave here, and I think the time has come when you should tell him quite candidly that you do not think him well enough to leave, and that much depends on his own conduct. I think also you should not write to him so often, and when you do, just acknowledge his letters and say something to the effect that all are well at home, that the weather is fine or wet, as the case may be, but do not allude to any of his questions or comments. I still think that Peter's value in the outside world amounts to nothing. He does not seem to realise the difficulties outside, nor his own unfortunate state.'

After refusing to bow any longer to Syria's censorship, Patricia carried on a regular correspondence with him for many years. It was clear that the psychotic storms of his early breakdown had cleared. He had recovered rational capacity and had worked out some of the causes of his troubles, though he never ceased to blame himself for his fate, an attitude in which he had the backing of both the Superintendent and Syria. He still had occasional outbreaks of rage with the staff and inmates, which he reported back shamefacedly to Patricia, remarking how right his mother had been to scold him for it. Patricia thought it was the natural reaction of a man who was being treated like a young child, and living among people with whom he had little in common but misfortune.

'This morning,' he wrote, 'I landed myself in bed again. It is a sort of mental derangement, though I realise how imprudent. I think it is born of loneliness and past memories that were better forgotten. I feel truly sorry for my troubles. It seems to bring it home that unkindness and other misdemeanours are a self-infliction, and make it harder for oneself. One or two of these mistaken ideas of mine, from the war years and since, still linger persistently. So for that reason I sometimes wish I could be home again and start afresh.' The fresh start he longed for was something Syria never allowed him to attempt. She would have been the last person capable of helping him, since the "mistaken ideas" with their load of guilt and distortion had been conditioned into Peter since childhood by Syria herself. She strove to prevent anyone from visiting him without her permission, which was not available to Patricia, nor even Georgy, who was by now a general practitioner. To his credit, for it was important to him not to displease Syria, he decided that as a medical man he was entitled to visit Peter without her permission, and he did so. Syria was indignant, and begged him not to go again, claiming that he had seriously unsettled Peter.

She claimed the backing of the hospital, but Patricia suspected that she had been labelled a difficult relative, whom it was simpler to placate. Syria must have been terrified that some new visitor might question whether his continued detention was justified. She was well aware that Patricia was critical of her acceptance of a life sentence for Peter. She remained adamant that she could not have him to live with her. He stood little chance of getting work, except possibly as a gardener, and he had reverted to the appearance and style of a Norfolk rustic. Sensitive as Syria was to social pressures, this must have been a big obstacle in the way of Peter's release. Soon after the end of World War II, the Captain had died, leaving Syria as small a portion of his assets as he could legally get away with, and she had moved to a small rural cottage on the other side of England. Patricia thought that perhaps she could not be blamed for feeling that she had at last earned the right to lead the rest of her life free from the cares that Peter would have brought with him.

The National Health Service arrived, and life at the hospital became as humane as such circumstances permitted. Wards were unlocked and conditions became more liberal. There was a large garden where Peter painted watercolour sketches and made pets of the cats that inhabited various sheds and had their kittens there. Somehow he acquired the tools with which he fashioned a set of keys that fitted most of the hospital locks, not that they were much needed by then. He enjoyed the market gardening which the hospital had set up in its grounds, and for which he received a small wage. He saved enough to buy Syria a costly Ronson cigarette lighter, which he proudly posted off to her. She sent it straight back, with a scolding for wasting money. She pointed out that it was not for him to indulge in the luxury of giving expensive presents.

Peter was mortified, and wrote sadly to Patricia. It was the kind of letter he used to write to Syria when he was at school, berating himself for general wrong-headedness. He now realised, he told Patricia, how foolish and and extravagant he had been. It was not for him to presume to send his mother an expensive present.

Patricia wrote back to ask if he would give it to her instead, as there was nothing she would like more. She hoped it would help to heal the hurt, if only a little. And so she came to possess a very fine lighter during her smoking years.

Shortly before Syria's death in 1968, Peter began complaining again about having to remain an inmate in a mental hospital. He was getting restless, decided Syria, and might even now land on her doorstep. She wrote to the hospital, offering them her permission to carry out a second lobotomy should they wish to do so. Before they had time to consider this, Syria dropped dead one cold winter's morning of a massive coronary.

Patricia found it hard to take in that this powerful force existed no longer. There had been so much ill will. The effort to sustain their relationship had been strained almost to breaking point. Yet she remained aware that the longing to give and receive love had struggled on in her mother's strange, severe nature, and that there was much that had needed to be expressed between them for which the right words, the right time, had never been found.

She crossed the country two days before Christmas to spend half an hour sitting with her dead mother in the village funeral parlour. She was the only one of her siblings to come near. Outside the open window, an unseasonal blackbird sang insistently.

Soon afterwards, the phone rang in Patricia's home in London, and she heard Peter's living voice for the first time in thirty years. He told her that the hospital had released him into a private hostel in Norwich. It was an ordinary house in an ordinary street, owned by a family who lived downstairs, and let three upper rooms to long-term ex-patients. They lived with the family. There was a fire, and cats in the kitchen, there was a mother and father, a grandmother, and a little girl of six. Peter could go to the hospital every day to continue his market-gardening job there, and keep an eye on the outdoor cats. He could come and go as he pleased.

Patricia drove to Norwich, and there they met. She embraced the big, shabbily-dressed man with thick grey crew-cut hair who stood waiting in the forecourt of the hospital. He had changed out of all recognition, but his eyes were still the jewel-like blue that she remembered.

'Patricia, you've lost your golden hair,' were his first words to her. She had. Her hair was now quite white.

They went to the seaside for the afternoon, and began the work of building a bridge over the gap of so many years; to make a connection between the person each of them saw now and the image that, until that day, they had carried in their minds from long ago. Peter still bore, and always would, the big round scar marks of the lobotomy, where the rod had been driven in and out of his brain.

Not long after this, the first of many meetings and visits until he died, Peter handed over to Patricia the set of metal keys he had secretly made, in the years of his incarceration, for unlocking hospital doors.

Syria in Lubumbashi, shortly before meeting Arthur

Arthur at the time of his marriage to Syria in 1911

Syria distancing herself from sister-in-law May.

Grey and Peter; Studio portrait sent to their parents in Africa during World War I

"She was not a weak vessel."

"For Grey, at least, there were the good times."

Syria's Father, Rector of Tunstall Rectory, Suffolk.

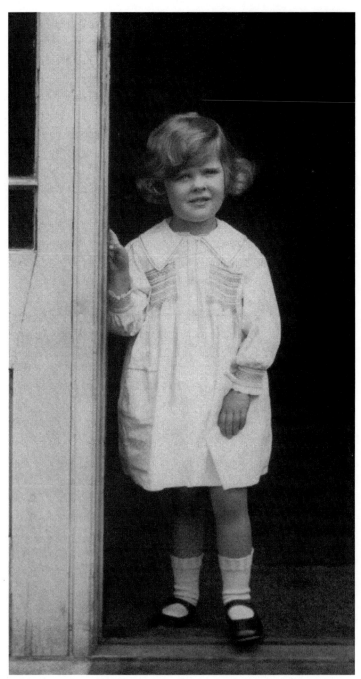

Patricia at four years old.

Grey looked very like pictures of Patricia's missing father.

Glovie disliked this picture because she said it left out her creases, which were, indeed, many.

Stepsister Bryn. Patricia thought her both beautiful and kind.

Patricia thought her mother looked as lovely as the lady in the big chocolate box with silk sides, in which she kept her handkerchiefs.

MISTRESS IN HER OWN HOUSE

Syria, Peter, Jane, Grey, Meredith, the Captain.

The ruined Church at Great Hautbois stood alone among the woods and fields bordering the wetlands, the churchyard was gay with wild flowers and butterflies, a favourite place.

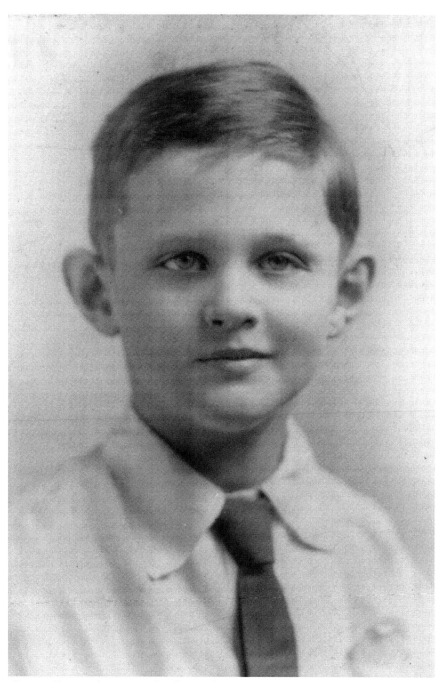

Georgy, Patricia's youngest brother and constant companion.

Maud, who made Patricia's secret iced cherry cake for her Midnight Feast.

Peter aged twenty-two, the year he was incarcerated for the next thirty-three years, under sentence of alleged schizophrenia.

Patricia's husband, Paul.